WHERE TO LOOK
FOR HARD-TO-FIND
GERMAN-SPEAKING ANCESTORS
IN EASTERN EUROPE

Second Edition

Index to 19,720 Surnames in 13 Books, with Historical Background on Each Settlement

Compiled by

Bruce Brandt

and

Edward Reimer Brandt

CLEARFIELD COMPANY

Printed for
Clearfield Company, Inc. by
Genealogical Publishing Co., Inc.
Baltimore, Maryland
1993

Reprinted for
Clearfield Company, Inc. by
Genealogical Publishing Co., Inc.
Baltimore, Maryland
1994, 1995, 1998

International Standard Book Number: 0-8063-4530-6

Made in the United States of America

TABLE OF CONTENTS

INTRODUCTION

First of all, it should be explained what this book attempts to do and what it does not attempt to do.

The "hard-to-find" in the title implies that users will already have taken the simple steps to locate their Germanic ancestors, and have not succeeded in finding them, but know or suspect that they came from Eastern Europe.

For novices, at least two such simple sources are very important. First, check with relatives and friends who might have some knowledge of your family, particularly older ones and those who have an interest in genealogy and history, to solicit whatever information they have. Even if this information turns out to be inaccurate, it can often be a very useful clue to help you find the right track.

Second, consult the International Genealogical Index (IGI) of the Church of Jesus Christ of Latter-Day Saints (Mormons, popularly referred to by genealogists as LDS). LDS has genealogical libraries in virtually every major city in the U.S. and Canada and in a great many others. You can view the IGI, which includes hundreds of thousands of entries for Germans alone, at any of these libraries. The IGI will give you a good clue to many of the localities where specific German surnames were found. Much new material on Eastern Europe has been added in recent years. This information is now accessible by computer, as well as on microfiche. This source is, of course, much more helpful for relatively rare names than for very common ones.

These entries, based largely on parish registers, include members of all religious groups, with Mormons being a minority.

If you want additional information on research steps to take, there are many good guidebooks. One of them is the *Research Guide to German-American Genealogy*, which may be purchased from the Germanic Genealogy Society, P.O. Box 16312, St. Paul, MN 55116, for the price of $16.50 postpaid.

The first edition of this book indexed surnames culled from five books which contain genealogically relevant information about Germans in Eastern Europe, especially the initial settlers. The project of writing this index was suggested to the compiler (Bruce) by his father (the co-compiler), Edward Reimer Brandt, who is an accredited genealogist specializing in German research. The compiler had the time to enter the names into the computer and the programming skills to sort and merge the names.

The first edition indexed the following books (see the section on the historical background of these settlements for the full citation, including publisher and date):

1. Benjamin Heinrich Unruh, *Die niederländisch-niederdeutschen Hintergründe der mennonitischen Ostwanderungen im 16., 18. und 19. Jahrhundert* [The Dutch-Lower German Background of the Mennonite Eastward Migrations in the 16th, 18th, and 19th Centuries], which has 513 indexed surnames

2. Dr. Oskar Kossmann, *Die Deutschen in Polen seit der Reformation: Historisch-Geographische Skizzen* [The Germans in Poland Since the Reformation: Historic-Geographical

Sketches], with 462 surnames included in this index

3. Ludwig Schneider, *Das Kolonisationswerk Josefs II. in Galizien* [The Settlement Activities of (Austrian Emperor) Joseph II in Galicia], with 3,404 surnames indexed in this book

4. Dr. Sophie Welisch, *Bukovina Villages/Towns/Cities and Their Germans*, with 422 surnames indexed in this book

5. Dr. Franz Wilhelm and Dr. Josef Kallbrunner, *Quellen zur deutschen Siedlungsgeschichte in Südosteuropa* [Sources Regarding the History of German Settlement in Southeastern Europe], with 13,201 surnames included in this index

In the second edition of this book we have added surnames from eight additional books, viz.:

6. Gustav Schedler, *Eben-Ezer: Eine Jahrhundertgeschichte der evangel. St. Trinitatisgemeinde zu Lodz* [Ebenezer: A Centennial History of the Evangelical (Lutheran) St. Trinity Congregation at Lodz], with 256 surnames included in this index

7. Hans Schmidt, *Die Geschichte des Deutschtums in Szamocin (Samotschin) und Umgebung* [The History of Germans in Szamocin (Samotschin) and the Surrounding Area], with 286 surnames included in this index

8. Irmgard Hein Ellingson, *The Bukovina Germans in Kansas: A 200 Year History of Lutheran Swabians*, with 258 surnames indexed in this book

9. Kurt Lück, *Die Geschichte des Deutschtums in Chodzież (Kolmar) und Umgebung* [The History of Germans in Chodzież (Kolmar) and the Surrounding Area], with 111 surnames included in this index

10. Martha Müller, *Mecklenburger in Osteuropa* [Mecklenburgers in Eastern Europe], with 2,233 indexed surnames

11. Gustav Adolf Famler, *Torzsa und Seine Ansiedlung* [Torzsa and Its Settlement (by Germans)], with 351 surnames included in this index

12. Georg Leibbrandt, Hansgeorg Leibbrandt and Otto G. Siegle, *Hoffnungstal und Seine Schwaben* [Hoffnungstal and Its Swabians], with 1,300 surnames included in this index

13. Herbert Weiss, *Colony Teplitz*, with 414 surnames indexed in this book

The Unruh, Schneider and Müller books have indexes, so no page numbers are given in this index. The Wilhelm and Kallbrunner book also has an index, but we discovered that it does not cover the first eight pages, so we have listed the page and line for these unindexed 585 surnames on these pages.
The first edition of this book indexed a total of 16,372

- iii -

different surnames, but included 18,587 references if we totalled the number of surnames appearing in each book.

The second edition indexes 19,720 different surnames, but has 23,796 references. The total number of individuals or families which are indexed is, of course, much greater.

You may wish to note that the maiden names of the wives have also been indexed, wherever they are listed.

The areas or groups of Germans, in terms of contemporary political jurisdictions, covered by each of these books is described here briefly. For more detailed information, see the historical section.

The genealogical data in Unruh consists of an almost complete list of Mennonites who moved from the Danzig area in Prussia (now Gdańsk in Poland) to Eastern Ukraine (then known as South Russia), beginning about 1789.

Kossmann's book focuses on Germans in Central and, to a lesser extent, Eastern Poland, i.e., essentially the part of Poland ruled by Russia from 1815 to World War I. The list indexed here deals only with those German names which also had Polish or Polonized variations. Kossmann cites the original sources from which he compiled this list.

Schneider deals with the settlement of Germans in Galicia, chiefly in 1782-85, after this area had come under Austrian rule pursuant to the First Partition of Poland in 1772. It became part of Poland again after World War I and has been divided between Poland and Ukraine (formerly the Soviet Union) since World War II. A substantial majority of the Germans settled in Eastern Galicia, now part of Western Ukraine, near Lemberg (Lwów in Polish; L'vov in Russian; L'viv in Ukrainian).

Welisch records the history of various German settlements in the Bukovina (Bukowina or Buchenland in German; Bucovina in Romanian), which is now divided between Romania (in the south) and Ukraine (in the north). The area was ceded to the Austrian Empire in 1775 as a result of one of the many Russo-Turkish Wars. (In the historic balance-of-power politics of Europe, third parties often profited from wars between others.) Immigration of German-speakers began in the late 1780s.

Wilhelm and Kallbrunner's book is by far the most comprehensive volume, in terms of its geographic scope and the number of names recorded in it, which is included in this index. The smaller portion of names deals with the German migrants to Galicia; the larger number pertains to Germans who settled in the Lower Danubian region, historically Southern Hungary, after that territory had been regained from the Ottoman Turks. Today most of that territory is part of Romania or the Vojvodina, a nominally autonomous Serbian province.

The Rev. Schedler records the centennial history of the German Lutheran mother church in Lodz (Polish: Łódź). This region had by far the largest number of Germans in the portion of Poland which was ruled by Russia between the Napoleonic Wars and World War I (1815-1914).

The Schmidt and Lück books deal with the Eastern Netze (Noteć) River district in Northern Posen (Poznań), from where many people emigrated to Central Poland. The Eastern Netze area had a large German minority prior until 1945, with the Western Netze region, which remained within the borders of interwar Germany, populated predominantly by Germans until then.

Müller has an extensive indexed list of Mecklenburgers who emigrated to many parts of Eastern Europe, but especially in a more or less directly easterly direction, i.e., to Pomerania, Northern Posen, West Prussia, East Prussia and the Baltic lands. The Ellingson book is a useful supplement for Welisch's. Together, the two books cover the original German settlers in the Bukovina almost as thoroughly as the settlers in Galicia and the Banat are covered by the Schneider and Wilhelm & Kallbrunner books and the Prussian Mennonites who migrated to Eastern Ukraine are recorded by Unruh.

The immense tome by Karl Stumpp, *The Emigration from Germany to Russia in the Years 1763 to 1862*, has not been included, because indexing it would be a task of such magnitude that another volume of comparable size would be needed.

However, since it is available in English, it is a primary reference tool for those whose German ancestors emigrated from the former Russian Empire, but not from one of the areas covered by this index. Since the names in Stumpp's book are only partially alphabetized and are listed by colony for the most part, it may take a considerable period of time to find your ancestors in this 1018-page book, unless you have a fairly accurate idea as to the specific place of origin. There was some migration from one colony to another during the period of residence in the Russian Empire, but a substantial majority of the families remained in the same area.

To index all of the information on German settlers in Eastern Europe which has been published in books would require at least half a dozen volumes of a comparable size (far more if the Germans in the Czech Republic were included), so this book, despite its extensiveness, represents only a beginning. It is by no means a comprehensive list of the surnames of all the Germans who settled in the East, much less all the individual settlers.

To give you an idea of the magnitude of German settlements in Eastern Europe, there were 1,790,489 ethnic Germans counted in the 1897 census of the Russian Empire (by which time many had already emigrated to the New World) and about 900,000 in post-World War I Romania (although nearly all of them had been under Hungarian or, in the case of Bessarabia, under Russian rule before the war).

Leibbrandt and his co-workers deal with Hoffnungstal, one of the larger colonies in the Western Black Sea region near Odessa. Most of its settlers were Lutheran Separatists from Württemberg. Quite a few of the descendants of these settlers migrated southward to Bessarabia, eastward to other parts of the Russian Empire and westward across the Atlantic. Many German-Americans (especially those whose immigrant ancestors settled in the Dakotas) have ancestors who are listed in this book.

Weiss's book provides a comprehensive and detailed history of Teplitz, one of the larger German colonies in South Central Bessarabia. Bessarabia was taken from the Ottoman Turks by the Russians shortly before the immigration of Germans. After World War I it became a Romanian province. It was transferred to the Soviet Union as a result of World War II. It is now split between Moldova (formerly Moldavia), which has a predominantly Romanian-speaking population, and Ukraine. Teplitz is located in Ukrainian South Bessarabia.

The Hoffnungstal and Teplitz colonies were founded by members of the same group of Separatist emigrants from Württemberg.

The Rev. Famler deals with the first (1784) and one of the more significant German settlements (Torzsa in Hungarian; Torschau in German) in the Batschka. Relatively little has been published about the Germans in what used to be Yugoslavia, so the inclusion of this book in our index represents at least a beginning with respect to genealogical research in an area from which it has been particularly difficult to obtain records.

Why did we select these particular books out of a hundred or more which it would be useful to index?

There are basically three reasons.

First, approximately half of the books involve areas which the co-compiler has researched in tracing his and his wife's ancestry. Personal interest is often the core of what becomes a broader interest.

Second, since the first edition focused heavily on the Germans in the eastern reaches of what used to be the Austro-Hungarian Empire, a deliberate effort was made to provide greater balance in the second edition by including more books which dealt with the former Russian and German Empires (but not those parts of the latter which had German-speaking majorities until 1945). The inclusion of the Torzsa book also falls into the category of expanding the geographic coverage.

Third, convenience and happenstance also played a role. Ten of the listed books are in our personal library. The Famler, Leibbrandt, and Weiss books are readily accessible at the library of the North Star Chapter of the American Historical Society of Germans from Russia, located here.

The surnames have been listed in this index exactly as they appear. But according to the above-mentioned *Research Guide*, "since German spelling wasn't standardized until the early 1800s, ... spelling variations are common ... when researching older records." (p. 21) A list in the *Research Guide*, supplemented by Edward Reimer Brandt (one of its co-authors), gives some letters that were often interchanged:

        i-j-y   f-v-w   ei-ai   d-t-th-tt   b-p   g-k-ch-c-qu
        z-tz-ts   s-sch-sz   a-ä-e   ü-i   a-o   ö-e

In the old Gothic script, capital I and capital J were printed so as to be identical or very nearly so. And although this wasn't a problem in compiling this index, often it is not at all obvious which letter is meant. The two letters may be listed together or separately in dictionaries or indexes.

Furthermore, since "h" is silent, except at the beginning of a syllable, it is sometimes missing and sometimes included; generally Germans tended to use a "th" spelling in the nineteenth century for names and other words which are usually spelled with only a "t" today (e.g., "Thal" vs. "Tal").

In early records, you may find an interchangeable use of single and double consonants, and long vowels may be single, double, or followed by an "h."

Thus if your name is "Schmidt," your ancestor's name may be listed as "Schmid," "Smidt," "Schmitt," or "Szmid" or "Szmit" in Slavic areas (especially Poland).

A related fact is that an "-in" ending simply referred to the female form of the name in most, but not all, cases. However, the actual surname which was used is not always clear. In a few cases the feminine ending became part of the permanent surname.

Thus "Wackerlin" probably means "Mrs. Wackerl" (if from Bavaria) or "Mrs. Wackerle" (if from Württemberg), referring to a widow, but it could conceivably have become a permanent name for the family.

Don't be fooled by the "ß" character. It is not a "B," but an "es-zet." Today it would be spelled "ss" in German if you did not have this character available. In earlier times, it was "sz" (which is what it literally means). The latter spelling was retained by the Germans in Eastern Europe much longer than in the Germanic countries themselves.

Names with an *Umlaut* would be spelled with an "e" following the letter in question, if this character was not available. For example, "Schäfer" would become "Schaefer." This usually happened in North America, but in some cases the *Umlaut* or "e" would simply be dropped, making it "Schafer." Of course, it could have been altered further to make it "Shafer" of "Shaver."

George Jones, in *German-American Names* (Baltimore: Genealogical Publishing Co., Inc., 1990) provides a lot of information on how various German names were Anglicized (with a changed spelling and/or pronunciation or by translating the meaning, so that a "Schneider" became a "Taylor") or corrupted on this side of the Atlantic.

Some of the names in the indexed book may be unclear or incorrect because of the poor quality of printing or mistakes made by the original recorder of information. For example, in the Torzsa book, it is not always possible to distinguish between "u" and "n," which closely resemble each other in the printed Gothic script and which could both fit in a given case. Where this occurred, we listed both possibilities, e.g., "Zenner" and "Zeuner."

There are also a few Hungarian names, which may be those of Hungarian ministers, for example, but could also be a Magyarized (i.e., Hungarianized) version of a German name. In such cases, it is not always clear whether the proper diacritical mark is the *Umlaut* (¨), which is used in both German and Hungarian, or the uniquely Hungarian diacritical mark (˝).

Furthermore, certain German letters are so similar that a mistake in proofreading the original book could easily have occurred. For instance, there is a reference to "Vernhard" (a very unusual name, if it exists), but this could easily have been the common "Bernhard," since the printed Gothic "V" and "B" look so much alike that even knowledgeable authors may make mistakes. We have listed both names in such cases.

Edward Reimer Brandt
Bruce Brandt
13 - 27th Ave SE
Minneapolis, MN 55414-3101

HISTORY OF THOSE GERMAN SETTLEMENTS IN EASTERN EUROPE WHICH ARE COVERED BY BOOKS INCLUDED IN THIS INDEX

The books which have been reviewed for surnames for this index are described here in alphabetical order, according to the surname of the author (which has been underlined for the convenience of readers). There is, of necessity, some repetition of information, because some of the books overlap each other in geographic terms.

(1) The first two of five chapters in Irmgard Hein Ellingson's *The Bukovina Germans in Kansas: A 200 Year History of the Lutheran Swabians* (Fort Hays, KS: Fort Hays State University, Ethnic Heritage Studies, No. 6, December 1987) cover the history of the pre-immigrant Germans in the Bukovina. The second two chapters deal with the Bukovina Germans in Kansas. The final chapter covers the post-immigrant history of the Bukovina. Most of the appendices (A-G) list the surnames (and in some cases, the first names) of those who emigrated to the Bukovina and those who later emigrated to Kansas, with later membership and clergy lists for the Bukovina Germans in Kansas.

You should be aware of the fact that the term "Swabian" became a virtual synonym for "South German" (in Prussian/German- and Russian-ruled areas) or for Germans in general (in much of what became the Austro-Hungarian Empire in 1867), although this simple statement does not do full justice to all the nuances involved. The majority of so-called "Swabians" did not come from Swabia, which is roughly identical with Württemberg, although it also includes the southwestern part of Bavaria. Moreover, the boundaries of "Swabia" did not remain constant throughout history.

Those who settled in areas regained from the Ottoman Turks in historic Hungary (including Romania and Yugoslavia after World War I) after 1699 were known initially as "Hungarian Germans." In the 1920s the term "Danube Swabians" came into general usage because (1) the majority of these Germans did not live in postwar Hungary and (2) most of the settlers had embarked at Ulm in Swabia and sailed down the Danube to what was then Southern Hungary.

However, the Bukovina (also known as "Buchenland," meaning the "land of beeches," in German) lies far to the north of the Danube and has a somewhat different history. It fell under Austrian rule in 1775, following one of the many Russian-Turkish wars. It is to the southeast of Galicia, from which a sizeable portion of its German settlers came, even though they had lived in Galicia only briefly. Galicia was the portion of Southern Poland which fell under Austrian rule in 1772 in the First Partition of Poland.

The Bukovina was an Austrian crown province, not a part of Hungary, when the Dual Monarchy was established in 1867. After World War I the Bukovina became part of Romania. Since World War II it has been divided between Romania and the Soviet Union (now Ukraine). However, the overwhelming majority of Germans lived in the Southern Bukovina (Bucovina in Romanian), which remained under Romanian rule.

According to *Meyers Kleines Konversations-Lexikon*, 7th ed. (Leipzig and Vienna: Bibliographisches Institut, 1908-09), which is a six-volume encyclopedia despite its modest title, the Bukovina's population in 1900 was 41.2% Ruthenian (Ukrainian),

31.6% Romanian, 22.1% German, 3.7% Polish and 1.3% Magyar (Hungarian).

One should note, however, that the figures for the "German" population in various parts of Eastern Europe, including the Bukovina, can vary a lot, depending upon whether or not the Jewish inhabitants were counted as Germans.

The first German Christian settlers arrived in Bukovina in 1787. The migration to Kansas began in 1886. Bukovina Germans migrated to other states and Western Canada as well.

Ellingson states (p. 9) that two-thirds of the Bukovina Germans were Roman Catholics. However, *Meyers Kleines Konversations-Lexikon* indicates that 15.1% of the total population in 1900 was Roman Catholic, while 13.2% were Jewish. Many of the Catholics were Poles or Hungarians. Welisch (discussed later) states that only 8.9% of the people in the Bukovina in 1930 were Germans. Even if one allows for the effect of emigration between 1900 and 1930, these figures can only be reconciled by the assumption that the Jews were counted as Germans in the 1900 census and that two-thirds of the German Christians were Roman Catholics.

According to Ellingson (p. 9), nearly all of the "Swabians" and two-thirds of the Zipsers (see Welisch) were Lutherans. Therefore, they must have been overwhelmed by German Catholics from Bohemia.

(2) *Torzsa und seine Ansiedlung* [Torzsa and Its Settlement] by Gustav Adolf Famler, a Protestant pastor, published by the Buchdruckerei V. A. Pajevics in Neusatz (Novi Sad in Serbian) in 1884, is one of the few available works dealing with the Germans in what used to be Yugoslavia. Novi Sad was known as the "Swabian capital" of Yugoslavia. Both Torzsa (Torschau in German) and Novi Sad are in the Vojvodina, a nominally autonomous province of Serbia, lying north of Belgrade.

The Vojvodina had large German and Hungarian minorities until the Germans were forced out after World War II in retaliation for the harsh treatment of the Yugoslavs (which means South Slavs) as a result of the guerilla warfare during the war.

This area was wrested from the Turks in 1697 and became the eastern part of Slavonia (not to be confused with Slovenia, which lies farther to the northwest). It was ruled by Hungary during the period of the Dual Monarchy (1867-1920).

Famler's book deals with only one of the German settlements in this specific area, which was historically known to Germans as the Batschka (Bácska in Hungarian, Bačka in Serbian). However, it was the first permanent settlement (established in 1784 by Protestants, mostly Lutherans but including some Reformed, from the Palatinate) and one of the larger ones. Famler's book briefly mentions other German settlements.

Actually, repopulation of the ex-Turkish lands had begun much earlier, but most of the early settlers were wiped out by the continuing border skirmishes and the first lasting settlements were in the Banat region to the east of the Batschka.

Besides Germans, the new settlers included Serbs, Hungarians, Slovaks, Russians, and members of smaller, lesser known ethnic groups.

Famler's book is essentially a history in story-book form, intended to pass on the heritage of the settlers to their descendants. However, he lists all of the 223 original settlers

(pp. 91-93), as well as well as the names of 71 families which
migrated onward to the Russian Empire between 1794 and 1807 (pp.
95-96). Beginning on p. 129, he also lists the heads of German
households belonging to the Torzsa Lutheran church in 1884.
However, the last page or two is missing from the LDS copy, so
this list includes 386 families, ending with Steinmetz.
The other name lists are those of pastors, judges, etc.

(3) *Die Deutschen in Polen seit der Reformation* [The Germans
in Poland Since the Reformation] is the major work of Dr. Oskar
Kossmann, the leading German expert on the Germans in Central
Poland. This book, published by the Johann Gottfried Herder-
Institut in Marburg/Lahn in 1978, concentrates primarily on
Central Poland, with some references to Posen and Eastern
Poland.
However, while it has tremendous value in identifying the
more than 1,000 localities in Congress Poland (i.e., Russian-
ruled Poland after 1815) in which Germans settled, it includes
relatively few references to individuals. The only surnames
incorporated into this index are those in the list of names (pp.
165-168) which also had Polonized forms. Some members of these
families may have become Polonized. On the other hand, even
German parish registers in this area were kept in Polish until
about 1865, when the use of Russian was made mandatory. Thus
the Polish spelling may simply reflect the way the name appears
in the registers.
Kossmann lists 15 different sources for this information,
some of which deal with specific colonies. Three are concerned
primarily with Posen, rather than Central Poland. This
information may thus help identify unknown ancestral places of
origin for those surnames which were not so common as to be
found in many places.

(4) *Hoffnungstal und seine Schwaben* [Hoffnungstal and Its
Swabians], by Georg Leibbrandt, Hansgeorg Leibbrandt and Otto
Siegle, 2nd ed. (published by Georg Leibbrandt, Bonn, 1980)
covers one of the more significant German colonies in the Odessa
area of Western Ukraine. According to Karl Stumpp, *The
Emigration from Germany to Russia in the Years 1763 to 1862*
(Lincoln, NE: American History Society of Germans from Russia,
reprinted 1982), Hoffnungstal was settled exclusively by
immigrants from Württemberg (p.100). However, a few other
Germans moved into the parish later. Adam Giesinger, in *From
Catherine to Khrushchev: The Story of Russia's Germans*
(published by the author in Winnipeg and printed by Marian
Press, Battleford, Sakatchewan), states (p. 167) that it was
founded by Separatists, most of them pietists who were at odds
with the prevailing rationalism of the established Lutheran
Church back home. Leibbrandt lists a population of 280 in 1817
already (p. 71), although some sources list 1818 as the founding
date.
Separatists also migrated to Bessarabia, the Crimean
peninsula, Eastern Ukraine and the Transcaucasus region east of
the Black Sea.
Part 2 B of the book (pp. 179-511) provides apparently
complete genealogical data on all the original settlers, as well
as some of the later ones, and their descendants, at least
insofar as they remained in Hoffnungstal. In numerous

instances, it specifies which families emigrated to the United States, sometimes specifying the locality, sometimes the state and sometimes without further specification, but there is no separate list of emigrants to America. Some of the children born in the United States are also listed.

The 64 founding families of Hoffnungstal are listed on pp. 171-172, with the specific village of origin given in each case.

There are maps showing the village lots of each property owner in Hoffnungstal (date not specified, but apparently in the early twentieth century; pp. 68-69), as well as in the nearby daughter colony of Hoffnungsfeld (p. 112). The 27 families who founded Hoffnungsfeld in 1856 are listed on p. 107. Other daughter colonies are listed on p. 113, but without specification of the names of the settlers.

The other name lists in the book are those of pastors, mayors, etc.

A major emigration from Hoffnungstal to America began in 1872, although 23 families had moved to Ohio in 1848 already. There was also a strong interest in joining the Templers in Palestine (1858-72) after the predicted coming of the millenium in 1836 turned out to be wrong, but apparently none of the residents of Hoffnungstal actually moved there.

It is recommended that those requesting a surname search specify whether they want only the genealogical tables, or the entire book, searched. Transcribing all of the entries for a popular surname is likely to take quite a long time.

Genealogists who desire a search for only certain first names in order to save research time and customer expense may so specify.

(5) *Die Geschichte des Deutschtums in Chodzież (Kolmar) und Umgebung* [The History of the Germans in Chodzież (Kolmar) and the Surrounding Area] by Kurt <u>Lück</u> is Booklet 1 of the series, *Unsere Heimat: Volkstümliche Schriftenreihe zur Förderung der deutschen Heimatbildung und Familienüberlieferung in Polen*, edited by Dr. Kurt Lück and Dr. Alfred Lattermann. It is an expanded special reprint by the Verlag "Deutscher Bücherei-Verein" E.V., Posen (1937) of an article in the 1937 issue of the "Landwirtschaftlichen Kalender für Polen."

This publication focuses on Kolmar in Northern Posen, formerly the seat of the county bearing the same name, which is located just south of the Netze River, although numerous other villages, especially to the south toward Budsin, are mentioned. (It is common in both Poland and Germany for the county to be named after the county seat.)

The most substantial immigration of Germans to Chodzież (also referred to in German books as Chodziesen, since the name "Kolmar" was not adopted until 1877) occurred in the seventeenth and eighteenth centuries, beginning in the 1630s, and especially as a result of the recruitment of German settlers by Polish noblemen to rehabilitate the area after the destructive war with Sweden (1655-60).

Many, but not all, of the weavers and those in other textile trades apparently came to this area from Silesia. However, many of the rural villagers came from borderlands of East Pomerania, an area which had once been the Duchy of Kashubia (Cassubien or Kaschubei in German), while others came from Brandenburg, especially from the area around Landsberg (now Gorzów

Wielkopolski). The term "Kashubians" was used, with a derogatory connotation, to describe these Germans in Northern Posen, particularly in Central Poland, Volhynia, and even Bessarabia, areas to which many of them migrated. In fact, "Kashubian" became virtually synonymous with "North German," and "Swabian" with "South German," in Central Poland and Volhynia.

Lück states that the belief, still common in the 1930s, that the ancestors of these settlers had come from Holland was erroneous. They often lived in so-called "Holländereien" (a term which came to be used interchangeably with "Hauländereien," a word which sounds similar, but has an entirely different meaning). However, this merely indicated that their settlements and farms reflected the style of the Netherlanders who did, in fact, flee to West Prussia in the sixteenth century and pioneered in draining swamplands and farming lowlands.

Nevertheless, it is an established fact that there were weavers from Flanders in this area in the early modern era, because a row of their Flemish-style houses in Chodzież is among the sites on the Polish historic preservation register today.

In 1763 there were 833 Catholics (half of them presumably Germans), 536 Protestants (virtually all Germans) and about 500 Jews in Chodzież -- a remarkably diverse and balanced population. Although some Germans settled in the area after the Prussian takeover in 1772, there was a substantial emigration, especially of weavers and other artisans, to Central Poland. This began during the days of the Grand Duchy of Warsaw (1807-15), but assumed large proportions after 1815, when Central Poland came under Russian rule, the chief attraction being access to the huge Eastern textile market.

About 200 Germans from the all-Protestant village of Podanin emigrated to America between 1856 and 1887. By 1910 the village had almost as many Catholics (mostly Poles) as Protestants.

According to the 1931 Polish census, only 15% of the residents of the city of Chodzież were Germans and only 28% of those in the surrounding rural county were non-Poles, i.e., chiefly Germans and Jews.

There are no name lists in the Lück book, but the names of mayors, pastors, teachers, artisans, colonists (meaning pioneer farmers), etc., have been culled from the text and included in this index.

(6) *Mecklenbürger in Osteuropa: Ein Beitrag zu ihrer Auswanderung im 16. bis 19. Jahrhundert* [Mecklenburgers in Eastern Europe: A Contribution (to the Study of) their Emigration in the 16th through 19th Centuries] by Martha Müller (published in 1972 by Ernst Bahr, on behalf of the Johann Gottfried Herder-Institut, Marburg/Lahn, as No. 91 of the series, *Wissenschaftliche Beiträge zur Geschichte und Landeskunde Ost-Mitteleuropas*) has an indexed list (pp. 443-471) of the emigrants who are mentioned. Three maps suggest that the largest number of Mecklenburgers went to Latvia (formerly Livonia and Courland) and Estonia (which includes part of the former Livonia), Central Poland (mostly to the more northerly areas along and north of the Vistula and Bug Rivers) and South Central Bessarabia (in Ukrainian territory bordering on Moldova today). However, emigrants to Finland and Russia, as well as a few to America, are also listed.

The book contains valuable genealogical data on the

emigrants, but relatively little relating to their ancestors or descendants, although some of their parents and children are named.

The author appears to have made a rather exhaustive search of parish registers and archival documents.

(7) *Eben-Ezer: Eine Jahrhundertgeschichte der evang. St. Trinitatisgemeinde zu Lodz* [Eben-Ezer: A Centennial History of the Evangelical (=Lutheran) St. Trinity Church in Lodz] by the Rev. Gustav Schedler (Lodz, Poland: printed by "Libertas," Verlagsgesellschaft m. b. H., 1929) is the history of the German Lutheran mother church in Lodz (Polish: Łódź), which was the center of the largest concentration of Germans in Central Poland. The church was dedicated in 1829. However, German immigration to the rural area around Lodz had begun in the 1780s already, when this area was still a part of Poland, which had been truncated by the First Partition of 1772, but which continued to exist as an independent state until 1795. Prior to the establishment of St. Trinity, German births/baptisms, marriages and deaths were recorded in the Mileszki Catholic parish records.

By far the largest number of Germans came to this area after 1815, when it had already come under Russian rule. Many of the German residents of the city were artisans, especially weavers, who came from Silesia, as well as from Posen.

The majority of German rural residents were of Pomeranian origin, although many of these had moved to Central Poland from Northern Posen. A significant number of settlers also came from Western Posen (adjoining Brandenburg) and the Vistula River valley. Southwest of Lodz there were many Silesian Germans. In the 1830s a contingent of Hessians also moved to the Lodz area.

In 1897 German Christians accounted for 22.6% of the population of Lodz County and 23.5% were German-speaking Jews, according to Dr. Oskar Kossmann (*Die Deutschen in Polen seit der Reformation*, p. 270).

Many of the Lodz Germans moved to the Chelm (German: Cholm) area in Eastern Poland and to Volhynia (German: Wolhynien), primarily after the Second Polish Revolt (against the Russians) in 1863-64. Around the turn of the century, many of these (or their children) migrated to Western Canada.

The compilers have only a partial copy of the Schedler book, but it includes the names of all of those who served St. Trinity Church in some capacity (from grave-diggers and bell-ringers to pastors) in the appendix (pp. 89-91), as well as the list of all of those who voted for a pastor in 1827 (p. 14) and those who contributed to the church in 1832 (pp. 18-19). The text also includes the names of teachers and educational administrators (pp. 54-62).

(8) *Die Geschichte des Deutschtums in Szamocin (Samotschin) und Umgebung* [The History of the Germans in Szamocin (Samotschin) and the Surrounding Area] by Hans Schmidt (Poznań, Poland: Verlag "Historische Gesellschaft für Posen," 1939) is a special reprint of an article in the 1939 issue of the "Landwirtschaftlichen Kalender für Posen," expanded for publication as Booklet 6 in the series, *Unsere Heimat: Volkstümliche Schriftenreihe zur Förderung der deutschen Heimatbildung und Familienüberlieferung in Polen,* edited by Dr.

Kurt Lück and Dr. Alfred Lattermann. It covers the Szamocin (German: Samotschin) area in the northeastern part of what used to be Chodzież (German: Kolmar) County in the Noteć (German: Netze) River area in the former province of Poznań (German: Posen). The eastern part of this river valley, including Szamocin, became part of a re-established Poland in 1919, although the western part remained in Germany until 1945.

Six *Holländereien* (all German Protestant settlements) were established during the period between 1735 and the Prussian takeover of Posen in 1772 as a result of privileges and concessions, including freedom of religion and various economic inducements, promised by the Polish noblemen who owned the land.

During the first period of Prussian rule (1772-1806), which was interrupted by the short-lived (1807-15) Grand Duchy of Warsaw established by Napoleon before Prussia regained control of the area, the town of Samotschin in particular experienced a substantial influx of German linen weavers and other artisans.

The Bromberg (Polish: Bydgoszcz) Canal, completed in 1773-74, which made the Netze River navigable, also led to the establishment of a considerable number of new rural German villages, some during the period of the Grand Duchy.

The Jewish population of Samotschin likewise increased manifold during the nineteenth century.

Peasants from this area were among those who migrated to Central Poland as early as the 1780s. However, a much larger migration, chiefly to the Lodz area, began after 1815. The weavers had a particularly strong incentive to migrate across the Prussian-Russian border in order to have the whole Russian, and even Chinese, market open to them without having to pay substantial Russian customs duties. But they were joined by many peasants who founded a large number of farm villages in the vicinity of Lodz.

Schmidt does not mention any large migration from Samotschin directly to America. However, some of the descendants of those who migrated to Central Poland (and often onward to Eastern Poland and Volhynia) later crossed the Atlantic, mostly settling in the Canadian Prairie Provinces.

The Schmidt book has no list of names as such. However, the surnames of mayors, artisans, rural settlers and others which appear in the text have been included in this index.

(9) *Das Kolonisationswerk Josefs II. in Galizien: Darstellung und Namenlisten* [The Colonization Activities of (Hapsburg Emperor) Joseph II in Galicia: Description and Lists of Names] by Ludwig <u>Schneider</u> (Leipzig: Verlag von S. Hirzel, for the Historische Gesellschaft für Posen, Poznań, 1939) is the most comprehensive and authoritative work on the Germans who settled in Galicia (the southern part of Poland which came under Austrian rule in the First Partition of 1772).

Most of the settlers came in 1782-85, with some stragglers, and a smaller wavelet in 1802-05. A large majority came from the southwestern Germanic area, with the current German state of Rhineland-Palatinate (then divided into numerous principalities) accounting for the largest number, so that the Galician Germans spoke what was essentially a Palatine dialect.

Most of the Galician Germans were Protestants, chiefly Lutherans and Reformed, but with a small Mennonite minority. Cornelius J. Dyck, the editor of *An Introduction to Mennonite*

History (Scottdale, PA: Herald Press, 2nd ed., 1981) states (p. 163) that there were some Amish among the Mennonites, but there is no mention of an independent Amish congregation in Peter Bachmann, *Mennoniten in Kleinpolen* (Lemberg [now L'viv, Ukraine]: Verlag der Lemberger Mennonitengemeinde in Lemberg, 1934).

There was, however, a substantial Catholic minority among the Galician Germans.

Galicia also had a large number of German-speaking Jews, but they had a different migration history and are not covered in Schneider's book.

Schneider lists the names of the original colonists (most of the lists are dated 1787-90, several years after the actual settlement, so they may not include those who died in Galicia during the first few years), as well as places of origin, occupation and family size in most cases, for each village.

In addition, his book includes the famous Bredetzky lists of 1812, which are in the nature of a census and list the year of birth (pp. 308-327), and lists of property owners in 1820, with a few items bearing other dates.

The three main sets of lists (1787-90, 1812, 1820) do not include the same villages in every case, which may mean that some early settlements were vacated and others were established after 1790. The county and other local government unit (e.g., tax office) is listed in most cases.

(10) *Die niederländisch-niederdeutschen Hintergründe der mennonitischen Ostwanderungen im 16., 18. und 19. Jahrhundert* [The Dutch-Lower German Background of the Mennonite Eastward Migrations of the 16th, 18th and 19th Centuries], written and published by Benjamin Heinrich <u>Unruh</u> (Karlsruhe, Germany: 1955), includes the names of very nearly all the Mennonites who moved from West Prussia (previously and again now part of Poland) to the Chortitza and Molotschna colonies in South Russia (Eastern Ukraine) between 1789 and 1895, as well as a few who migrated directly to the Crimean peninsula or the Transcaucasus. The record seems to be more complete for the original settlers, who moved in large groups, than for the smaller numbers who moved after 1808, although he records a substantial wavelet in 1818-19. Only a handful are shown for after 1847.

The Unruh book also includes the 1795 revision list (a census of property owners, which, however, lists a few families which did not own a farmstead) for Chortitza (pp. 237-244) and the 1808 revision lists for Molotschna (pp. 304-330) and some Chortitza villages (pp. 257-277). These revision lists have an impressive amount of genealogical information, including the names and ages of all household members (both censuses) and the place of emigration and date of arrival (1808 only).

Data on the Chortitza settlements also include: (1) lists of heads of households in 1793 (pp. 210-212) and 1803 (pp. 213-215); (2) a list of *Feuerstellen* (homesteads served by the volunteer fire brigade), which is useful because it reflects changes in ownership between the date of original settlement and 1802; and (3) family lists, similar to the revision lists, for Neuendorf in 1802 (pp. 254-256) and for four Chortitza villages in 1814 (pp. 278-285).

There is also a family list for Rückenau, Molotschna, in 1811 (p. 330) and a list of Molotschna births, marriages and deaths

between August 25, 1812, and August 25, 1813.
Unruh's book does not deal with the much smaller Mennonite
settlements founded in the Volga River region in the 1850s.

(11) *Colony Teplitz* by Herbert Weiss (Bismarck: Germans from
Russia Heritage Society, English translation, 1978) is a history
of one of the more important German settlements in Bessarabia.
Teplitz (originally Colony No. 12, then Töplitz) was founded in
1817, mostly by Württemberg Separatists, who were part of the
same emigrant group which founded Hoffnungstal (see Leibbrandt
book). Some families came from Central Poland, Hungary and
Alsace, but most of these also appear to have had a Swabian
background. (The term, "Swabian," is often equated with
"Württemberger," but it does, in fact, have a somewhat broader
meaning.)
The original immigrants (including some who had died in 1817)
are listed on pp. 11-23. Later immigrants, mostly from
Württemberg and other Black Sea colonies (both in Bessarabia and
in the Odessa region) are listed on pp. 25-31.
The children are usually listed for the first-year
immigrants, but only the spouse is listed for the later
immigrants.
Those who moved to other locations are included on several
lists, beginning on p. 38. Emigration to the New World began in
1874. Those who left for America are listed on pp. 43-46, those
who went to Argentina on pp. 46-47, and those who migrated to
the Dobrudscha (Romanian: Dobrogea) in Romania, various places
farther east within the Russian Empire, and Germany are recorded
on pp. 38-39, 42-43 and 47-50. Those who moved to other
localities in Bessarabia can be found on pp. 39-41 and 51-54.
There are lists of judges, mayors and other public officials
on pp. 66-68. Owners of the same farms in 1818 and 1835,
respectively, are recorded on pp. 80-82. Other changes of
ownership are recorded on pp. 89-90. Those who owned farms
which had been expropriated by the Communists, but which were
returned to the owners in 1920-22 after Bessarabia came under
Romanian rule, are listed on pp. 87-88. The 31 craftsmen in
Teplitz in 1847 are listed on p. 112. The administrators and
auditors of the community store from 1905 to 1921 are mentioned
on pp. 124 to 125-A.
The sextons, who were also teachers, and the church trustees
are listed on pp. 179-180 and 207-208. Students of intermediate
and secondary schools in Sarata, Grossliebental, Teplitz (after
1919) and Tarutino are listed on pp. 210-213. Reservists who
had to report for military duty between 1889 and 1900 are named
on pp. 227-228. Soldiers who "died the hero's death for the
(Russian) fatherland," or were missing, taken prisoner or
invalided during World War I are listed on pp. 236-238.
Persons who died as a result of accidents, murder or suicide
are listed on pp. 240-243. Cholera victims in 1866 are recorded
on p. 244.
Some other names have also been culled from those parts of
the text which contained a significant number of names, but this
index does not include every textual reference.

(12) *Bukovina Villages/Towns/Cities and Their Germans* by
Sophie A. Welisch (Ellis, KS: Bukovina Society of the Americas,
1990) is an authoritative account of the history of 22 of the

more significant localities in which Germans lived. Many of the settlers originally came from Rhineland-Palatinate, Baden-Württemberg, Hesse (lumped together as the "Southwest Germans"), Southwestern Bohemia, and the Zips (Spiš) region of Eastern Slovakia, with a few from the Banat (today in Western Romania and the Vojvodina, a Serbian province). However, most of the Southwest Germans had already lived in Galicia (into which the Bukovina was incorporated for purposes of governmental administration until 1849) for a few years before migrating onward.

Today Southern Bukovina (where most of the rural Germans lived) belongs to Romania; Northern Bukovina, including the former capital city (German: Czernowitz; Romanian: Cernăuţi; Ukrainian: Černivci), where a German university was established in 1875, to Ukraine.

While Ellingson focuses on the Lutherans and emigration to Kansas, Welisch also discusses the German Catholics and mentions their emigration to the New York City area in 1890-1956 and to Bosnia after 1908 (pp. 17, 37, 48).

Welisch provides the surnames of many of the original settlers in the text of her book, but not in list form, which is why we considered it useful to include this English-language book in our index.

(13) *Quellen zur deutschen Siedlungsgeschichte in Südosteuropa* [Sources for the History of German Settlement in Southeastern Europe] by Dr. Franz <u>Wilhelm</u> and Dr. Josef <u>Kallbrunner</u>, published as No. 11 in the *Schriften der Deutschen Akademie* (Munich: Verlag von Ernst Reinhardt, 1938), is by far the most encyclopedic work included in our index insofar as the number of personal names is concerned.

The entire book consists almost exclusively of lists of Germans who settled in Southeastern Europe in 1749-1803. (Actually, some of the families from Alsace-Lorraine and Luxembourg were either French or a mixture of French and German.)

The authors made a thorough search of the contents of the Austrian *Hofkammer* [Exchequer] Archives for data on the immigrants who settled either in the historically Hungarian territory regained from the Turks in 1699-1718 or in Galicia, which came under Austrian rule in the First Partition of Poland in 1772. Only a small number of the name lists they found predate 1763.

Most of those listed migrated to the Banat (an area along the Lower Rhine which is now divided between Romania and the Vojvodina, with 3 villages remaining in Hungary) or to Galicia. Those who migrated to Galicia will also be found in Ludwig Schneider's book; thus those who are not mentioned in both books went to Hungary.

The book also lists those who went to the Batschka region (just west of the Banat) in 1763-68 (pp. 14-29).

Also included are several lists (pp. 315-326) of Germans who migrated to Transylvania (*Siebenbürgen*), where there were centuries-old German settlements which had become Lutheran while under Turkish dominance. Most of these were Lutherans who were expelled from Austria in the 1750s, but there were also a few voluntary immigrants who came from Hanau (near Frankfurt) and the Liechtenstein district of the Grand Duchy of Hesse-Darmstadt in 1770.

The major migrations to Southern Hungary occurred in 1763-72 and 1784-86. The migration to Galicia took place mostly in 1782-85. A smaller number of migrants (pp. 298-314) went to both Hungary and Galicia in 1802-03 as a result of the Napoleonic Wars.

The authors tried to identify the village of origin, which is given in most, but not all, cases. Due to misspellings in the original records and the fact that many German villages often bear identical or very similar names, there are a lot of misidentifications.

If you have researched the vital records of the village from which your ancestors are supposed to have come, but do not find relevant entries there, try writing to the following institute (English letters are acceptable), since it has the most comprehensive list of locality corrections:

> Institut für pfälzische Geschichte und Volkskunde
> Benzinoring 6
> Postfach 2860
> D-67657 Kaiserslautern
> Germany

Despite these errors, the book's statistical tables can be assumed to be accurate enough to say with certainty that the largest number of immigrants to Hungary came from Lorraine and the largest number of those going to Galicia, from Rhineland-Palatinate. Most of the others came from Alsace and the present German states of Hesse and Baden-Württemberg.

The amount of detail varies from one list to another, but besides the place of origin, the lists usually give the number of persons in the family and frequently the occupation of the head of household (which is peasant in the vast majority of cases).

It is also important to note that religious freedom was decreed in the Austrian Empire in 1781. Thus all immigrants prior to that date would have been Catholics, except for those going to Transylvania, which was a deviant case.

The vast majority of immigrants were recruited and subsidized by the Austrian government, but a few settled in the so-called "free cities" of Hungary (meaning that the cities had no overlord, except for the emperor himself) at their own expense.

Most of the immigrants received their documents and subsidies in Vienna, but for a minority of those going to Galicia, Mährisch-Neustadt (in Moravia, on the overland route to Galicia, as contrasted with sailing down the Danube to Vienna) was the processing point.

HOW TO OBTAIN INFORMATION INDEXED IN THIS BOOK

Some genealogists who consult this book may have convenient access to libraries which have the indexed books and either know sufficient German to use them or know someone else who does. Note, however, that the older German books listed here are not only out-of-print, but are also printed in the Gothic script. But many other genealogists are unlikely to be in this position and may want to know how to get the pertinent information. We either have, or have local access to, all these books and will provide information on any surname(s). However, prompt responses cannot be guaranteed. Should you wish to use this research service, please specify which of the following you desire:

(1) only a transcript of the German entries, but in Roman script (available only for English-language books and for data in German books which is in list form)

(2) a transcript of the German entries and a translation of the information

The explanation for the difference is that the compiler (Bruce), with only a limited knowledge of German, can handle data in the first category, but the co-compiler's involvement is required in other cases.

You should know that the number of entries for a given surname, as well as the amount of detail provided, varies considerably not only between books, but also within books.

Furthermore, there may be various spellings of the same surname (e.g., Brauvogel, Breuvogel and Breyvogel) which only an expert genealogist or other person who has done a considerable amount of relevant research might recognize. (For example, the co-compiler, through his own research, has discovered that Preytegl was a mistranscription of the same name and Breivogel was a common spelling before emigration to Eastern Europe, although we cannot guarantee to recognize all such mistakes or variations.)

It is very time-inefficient to engage in very small research tasks, because even the smallest search involves examining the book not only to find the surname but also to look for the list title or section heading which may be necessary in order to provide meaningful information; putting the information on the word processor; printing it; and mailing it. For this reason, the minimum charge is $10 for each request involving transcription only and $30 for transcription plus translation.

This minimum does not apply to searches involving only entries in the Kossmann book, since this lists only Polonized surnames, along with the original German version, and the book or other source from which this information was obtained. Only $5 will be charged for requests of up to 3 surnames.

Should anyone seek to determine only whether a particular first name is listed (e.g., whether there is a Wilhelm listed under the Spindeln surname), only $5 will be charged for a negative reply. However, in most cases, it would be unwise to make such a request, because nearly all of these Germans lived in Eastern Europe for at least two generations and some for more than two centuries, so it is very doubtful that the first name of the original migrant to Eastern Europe was the same as that of the immigrant to North America.

The places from which, and to which, Germans migrated, and

when they moved to Eastern Europe, are sometimes listed very specifically, sometimes only in terms of the principality (large or, more often, small) or settlement area involved, and sometimes no place of origin is given. Therefore, we may charge less than the specified minimum if only a very limited amount of information can be provided.

If you wish, you may request that only a particular book or two be checked where a surname appears in most of the books, as is likely to be the case with very common surnames. This would certainly be applicable if you have some idea as to the region in Eastern Europe from which your ancestors came.

You may also request that you be given an estimate if the cost exceeds some amount you specify. This will usually be applicable only if you want a number of surnames checked, if you are asking for information about a common surname like Schmidt (for which there may be dozens of entries), or if you are asking for information from such books as those by Leibbrandt and Unruh (where there may be a large number of entries for surnames which were common only among the respective groups of migrants). It is impractical to provide estimates for assignments that are likely to take no more than 2-3 hours. The fee for a lengthy or extensive search is $10 per hour for transcription and $20 per hour for translation. A fee of more than $50 will not be charged, unless you have been provided with an estimate or specifically pre-authorized a larger amount.

In the case of the Leibbrandt and Weiss books, where many of the surnames recur very frequently, we have simply listed the number of entries where there were 5 or more.

The co-compiler checked the frequency of surnames in several of the other books in order to:

(1) give you an idea as to which surnames were very common;
(2) give you an idea as to which transpositions of letters, and which spelling variations, occurred frequently in old records; and
(3) promote his own development as a genealogist.

The transposition of "c" for "z" in one case (Celler/Zeller) reflects a Latin influence. A "c" is never soft in words of German origin. Such names were, however, borrowed from the Latin; the "c" usually became a "z" in German spelling sooner or later.

The "cz" letter combination is invariably due to Slavic influence. Either the Germans lived in a Slavic area (e.g., Bohemia) or the recorder was Slavic.

The most common names in Wilhelm and Kallbrunner, the most voluminous book, are: Bauer/Pauer; Becker/Böcker/Pecker, etc.; Braun(n)/Praun; Diet(e)rich/Titrich, etc.; Fischer; Hof(f)man(n); Jung; Keller; Klein; Meyer/Maier/May(e)r, etc.; Miller/Müller; Schäf(f)er/Schaef(f)er; Schmid(t)/Smidt, etc.; Schneider; Wagner; Weber/Weeber; and Wol(l)f(f)/Volf. There are at least 10 entries for each of these names in the Schneider book also.

Other names for which there are more than 10 entries in Wilhelm and Kallbrunner, with "(S)" indicating that there are also more than 10 entries in Schneider, are: Ackermann (S); Adam; Albrecht; Andres(s) (S); Arnold; Bart(h); Bachmann/ Pachmann; Bastian; Bauman(n)/Pauman; Bayer; Be(c)k (S); Bender (S); Berg (S); Berger; Bergmann/Pergmann; Bern(h)ard(t); Betz/ Petz; Blum(m)/Plum; Böhm(e)(r) (S); Brand/Prand; Brun(n)er/

- xx -

Prunner; Burger/Purger; Burg(h)ard, Bur(c)k(h)ard(t), etc. (S); Carl(e)/Karl; Caspar/Kaspar; Celler/Zeller; Christ/Krist; Claus/ Klaus; Clement(s); Conrad/Konrad; Cramer/Kramer; Czi(e)gler/ Zi(e)gler; De(c)k(h)er; Diehl/Dill/Till, etc.; Deys/T(h)eis, etc.; Di(e)tz/Titz, etc.; Dreher/Treer, etc.; Dur(c)k/Tür(c)k; Eberhard; Ebner; Eder; Eng(e)l (S); E(h)rhard(t); Faber; Finck/ Fing; Fle(c)kenstein; Frank(h); Franz; Frey/Frei (S); Fri(e)d(e)rich/Fridrik; Fries/Frieß; Fritz (S); Fuchs (S); Gabriel; Geiger; Gerber; Gerhard(t) (S); Geyer/Gayer, etc.; Ginter/Gunt(h)er; Gö(t)z; Graf(f); Gremer/Kremer/Kre(h)m(m)er (S: Krämer), etc.; Groß; Gruber (S).
    Also: Haan/Hahn/Hann, etc. (S); Hass/Haaß (S); Ham(m)an(n); Hartman(n) (S); Haus(s)er (S); Hein/Hayn, etc.; He(i)nrich; Hein(t)z/Heincz; Hen(n); Her(r)man(n) (S); Herzog; Heß/Häß; Hirsch; Hi(e)rt(h)/Hürth; Hittmay(e)r/Hüttmayer; Hoch; Hol(t)z/ Holcz; Horn(n); Huber/Hueber (S); Hubert/Hupert; Hum(m)(e)l; Jacob; Jäger; Jost; Jun(c)ker/Jungker; Kaiser/Kayser, etc.; Kauf(f)man(n); Kern; Keßler; Ki(e)f(f)er, etc.; Koch (S); Kohl/ Koll; Kohler/Koller; Köhler/Köller; Kolb; König; Kop(p)/Koob; Kram(m)er; Kraus/Krauß (S); Krebs/Kreps; Kri(e)ger/Krüger; Ku(h)n; Kunz; Kur(t)z (S); Lambert; Lang (S); Lauer; Lehmann/ Leeman, etc.; Le(h)nhard(t)/Lehnhart; Lehr/Löhr; Leit(t)ner/ Leuthner; Lin(c)k; Loren(t)z/Lorencz (S); Ludwig; Lu(t)z/Lucz (S); Man(n) (S); Marschall; Martin (S); Marx (S); Mathes/Mattes, etc.; Maurer (S); May; Mer(t)z/Mercz; Metz; Me(t)zger/Meczker; Mich(e)l; Mohr (S); Moser;
    Furthermore: Nag(e)l; Neu/Ney; Oswald, etc.; Ott/Oth; Paul; Pauli; Peter; Petri/Petry (S); Pfeif(f)er/Pfeyffer (S); Philipp/ Phillip; Ployer; Reder/Röder; Reinhard(t)/Reinhart; Reis/Reiß, etc.; Reiter; Resch/Rösch; Reut(h)er/Reutter; Ries/Ri(e)ß; Ritter; Rohr; Roß (S); Roth (S); Rudolf (S); Rup(p)ert; Sauer (S); Schef(f)er; Scheid(t); Scherer; Schilling; Schil(t)z; Schisler/Schüßler, etc,; Schlosser; Schmi(t)z; Schram(m) (S); Schreiber; Schreier/Schreyer (S); Schreiner; Schröder/Schröter; Schu(h)macher, etc. (S); Schul(l)er; Sc(h)ulte; Schul(t)z/ Schulcz; Schuster (S); Schütz; Schwa(a)b, etc.; Schwarz; Schwei(t)zer (S); Seil(l)er; Seibert(h)/Seybert; Simon (S); Som(m)er; Staub; Stein; Steiner; Steinmetz; Stenger; Stephan/ Ste(p)fan; Straub; Stumpf; Thiel(l)/Thil(l); T(h)omas (S); Uhl/Ull (S); Ulrich; Veit(h); Vetter; Vog(e)l; Vogt; Walt(h)er (S); Weil(l)er; Weis/Weiß, etc. (S); Weisgärber/Weisgerber, etc.; Wel(c)ker; Wen(t)z(e)l/Venczl; Werner (S); Wild/Vild; Wil(l)helm/Vil(l)helm; Win(c)kler/Vingler; Wirth/Würth; Zimmer (S); and Zimmermann (S).
    The Schneider book, which has some data up to 1820, has more than 10 entries for the following names, which also appear in Wilhelm and Kallbrunner, but in lesser numbers: Buch, Butz, Fastnacht, Fröhlich, Ganz, Haber, Hell, Huth, Knecht, Laubenstein, Manz, Matern, Rech, Reichert, Rol(l)and, Rupp, Schick, Schott, Trautman, Wagemann, Wendel, and Windisch. This indicates that these families (and certainly some others) had increased in numbers in Galicia within the first 35 years.
    On the other hand, Schneider also has more than 10 entries for Bisanz and Christel, for which no recognizable equivalent could be found in Wilhelm and Kallbrunner. This means either that the surname was badly misspelled in the original archival records or that these families were among the few who migrated to Galicia after 1785.

The Unruh book contains only a few of the same names. Those listed more than 10 times include: A(h)rend(s)/Arent; Baerg/Berg/Burg; van/von Bergen; Barkmann/Bergmann; Braun/Bruhn; Cla(a)ssen/Kla(a)ssen; Die(c)k/Dick/Dueck/Dyck; Dirksen/Doerksen/Duercksen; Dried(i)ger/Druedger; En(n)s/En(t)z, etc.; Epp; Ewert; Fast; Friesen/von Riesen; Froese; Fun(c)k; Gisbrecht; Gehrts/Goertz; Gertsen/Goertzen; Go(o)ssen; Ginter/Guent(h)er; Hamm; Harder; Harms; Heud(e)brecht/Heydebrecht; Hi(e)bert/Hübert; Hil(de)brand(t); Isaak; Jantzen; K(a)ehler/K(a)ethler, etc.; Krahn; Kroe(c)ker; Lemke; Lepp/Loepp; Löven/Löwen; Ma(e)rtens, etc.; Neufeld(t); Neustae(d)ter, etc.; Nickel; Pauls; Penner; Peters; Preis(z)/Pries(s)/Preuss; Redekopp; Regehr/Regier, etc.; Reimer; Rempel; Sawatsky/Sawatzki; Siemens/Ziemens; Sudermann/Zuthermann; Schellenberg/Schöllenberg; Schmi(d)t/Schmitt/Schmied; Schröder/Schröter; Teichgräf(f)/Teichgräb/Teichgräw, etc.; T(h)iessen; Tilitzki/Tillieke, etc.; Toews; Unger; Vogt/Voth/Foth; Wall; War(c)kentin; Wieb(e); Wie(h)ler; Wiens(s); and Will(e)ms.

In contrast, the Müller book has more than 10 page references only to Lange, (von) Meyer, Müller, von Peters(s)en, S(ch)mi(d)t, (von) Schröder, Schul(t)ze, Schwar(t)z, and (von) Walt(h)er.

Some of the entries may provide considerable information about the family migrating to Eastern Europe (which may include, for example, the number of children, or even the children's names in Unruh and Leibbrandt; the father's occupation, and in the Unruh book sometimes a specific inventory of farm property; and/or the age(s) of the husband, couple, or entire family). If you desire to have these books checked for only certain information, with other information to be omitted from the transcription, you may specify this.

There is an order form on the next page which you may use or xerox. Please don't tear out the form if you are using a library copy of this book.

Bruce will handle transcription-only requests, in consultation with Ed regarding varying spellings where this seems necessary. Ed will provide the other services. For simplicity, please mail all requests to:

Edward R. Brandt
13 - 27th Ave. S.E.
Minneapolis, MN 55414-3101

ORDER FORM

(Please xerox the form if this book is not your own copy. It is
highly advisable to read the foregoing material before
requesting information. We cannot promise fast service.)

Name_____

Address_____

_____

I would like to have information on the following surnames
indexed in the 2nd edition of *Where to Look for Hard-to-Find
German-Speaking Ancestors in Eastern Europe*:

_____ _____ _____

_____ _____ _____

____ I would like to have all the books in which this surname
       (these surnames) appear(s) searched.

____ I would like to have all the pages in the following book(s)
       searched. (List abbreviations used in this book.)

_____ _____ _____ _____ _____ _____ _____ _____

____ I would like to have only the following pages of the books
       specified here searched.

         _____, pp. _____   _____, pp. _____   _____, pp. _____

I request

____ only a transcript of the pertinent entries (minimum fee
       $10); applies only to data in list form and English books

____ a transcript and a translation of the pertinent entries
       (minimum fee $30)

(While the simplicity/complexity of the different books varies
greatly, you can assume that the minimum fee will cover at least
10 entries in the indexed books, which does not mean 10 names;
there may be many entries for one name.) I request that I be
provided with an estimate if the cost will exceed $_____.

Use the reverse side or add an additional sheet for special
requests or comments (e.g., if the name you are researching
appears in the Leibbrandt book, you may wish to specify that
only entries in the genealogical tables be checked). Check here
if reverse side is used_____

Mail to: Edward R. Brandt
         13 - 27th Ave. S.E.
         Minneapolis, MN 55414-3101
         U.S.A.

The symbols, in alphabetical order, refer to surnames found in the following books (see historical section for full citation):

BU   Benjamin Heinrich Unruh, *Die niederländisch-niederdeutschen Hintergründe der mennonitischen Ostwanderungen im 16., 18. und 19. Jahrhundert* [The Dutch-Lower German Background of the Mennonite Eastward Migrations in the 16th, 18th, and 19th Centuries]

GF   Gustav Adolf Famler, *Torzsa und Seine Ansiedlung* [Torzsa and Its Settlement (by Germans)]

GL   Georg Leibbrandt, Hansgeorg Leibbrandt and Otto G. Siegle, *Hoffnungstal und Seine Schwaben* [Hoffnungstal and Its Swabians]

GS   Gustav Schedler, *Eben-Ezer: Eine Jahrhundertgeschichte der evangel. St. Trinitatisgemeinde zu Lodz* [Ebenezer: A Centennial History of the Evangelical (Lutheran) St. Trinity Congregation at Lodz]

HS   Hans Schmidt, *Die Geschichte des Deutschtums in Szamocin (Samotschin) und Umgebung* [The History of Germans in Szamocin (Samotschin) and the Surrounding Area]

HW   Herbert Weiss, *Colony Teplitz*

IE   Irmgard Hein Ellingson, *The Bukovina Germans in Kansas: A 200 Year History of Lutheran Swabians*

K1   Dr. Oskar Kossmann, *Die Deutschen in Polen seit der Reformation: Historisch-Geographische Skizzen* [The Germans in Poland Since the Reformation: Historic-Geographical Sketches]

KL   Kurt Lück, *Die Geschichte des Deutschtums in Chodzież (Kolmar) und Umgebung* [The History of Germans in Chodzież (Kolmar) and the Surrounding Area]

LS   Ludwig Schneider, *Das Kolonisationswerk Josefs II. in Galizien* [The Settlement Activities of (Austrian Emperor) Joseph II in Galicia]

MM   Martha Müller, *Mecklenburger in Osteuropa* [Mecklenburgers in Eastern Europe]

SW   Dr. Sophie Welisch, *Bukovina Villages/Towns/Cities and Their Germans*

WK   Dr. Franz Wilhelm and Dr. Josef Kallbrunner, *Quellen zur deutschen Siedlungsgeschichte in Südosteuropa* [Sources Regarding the History of German Settlement in Southeastern Europe]

W#   Unindexed portion of Wilhelm and Kallbrunner book

The symbols represent the initials of the chief author,
except that K1 has been used for Dr. Kossmann because he has
published many books and we considered the possibility that we
might want to index some of the others at some time, and WK
represents the initials of the surnames of both co-authors.

The Unruh (BU), Schneider (LS), Wilhelm and Kallbrunner (WK),
and Müller (MM) books have indexes, so the pages on which the
name occurs are not given. But we discovered that Wilhelm &
Kallbrunner's index does not cover the first eight pages.
Therefore, the abbreviation W# is used to denote the entries on
these pages, followed by the page, a dot, and the line. Thus
W#(7.21) means that the name occurs on line 21 of page 7. The
line is given only for the Wilhelm and Kallbrunner book, because
it is indexed that way.

The letters A and B have been used to denote the column where
the authors have listed the names in double columns.

ALPHABETICAL INDEX

OF SURNAMES

Altmajer,WK
Altmann,LS,MM,
  SW(24),W#(8.91),
  WK
Altmayer,WK
Altmeyer,WK
Altmüller,WK
Altner,WK
Altschinger,WK
Altschwager,MM
Altstädter,WK
Altstätter,WK
Alunse,MM
Alvenz,WK
Alwerdt,MM
Alznauer,SW(21)
Aman,WK
Amandus,WK
Amann,WK
Amannin,WK
Ambach,WK
Amberg,WK
Ambert,WK
Amblacherin,WK
Amboster,LS
Ambros,MM
Ambrosi,LS
Ambrosius,LS,WK
Ambrüster,SW(19)
Ambs,WK
Ambsin,WK
Ambstetter,WK
Amburger,MM
Amelung,MM
Amend,WK
Ament,WK
Amering,WK
Ameringerin,WK
Ammann,WK
Ammer,GL(212)
Ammon,HW(31,89)
Amnitschin,WK
Amon,WK
Amorbacher,WK
Amos,LS,WK
Amrein,WK
Amrhein,LS,WK
Amsmann,WK
Amstadt,WK
Amstätter,LS
Anacher,GL(371)
Ancelle,WK
Anden,WK
Anders,K1(165A),LS,
  MM,WK
Anderson,MM
Anderst,HW(31,42,90)
Anderthamerin,WK

Anderzamin,WK
Andes,LS
Andeß,LS
Andhall,WK
Andler,LS,WK
Andorfer,WK
Andrä,WK
Andracsek,WK
Andre,WK
Andreae,MM
Andreas,BU,LS
Andree,WK
Andrekovics,WK
Andres,BU,GF(92A),
  LS,MM,SW(2),WK
Andresen,MM
Andreß,WK
Andrioll,WK
Androski,LS
Andrzej,K1(165A)
Andzeikovics,WK
Anebring,WK
Anen,WK
von Anen,MM
Angel,LS,WK
de Angelroth,WK
Anger,WK
Angerbauer,WK
Angerman,WK
Angermanin,WK
Angermann,LS,MM,WK
Angerstein,MM
Angl,WK
Angner,WK
Angroß,WK
Angst,WK
Anheiser,WK
Ankenmann,MM
Anker,LS,WK
Ankerstein,MM
Anmes,WK
Annau,W#(2.5)
Annen,LS,WK
Annit,WK
Anofrienko,GL(453)
Anreid,WK
Anreims,WK
Anschuberin,WK
Ansel,WK
Anselm,WK
Anselmo,WK
Anstoß,WK
Anteis,WK
Antes,LS
Anthes,WK
Antler,WK
Antoine,WK
Antoinell,WK

Anton,GL(409),LS,WK
d'Antonel,WK
Antoni,LS,WK
Antonie,WK
Antoniewicz,K1(165A)
Antony,LS,WK
Antres,WK
Antriota,WK
Antus,WK
Anweiler,GF(93B),LS,
  WK
Anzeiger,WK
Apell,WK
Apelt,GS(18)
Apfel,LS
Apol,WK
Appel,GF(93A),LS,WK
Appelmann,LS
Appenheimer,LS,WK
Appersheimer,LS
Appert,WK
Appler,WK
Aprel,WK
Aramund,WK
Arbokasch,WK
Arby,WK
Archi,WK
Arend,BU,IE(89),LS,
  SW(31),WK
Arends,BU,MM,WK
Arendsee,HS(26)
Arens,MM,WK
von Arensköld,MM
Arent,BU,KL(14),LS,
  WK
Areus,WK
Arger,WK
Arlen,WK
Armbriester,IE(95)
Armbrister,WK
Armbruger,WK
Armbrust,WK
Armbruster,LS,WK
Armbrüster,IE(93,96,
  97),LS,WK
Armburst,HW(15)
Armbuster,LS
Armengast,WK
Armknecht,LS
Arnal,W#(1.71)
Arnald,WK
Arnbrust,WK
Arnd,MM
Arndt,HS(38,44,65,
  75),KL(14,54),MM
Arnecker,WK
Arned,WK
Arnet,WK

Bahnmüller,GL(188,
   315,406),HW(19
   entries)
Bahr,MM
Bähr,SW(16),W#(3.6,
   3.13,7.45),WK
von Bähr,MM
Bahrdt,MM
Bährl,GL(382)
Bährmann,WK
Baier,WK
Baierle,WK
Baijer,LS
Bailke,WK
Bailler,WK
Bailleux,MM
Baisch,LS,WK
Baiser,GL(212)
Baitinger,GL(409)
Baitner,LS
Baitz,WK
Bajar,WK
Bajer,LS
Bak,WK
Bakas,WK
Bäker,WK
Bakes,WK
Bakin,GL(285)
Baky,WK
Balan,WK
Balauf,WK
Balbach,WK
Balbier,LS
Balbierer,LS
Balck,MM
Baldauf,WK
Baldauffin,WK
Balder,MM
Baldera,WK
Balderes,WK
Baldes,WK
Baldreich,GL(416)
Baleß,LS
Balg,WK
Balinger,LS,WK
Baljard,GL(108)
Ball,GF(91B),WK
Ballausch,WK
Balle,WK
Ballenbach,WK
Balles,GL(411)
Balling,WK
Ballivi,MM
Balm,WK
Balma,WK
Balmann,BU,WK
Balmer,HW(33
   entries)

Balser,WK
Balt,BU,WK
Baltauf,WK
Baltes,WK
Balthasar,WK
Baltisberger,GL(276)
Baltz,WK
Baltzer,LS
Baltzert,LS
Balwir,LS
Balwirer,WK
Balzer,BU,WK
Balzert,LS,WK
Balzk,GL(351)
Bälzner,HW(12)
Bambach,WK
Bamberger,LS
Bambole,WK
Bamburg,WK
Bamesberger,GL(75
   entries)
Bämler,WK
Banabel,WK
Banbehön,WK
Banck,WK
Bandel,GL(511)
Bändel,WK
Bandelau,GS(22)
Bandenburg,WK
Bander,LS,WK
Bando,GS(12,14)
Baneker,WK
Baner,GL(317),WK
Bangert,WK
Baniset,WK
Bank,LS,WK
Banmann,BU
Banmüller,GL(68)
Bannert,LS,WK
Bannier,MM
Bannmann,BU
Banno,WK
Banó,WK
Bantgartner,WK
Bantle,WK
Bantleon,WK
Banzlof,WK
Bapp,WK
Baptiste,WK
Bär,WK
von Baranoff,MM
Barantin,WK
Barba,LS,WK
Barbasan,WK
Barbet,GL(340),LS
Barbich,LS
Barbie,WK
Barbier,WK

Barbierer,WK
Bärbierer,WK
Barbig,WK
Barbisch,WK
Barchewitz,MM
Barck,BU
Barckmann,BU
Barclay de Tolly,MM
Barcnerl,MM
Bardell,WK
Bardemann,MM
Barden,BU
Bardo,WK
Bardonok,WK
Bardosch,LS
Bardua,LS
Bareiter,GL(287)
Bareither,GL(480)
Barell,WK
Bärenfeldt,MM
Bäreng,WK
Bareuther,GL(231,
   254)
Barfuß,WK
Barg,BU
Bargehen,BU
Bargen,BU
von Bargen,BU
Barget,WK
Barginion,WK
Bargoschno,WK
Bargs,BU
Barier,LS,WK
Barisio,WK
Bark,BU
Barker,LS
Barkhausen,MM
Barkholz,MM
Barkmann,BU
Barkuß,WK
Barlacher,LS
Barleon,WK
Barmathe,WK
Barn,BU
Barnehl,MM
Baro,WK
Baroisse,WK
Baroky,WK
Barold,MM
Baron,LS,WK
Barondour,WK
Baroth,MM
Bärr,WK
Bars,MM
Barsau,MM
Barsch,WK
Barschel,WK
Bart,K1(167B),LS,WK

Bechthold,GF(104A, 127A)
Bechtlof,LS
Bechtloff,LS
Bechtold,GF(93B, 129A),GS(89B, 90A),LS,WK
Beck,GF(91A,125A, 129A,129B),GL(24 entries),HW(14), LS,W#(2.27),WK
Beckbißinger,GL(296)
Beckel,WK
Becken,WK
Beckenbach,LS
Becker,GF(92A,96B, 112,118,129B), GL(16 entries), HS(65),LS,MM,WK
Beckerin,WK
Beckers,WK
Beckersch,WK
Beckert,WK
Beckes,LS
Beckher,WK
Beckier,WK
Beckmann,GF(93A),MM, WK
Beckoll,WK
Beczkowski,K1(165A)
Bedel,WK
Bedenbach,WK
Bedler,WK
Bednarczyk,K1(165A)
Bedy,WK
Beeck,WK
Beek,WK
Beer,LS,SW(29),WK
Began,WK
Bege,WK
Beh,GL(371)
Beham,WK
Behe,WK
Behl,WK
Behm,GS(60),LS,WK
Behmer,IE(88),LS
Behncke,MM
Behnke,GL(372),MM
Behr,HS(44),MM,WK
Behrens,MM
Behring,MM
Beicht,WK
Beichtloff,WK
Beide,GL(40)
Beidel,GL(488)
Beidl,LS,WK
Beidlmann,WK

Beier,GL(356),LS,MM, WK
Beiffer,WK
Beigli,WK
Beijer,LS
Beil,LS,WK
Beill,LS,WK
Beillmann,WK
Beilstein,WK
Beis,LS
Beisch,LS
Beischel,WK
Beischer,LS
Beiser,WK
Beissart,K1(166A)
Beitel,LS
Beitl,LS,SW(16), W#(6.78),WK
Beitlhauser,WK
Beitz,WK
Bek,LS,WK
Bekelehner,WK
Bekenbach,WK
Bekenbronk,WK
Beker,LS,WK
Beketova,MM
Bekl,WK
Belbo,WK
Beldie,WK
Beldighofer,WK
Belesas,WK
Belgium,WK
Belindier,GL(450)
Belion,WK
Beljaeva,MM
Bell,WK
Beller,GL(439),WK
Belley,WK
Belohorßky,GF(119A)
Below,MM
Belser,LS,WK
Belß,WK
Belstler,WK
Beltier,WK
Belusch,GL(396)
Belwion,WK
Belz,GL(184,326, 464),LS
Belzer,LS
Bemble,WK
Bemens,WK
Bemler,LS
Benaudin,WK
Bench,BU
Bencken,MM
Bendel,WK

Bender,GL(234,407), HW(7 entries),LS, WK
Benderin,WK
Benderot,WK
Bendling,WK
Bendre,WK
Benedik,MM
Benedikt,WK
Benek,LS
Beneke,MM
Bener,LS
Benera,WK
Beng,WK
Bengel,WK
Benger,LS
Bengler,WK
Benicke,KL(20)
Benicken,MM
Benike,KL(47,49)
Benjamen,WK
Benjawitz,WK
Benke,GL(372), GS(19),MM
Benker,WK
Benn,LS,WK
Benner,LS,WK
Benni,GS(26),WK
Benninger,W#(7.89)
Benoit,WK
Benrad,WK
Benrod,LS
Bens,LS
Bensel,KL(44,51)
Bensinger,HW(27,82)
Bensler,WK
Bentz,GL(225),LS, W#(4.33,5.67),WK
Bentzin,WK
Bentzinger,W#(5.62)
Benz,GL(437),HW(8 entries),LS,WK
Benzbey,LS
Benzel,LS
Benzenhöfer,GL(257)
Benzing,WK
Benzinger,HW(6 entries)
Beppel,WK
Bequet,WK
Ber,WK
Berang,WK
Berauer,WK
Berbaum,MM
Berberich,WK
Berbrich,WK
Berbrig,WK
Berch,WK

Bezille,GS(55)
Bezner,WK
Bezylle,GS(18)
Biar,WK
Biba,LS
Bibel,LS,WK
Bibell,WK
Biber,WK
Biberher,WK
Bibert,WK
Bibow,MM
Bichler,WK
Bichlerin,WK
Bickel,LS,W#(5.20)
Bickerich,LS
Bickert,BU
Bickle,WK
Bickler,WK
Bicklin,WK
Bickmann,GL(256)
Bickrel,WK
Bickring,LS,WK
Bidder,MM
Bidel,WK
Bider,WK
Bidermann,WK
Bidthart,WK
Bieber,GF(91B,104B),
  GL(7 entries),LS
Biederböck,WK
Biedermann,GL(40),
  GS(89A,90B)
Biederstadt,GL(285)
Biederstädt,GL(285),
  MM
Biedlingmaier,GL(5
  entries)
Bieger,WK
Biegler,GL(400)
Biel,MM,WK
Bieler,GL(461),LS,WK
Bienert,BU,MM
Bier,WK
Bierbrauer,WK
Bierbreyer,WK
Bierbrunner,GF(122B)
Bierenbaum,WK
Bierfit,WK
Biermann,GF(91B,
  129B),WK
Biermayer,WK
Biernbaum,WK
Bierson,WK
Biersteet,MM
Bieschwang,MM
Bieser,MM
Biesinger,WK

Bietsch,GL(6
  entries)
Biffert,GL(507)
Bifili,W#(5.50)
Bigalke,KL(18)
Bigau,WK
Bigenhoch,WK
Bigler,WK
Bihen,WK
Bihlmaier,GL(509)
Bihlmayer,GL(442)
Bihlmeyer,GL(246)
Bihn,LS,WK
Bihner,WK
Bikar,WK
Bikel,LS
Bikert,BU
Bilar,WK
Bilawski,SW(12)
Bilchen,WK
Bilcher,LS
Bild,WK
Bildhauer,WK
Bili,WK
Biliński,LS
Bilion,WK
Bilke,GS(14)
Bilkenroth,MM
Bill,LS,WK
Billete,WK
Billger,WK
Billharz,WK
Billi,WK
Billich,WK
Billiger,WK
Billing,WK
Billmann,WK
Billmayer,WK
Billon,WK
Billy,WK
Bilo,WK
Bilpert,WK
Binck,WK
Binckel,WK
Binder,GF(129B,
  130A),GL(7
  entries),HW(66,
  82,89,90),LS,
  SW(38),WK
Bindewald,GL(451,
  457,492,509)
Bindmann,WK
Bindner,WK
Biney,WK
Bing,MM
Bingel,WK
Bingener,WK
Bingenheimer,WK

Binger,MM,WK
Bingert,WK
Binges,LS
Bingis,LS
Bingulis,LS,WK
Bingwa,WK
Binkh,WK
Binn,WK
Binnbach,WK
Binno,WK
Binz,GL(326)
Binzi,WK
Biot,WK
Biou,WK
Bir,WK
Birchemayer,WK
Bircke,WK
Birckenfeld,WK
Birckmayer,WK
Birdhof,WK
Birerl,WK
Birgel,WK
Birger,WK
Birgham,LS
Birhand,LS
Birin,WK
Birk,GL(239)
Birkel,WK
Birkene,WK
Birkenmayer,WK
Birkenstädt,MM
Birkholz,HS(26,38),
  K1(165A)
Birkle,GL(13
  entries)
Birkmayer,LS,WK
Birky,WK
Birl,LS
Birli,W#(5.77)
Birling,WK
Birman,GF(125A)
Birmann,GF(104A,
  104B)
Birn,LS
Birnbach,LS,WK
Birner,WK
Birnstil,WK
Birobri,WK
Biron,WK
von Biron,MM
Birr,WK
Birsch,LS
Birschen,WK
Bisang,LS,WK
Bisanz,LS
Bisay,LS
Bisch,LS,WK
Bischau,WK

Bode,WK
Bodenstein,WK
Bodesheim,WK
Bodin,WK
Bodmann,WK
Bodmischel,W#(8.51)
Bodnaruk,SW(15)
Bodner,WK
Bodsohn,WK
Boeck,LS,WK
Boeckel,MM
Boehm,LS
Boekerle,WK
Boelter,HS(26)
Boemler,WK
Boepple,GL(26)
Boerhave,MM
Boerner,GS(22)
Boerst,MM
Boeteführ,MM
Boettcher,GS(89B)
Bogatka,LS
Bogdański,K1(165A)
Boge,WK
Bogenritter,LS,WK
Bogenschütz,WK
Bögle,WK
Bognar,WK
Bogner,HW(208),WK
Bogomir,WK
Bohacs,W#(7.102)
Bohl,LS
Bohlander,WK
Bohlen,WK
Bohlenbach,LS
Bohler,WK
Böhler,LS,WK
Bohlin,W#(4.91)
Bohlleber,WK
Bohm,MM
Böhm,KL(37),LS,MM,WK
Böhme,WK
Bohmer,LS
Böhmer,IE(88),SW(4,
14),WK
Bohn,HS(75),MM,WK
Böhn,MM
Bohne,K1(165A),MM
Bohnenberger,WK
Böhner,WK
Bohnet,HW(207)
Bohnhof,MM
Bohni,WK
Bohnsack,MM
Bohr,LS,WK
Bohrer,K1(167B),WK
Bohrn,WK
Boht,MM

Bohusiewicz,SW(36)
Boiger,WK
Boiguin,WK
Boilo,WK
Boisch,WK
Boisseau,WK
Bojacsek,WK
Bojar,WK
Bok,W#(7.73),WK
Bök,LS
Bökkel,MM
Bokryß,WK
Bolander,WK
Bolch,WK
Boldt,BU,MM
Bolembach,LS
Bolenbach,LS
Bolender,WK
Bolich,MM
Bolick,MM
Bolio,WK
Boll,GL(334,337,
508),WK
Bolle,GL(493)
Bolleck,WK
Bollee,BU
Bollena,WK
Bollenbach,LS
Boller,SW(16)
Bollig,WK
Bollinger,GL(22
entries)
Bollingerin,WK
Bollinnerin,WK
Bollmann,WK
Bolmar,MM
Bolt,BU,LS
Bolte,MM
Boltz,MM,WK
Bolz,GF(91A)
Boma,WK
Bombach,LS
Bomersbach,WK
Bomesberger,GL(195)
Bomgort,K1(165A)
Bommersbach,LS,WK
Bommo,WK
Bon,WK
Bonacker,WK
Boncin,WK
Böncken,MM
Bonekemper,GL(117,
118)
Bonert,WK
Bonerth,LS
Bongard,WK
Bonge,MM
Bongelin,WK

Bongraz,WK
Bonichot,WK
Bonifer,WK
Bonik,GS(14)
Bonjongin,WK
Bonkel,WK
Bonkowski,K1(165A)
Bonn,WK
Bonnat,WK
Bonne,WK
Bonnelis,BU
Bonnellis,BU
Bonner,WK
Bonnertin,WK
Bonno,WK
Bonny,WK
Bono,GL(351,501)
Bonowicz,K1(165A)
Bonquaet,WK
Bonse,LS
Bonsler,WK
Bonstädt,MM
Bontemps,MM
Bonum,W#(2.69)
Bony,LS,WK
Boo,WK
Boon,WK
Boos,LS,WK
Boosin,WK
Booß,LS,WK
Böpple,HW(17
entries)
Bor,WK
Borat,WK
Borbonn,WK
Borchard,MM
Borchert,MM
Borchmann,MM
Borck,WK
Bord,WK
Borde,K1(165A)
Borden,WK
Bordind,MM
Bording,MM
Bordo,K1(165A)
Borg,WK
Borger,IE(88),LS,WK
Börger,WK
Borgert,LS
Borgmann,MM
Borgwardt,MM
Borgwedel,MM
Borie,WK
Boringer,WK
Borkowski,K1(165A)
Borkowsky,WK
Borkwitz,MM
Borm,BU

Borma,K1(165A)
Bormann,MM
Bormet,WK
Bormücher,MM
Born,BU,GL(196),
    K1(165A),LS,WK
Borna,WK
Borne,WK
Borner,WK
Börner,MM
Bornheimer,LS,WK
Bornikel,WK
Bornn,BU
Borowski,K1(165A)
Borr,GF(91A)
Börs,WK
Borsch,LS
Börsch,WK
Borschmann,BU
Börsing,WK
Börsler,LS
Borstler,LS
Borstling,LS
Bort,WK
Borten,WK
Borth,KL(38),LS
Bortner,GL(507)
Borty,WK
Bortz,WK
Boryta,MM
Borz,WK
Borzel,GL(223)
Bös,LS
Bösbier,LS
Bosch,WK
Bösch,WK
Boschee,GL(189)
Boschmann,BU
Boshe,GL(189)
Bösherz,GL(477)
Bösler,LS
Bosnik,WK
Bosowicki,IE(98)
Boß,WK
Böß,WK
Bossard,WK
Bößbier,WK
Bossert,GL(390,504),
    HW(207)
Bößle,WK
Boßler,W#(4.112)
Boßmann,WK
Bößmayer,WK
Bost,LS,WK
Bosten,MM
Bostyan,WK
Bötefeur,MM
Both,WK

Bothe,WK
Bothländer,WK
Bothmann,WK
Botke,HS(65)
Bott,LS
Böttcher,LS,MM
Bottelberger,LS,WK
Böttger,MM
Bottiel,WK
Bottiger,MM
Böttiger,GL(50)
Bötz,WK
Botzem,WK
Botzum,WK
Boudain,WK
Boudinet,WK
Bouillon,MM
Bouket,WK
Boulangeot,WK
Boulanger,WK
Bounert,WK
Bouquet,WK
Bour,WK
Bouren,WK
Bourg,WK
Bourgignion,WK
Bourgignon,WK
Bourgois,WK
Bourguignon,WK
Bourlo,WK
Bournotte,WK
Bourschun,WK
Boußle,WK
Boustedt,MM
Boutaile,WK
Boutor,WK
Bowman,GL(337)
Bowmann,BU
Boyen,WK
Boysa,WK
Braam,WK
Braatz,HS(75)
Brach,WK
Brachel,WK
Brack,WK
Brad,WK
Bradner,WK
Bradt,MM
Braetigam,MM
Brägel,WK
Brahmer,GL(498)
Brahn,BU
Braht,MM
Brain,W#(5.120),WK
Braitsch,WK
Braitviser,WK
Braknik,LS

Bram,WK
Bramburg,MM
Bramer,WK
Brand,LS,WK
Brandauer,LS
Brandbeck,WK
Brandel,LS,WK
Brandenburg,MM,WK
Brandenburger,MM
Brandenburgerin,WK
Brandl,SW(7,17),WK
Brandmann,WK
Brandmayer,WK
Brandmeyer,WK
Brandner,GL(399,400,
    506),WK
Brandscheid,WK
Brandstätter,WK
Brandstetter,WK
Brandt,BU,LS,MM,WK
Brankert,WK
Branner,WK
Brant,WK
Brasch,MM
Bräsch,WK
Braschill,LS
Braster,WK
Bratschi,W#(5.21)
Brattenberger,
    W#(6.24)
Bratviser,WK
Brau,WK
Brauberger,LS
Brauch,LS,WK
Brauchler,WK
Bräuel,BU
Brauer,HW(53),LS,MM
Braumetzer,WK
Braun,BU,GL(425,
    447),LS,MM,SW(17,
    53),WK
Braunberger,LS,WK
Braunecker,WK
Braunen,BU
Bräuner,WK
Braunersdorfer,WK
Braunewiser,WK
Bräunle,GL(408)
Braunn,WK
Braunschneider,WK
Braunschweig,MM
Braunschweiger,LS
Braunstan,WK
Brauntz,WK
Brausch,GF(92A,95B,
    130A)
Brause,HS(33),LS,WK
Braütling,HW(25)

Buges,HS(49)
Bügler,WK
Buhl,WK
Buhler,BU
Bühler,GL(474),LS,
   MM,WK
Bühlerin,WK
Bühn,WK
Buhr,BU,MM,WK
Buhrlen,WK
Buhse,MM
Bukowsky,GL(339,500)
Bulaier,WK
Bulange,WK
Bulay,WK
Bule,WK
Buleng,WK
Buler,LS
Bull,MM
Buller,BU,WK
Bullmann,LS
Bullus,WK
Bully,WK
Bulmann,LS,WK
Bulmer,HW(20),WK
von Bülow,MM
Bulz,WK
Bumbauer,WK
Bumer,LS
Bümler,LS
Bunde,WK
Bünder,LS,WK
Bundereck,WK
Bunding,GL(306),WK
Bundschuch,WK
Bundschuh,WK
Bungart,WK
Bunge,IE(99),MM
Bungert,WK
Bungerth,WK
Bungor,WK
Bunkert,SW(29)
Bünsow,MM
Buntschuch,WK
Bur,WK
Bürall,WK
Burbach,WK
Burchard,MM,WK
Burchardi,MM
Burchardius,MM
Burchardus,MM
Burcher,WK
Bürchy,WK
Burck,WK
Burckhard,WK
Bürckle,WK
Buresch,LS,W#(8.46)

Burg,BU,GF(91A),
   W#(1.20),WK
Bürg,WK
Burgard,WK
Burger,GF(93B,130A),
   LS,W#(5.59,5.90),
   WK
Bürger,MM,WK
Burgermeyer,LS
Burget,WK
Burgh,WK
Burghard,IE(89),LS,
   WK
Burghardt,LS,WK
Burghart,WK
Burgino,WK
Burgstaller,WK
Burgstallerin,WK
Burgund,WK
Burian,WK
Burik,WK
Burin,WK
Bürin,WK
Burk,HW(29)
Burkard,GL(336),WK
Burkart,WK
Bürkenring,WK
Bürker,WK
Burkhard,WK
Bürkhard,W#(7.101)
Burkhardin,W#(6.89)
Burkhardt,GL(417),
   HW(12,27),LS
Burkhart,WK
Burkheim,WK
Bürkle,GL(16
   entries)
Burlenbach,WK
Bürlin,WK
Burmann,GF(130A)
Burmeister,MM
Burner,WK
Burnoy,WK
Burns,GL(403)
Burr,GL(193),WK
Bürsch,WK
Bursche,GS(26,89A)
Burschet,WK
Burssin,WK
Burth,WK
Bury,WK
Burz,WK
Burzynski,HS(26)
Busch,GL(337),LS,MM,
   WK
Buschbach,WK
Buschbaum,WK
Busche,WK

Buscher,WK
Buschhauer,WK
Büsching,MM
Buschke,HS(26)
Büschke,K1(165B)
Buschmann,BU,GS(89A)
Buse,GS(89A),
   K1(165A),MM
Busek,SW(17)
Busen,WK
Buser,WK
Businger,WK
Buskupski,SW(15)
Busse,HS(24,25,26,
   33,65),HW(67),
   KL(49),MM
Buße,GF(122A)
Bußler,KL(18,21)
Bust,WK
Butländer,WK
Butsch,GL(409)
Butschek,LS
Butscher,WK
Butschke,BU
Butt,GL(409)
Buttel,WK
Büttel,LS
Butterfaß,WK
Buttion,WK
Buttländer,LS
Buttmann,GL(225)
Büttmann,WK
Büttner,WK
Buttstaedt,MM
Butz,GL(409),LS,WK
Bützow,MM
Buuck,MM
Buvange,WK
Büx,WK
von Buxhoevden,MM
Buz,GL(184)
Buza,K1(165A)
Buzik,SW(38)
Bych,K1(165A)
Byry,WK
Byśka,K1(165B)
Cadarius,WK
Caden,MM
Cadra,WK
Cahoon,IE(98)
Caillerin,WK
Calen,MM
Calvilius,WK
Cambe,WK
Camer,WK
Cameraria,MM
Cammer,WK
Canaper,WK

Candiol,WK
Canduel,WK
Cant,HS(24)
Canto,WK
Cantzler,MM
Cap,WK
Capel,WK
Capgen,WK
Capler,WK
Capobus,MM
Caps,WK
Caquis,WK
Carbach,WK
Carie,WK
Carillon,WK
Carl,WK
Carle,WK
Carli,W#(4.96),WK
Carlicz,WK
Carlitz,WK
Carnatz,MM
Carner,WK
Carpentier,WK
Carré,WK
Casdorf,BU
Case,GL(337)
Casidaenius,WK
Casimir,WK
Caspar,WK
Caspari,WK
Casparin,WK
Caspars,WK
Casper,BU,MM,WK
Caßner,WK
Casta,WK
Castar,WK
Castill,WK
Catharina,WK
Catis,WK
Cauenhowen,BU
Caufmon,WK
Cawossels,WK
Ceiter,LS
Celler,WK
Cender,K1(165B)
Cepper,WK
Cerbes,WK
Cerda,WK
Cerkasova,MM
Cervas,LS,WK
Cerveau,WK
Cesar,WK
Chaly,WK
Chambre,WK
Champenois,WK
Champier,WK
Chapie,WK
Chapuis,WK

Chardin,WK
Charie,WK
Charpentie,WK
Charpentier,WK
Chatne,WK
Cheh,WK
Chelius,LS,WK
Chene,WK
Chermont,WK
Chevalier,WK
Chlumecsky,WK
Chmel,LS
Chmielewski,K1(165B)
de Cholett,MM
Cholewicz,K1(165B)
Cholodetzkij,GL(134)
Chonter,WK
Chorowicz,LS
Chre,WK
Chreber,WK
Chreider,WK
Chretien,WK
Christ,GF(91B),LS,
  MM,WK
Christa,W#(6.74)
Christanner,WK
Christel,LS
Christen,WK
Christens,MM
Christian,GL(204),
  LS,WK
Christman,GF(95A),
  HW(227)
Christmann,GF(93A,
  95A),GL(322),LS,
  WK
Christner,HW(5
  entries)
Christoph,WK
Christophin,WK
Christophori,SW(27)
Chulas,WK
Chun,WK
Chustow,HS(35)
Chyträus,MM
Ciba,WK
Ciciet,HS(45)
Cicius,LS
Ciemny,K1(165B)
Cifrit,WK
Cilian,WK
Cinna,LS
Cirgoviz,WK
Ciriak,WK
Citius,WK
Claassen,BU
Claaßen,MM
Claire,WK

von Clapier,MM
Clar,WK
Claren,WK
Clasquin,WK
Classen,BU
Claudon,WK
Claus,WK
von Clausenstein,MM
Clauser,MM
Clauß,WK
Cleder,WK
Cleemann,MM
Clehr,WK
Clement,WK
Clements,WK
Clemmer,WK
Clemon,WK
Clen,WK
Cler,WK
Clir,WK
Clocovius,MM
von Clodt,MM
Cloo,WK
Clos,WK
Cloy,WK
Cnuppert,MM
Cobez,WK
Cocher,LS
Colberg,MM
Coler,MM
Coleri,MM
Colerius,MM
Colerus,MM
Colin,WK
Collard,LS,WK
Collel,WK
Colleng,WK
Collet,WK
Collignon,WK
Collin,WK
Colling,WK
Collins,MM
Collintz,WK
Collmann,WK
Colmann,LS
v. Colmar,KL(42)
Cologne,LS
de Colongue,MM
Colson,WK
Comenda,WK
Comte,WK
Concet,WK
Conczentius,WK
Conrad,BU,GL(12
  entries),LS,WK
Conraden,GL(154)
Conradi,MM,WK

Conradt,GL(64,157, 158),LS
Conradtin,GL(157, 158)
Conrardi,WK
Conrod,WK
Consele,WK
Contton,WK
Contz,WK
Coons,GL(495)
Cooper,GL(388,504)
Cordell,IE(98)
Cordes,MM
Cordie,WK
Cordier,WK
Cordt,MM
Corell,WK
Coret,WK
Corineth,WK
Corneli,WK
Cornelius,BU,LS,MM, WK
Cornelsen,BU
Corneltzen,BU
Cornet,WK
Cortaing,WK
Corte,WK
Cortero,WK
Cory,WK
Cosar,WK
Coschert,WK
Cosman,WK
von Cossel,MM
Coster von Rosenburg,MM
Cottingham,GL(337)
Courar,WK
Cozel,WK
Craim,WK
Crainer,WK
Cramer,WK
Crammer,WK
Cranz,WK
Crausin,WK
Crecherle,WK
Creder,WK
Creitz,WK
Cremon,WK
Crep,WK
Creper,WK
Cretien,WK
Creutz,LS,MM,WK
von Creutz,MM
Creutzer,WK
Creutzwatis,LS
Creuz,GL(267)
Cristics,WK
Cristmann,GF(95A)

von Crivitz,MM
Croellen,WK
Croix,WK
Crokisius,MM
Cron,WK
Cronau,WK
Cronbauer,WK
Croneberger,WK
Cronenberg,WK
Cronin,WK
Crosdemange,WK
Croy,LS,WK
Cruchten,WK
Crutschnig,WK
Csara,W#(8.47,8.48)
Cseh,WK
Cselikovics,WK
Cser,WK
Cserin,WK
Csermak,WK
Csernik,WK
Csias,WK
Csinak,WK
Csirak,WK
Cuba,WK
Cubelmann,WK
Cubuk,LS
Cullmann,WK
Cuman,WK
Cun,WK
Cunet,WK
Cuprian,WK
Cur,WK
Curdes,WK
Curios,WK
Curschmann,MM
Curwud,LS
Cusin,WK
Cussy,WK
Cybart,K1(165B)
Cygański,K1(165B)
Cyla,K1(165B)
Cylm,K1(165B)
Cymer,K1(165B)
Czarkowski,GS(11)
Czarnecki,K1(165B)
Czarniecki,KL(30)
Czech,K1(165B),LS
Czeigl,WK
Czeller,WK
Czengruber,WK
Czercza,WK
Czermak,LS
Czernecki,LS
Czerny,SW(38)
Czerwinski,KL(28)
Czerwiński,K1(165B)
Cziczek,SW(52,58,59)

Czieger,WK
Cziegler,WK
Czier,WK
Czigl,WK
Czigler,WK
Czimar,WK
Czimer,WK
Czimermon,WK
Czimpfer,WK
Czirek,WK
Czölf,WK
Czorn,WK
Czuzek,WK
Czybura,K1(165B)
Dabbert,MM
Dabelow,MM
Dabischa,HW(208)
Daborn,WK
Daboure,WK
Dach,K1(165B)
Dachs,LS
Daemfelser,GF(92A)
Daentler,MM
Dägele,GL(9 entries)
Dahl,MM
von Dahlen,MM
Dahlheiserin,WK
Dahlke,GL(496), HS(33)
Dahm,WK
Dahms,MM
Dahn,LS,WK
Dähn,GL(231)
Daickler,WK
Dainier,HS(65)
Dais,GL(239)
Daiwert,WK
Dalafus,WK
Dalheimer,GF(92B, 104B),WK
Dalke,MM
Daller,WK
Dallheimer,WK
Dallmang,WK
Dallmann,MM
Dalongeville,WK
Dam,LS,WK
Damar,WK
Damasch,WK
Damasius,MM
Dambacher,WK
Dambocher,WK
Dambrowski,K1(165B)
Dami,WK
Damian,WK
Daminger,WK
Damitschek,W#(8.1, 8.2)

Dämkusreither,WK
Damm,LS
Dammann,MM
Dammel,HW(7 entries)
Damp,LS,WK
Dampsch,WK
Damrau,GS(91B)
Danaberger,WK
Daneberger,WK
Danek,LS
Dänemark,MM
Danenfelser,GF(93B)
Danenheimer,LS,WK
Dangel,WK
Dangelmayer,WK
Dangler,WK
Daniel,LS,WK
Danielowski,K1(165B)
Daniels,BU
Danik,MM
Daninger,LS,WK
Danküf,WK
Dankwertz,MM
Dannecker,LS
Dännemark,MM
Dannenberger,WK
Danner,GL(334),
  W#(6.59)
Dannes,WK
Dannewitz,LS
Däntl,WK
Daper,WK
Darden,WK
Dardin,WK
Dargent,WK
Dargund,WK
Darmstädter,LS,WK
Darmstätter,LS
Darmstetter,LS
Darowski,K1(165B)
Darschan,WK
Dary,WK
Dasch,WK
Daschner,WK
Dase,MM
Dasing,WK
Dasinger,WK
Dassenbacher,WK
Daszkiewicz,K1(165B)
Datie,WK
Datter,WK
Dattle,WK
Dätzauer,WK
Daub,IE(88,89),LS,WK
Däuber,GL(361)
Dauberbacher,WK
Dauenhauer,WK
Dauenheimer,LS

Daum,WK
Daun,LS,WK
Daunenhauer,LS
Daunheimer,LS
Dauninger,LS
Dauran,WK
Daus,WK
Dauster,GF(93B,130A)
Daut,WK
Dautel,GL(373)
Dautermann,WK
Davenport,GL(408)
Daverne,LS
David,WK
Davids,MM
Deal,GL(391,504)
Debald,WK
Debel,MM,WK
Deber,WK
Debes,WK
Debois,WK
Debolt,LS
Debrell,WK
Dech,GF(130A,130B),
  LS,WK
Dechen,WK
Deck,GF(91A)
Decker,BU,HW(14,81),
  LS,MM,SW(13),WK
Deckert,WK
Deckh,W#(5.25)
Deckher,WK
Deckorsi,WK
Decrion,WK
Decumbee,WK
Dedich,LS
Dedinsky,GF(118)
Deeg,HW(29,30,67)
Dees,GL(424)
Defehr,BU
Defer,BU
Deffinger,HW(54)
Defort,LS
Deg,HW(13)
Degele,GL(228,495)
Degelow,MM
Degen,GF(91B),LS,MM,
  WK
Degener,MM
Degenhart,WK
Deger,GF(111)
Deggert,WK
Degler,LS
Dehan,SW(29),WK
Dehant,WK
Dehl,BU
Dehlsen,MM
Dehm,WK

Dehn,MM
von Dehn,MM
Dehrental,MM
Dehringer,WK
Deibel,WK
Deich,WK
Deichler,WK
Deichmann,WK
Deiff,WK
Deimbelfeld,WK
Deimberich,WK
Dein,WK
Deiser,WK
Deismann,WK
Deiss,HW(6 entries)
Deiß,WK
Deißmann,LS
Deisz,HW(123,180,
  208)
Deiter,GS(89B)
Deitsch,WK
Deitz,WK
Deixler,WK
Dejeruet,WK
Dekendorf,WK
Deker,WK
Dekinder,LS
Dekman,WK
Dekoff,LS
Del,BU
Delby,WK
Delert,KL(9)
Deleß,WK
Delfeil,WK
Deliram,LS
Delker,GL(349,501),
  LS
Dell,BU,WK
Della,LS
Dellastrada,LS,WK
D'Ellevaux,LS
Dellinger,WK
Delong,WK
Delvo,WK
Delwo,LS,WK
Dembowski,K1(165B)
Demel,WK
Demerle,WK
Demisard,WK
Demjanow,GL(68)
Demm,WK
Demogen,WK
Demon,LS
Demoyen,WK
Dempf,WK
Demuth,W#(2.90),WK
Demy,WK
Demzau,MM

Denat,GL(305)
Denck,WK
Dengel,LS
Dengl,WK
Dengler,LS,WK
Denicke,MM
Denier,WK
Denig,WK
Dening,GL(217)
Denis,WK
Denisard,WK
Denker,IE(97)
Denlingen,WK
Dennerer,WK
Dennich,LS,WK
Densel,LS,WK
Denser,WK
Denßky,WK
Dentzau,MM
Denus,WK
Denzau,MM
Denze,GS(18)
Denzel,WK
Denzinger,WK
Deocastulus,WK
Depal,LS
Depenbrok,MM
Depine,WK
Depisch,WK
Deppert,WK
Depre,WK
Depris,WK
Der,WK
Derbaluk,MM
Derflinger,WK
Derfuß,WK
Derheim,GL(69)
Deringer,WK
Deringerin,WK
Derink,WK
Derksen,BU
Derksin,BU
Derm,LS
Dern,LS,WK
Dernbach,WK
Dernehl,MM
Derner,WK
Dernst,HW(12)
v. Derschau,MM
Derth,WK
Deschan,WK
Deschou,WK
Deschu,WK
Deserf,WK
Desiles,WK
Desl,WK
Desoy,WK
Dessarek,W#(8.62)

Detambt,WK
Detampl,WK
Detar,WK
Detard,WK
Deterin,MM
Deters,MM
Detharding,MM
Dethloff,MM
Dethtloff,MM
Detich,WK
Detin,WK
Detloff,MM
Deton,WK
Dettich,LS,WK
Dettloff,MM
Detzel,GL(338)
Deufel,MM
Deutsch,LS,MM,WK
Deutscher,IE(90,95,
    96,98),SW(14,60)
Deutschmann,LS,WK
Dever,BU,WK
Deves,WK
De Wald,GL(496)
Dewald,LS,WK
Dewes,WK
Dewis,LS
Dewisch,LS
Dex,WK
Dexheim,LS,WK
Dexheimer,LS
Dey,MM
Deymann,LS,WK
Deys,WK
Deyseroth,WK
Dezi,WK
D'Hare,WK
Dialler,WK
Dibau,WK
Dibo,WK
Diboi,WK
Dibois,WK
Dibry,WK
Dichelborer,WK
Dick,BU,GF(92A),
    GL(410),LS,WK
Dickenscheid,WK
Dicker,LS
Dickes,LS
Dickmann,LS
Dickmeyer,LS
Dickrouin,WK
Dicks,WK
Didach,WK
Didchen,LS
Didenhoffer,WK
Dides,WK
Didie,WK

Didier,WK
Didihober,WK
Didio,WK
Didriß,WK
Die,WK
Diebald,LS
Diebert,MM
Diebold,W#(2.24),WK
Diebolt,LS
Dieck,BU
Diedl,WK
Diedorf,WK
Diefebach,WK
Diefenbach,LS
Dieffenbach,WK
Diegel,GL(14
    entries),HW(179)
Diehl,GL(78,407),LS,
    WK
Diehm,WK
Diek,BU
Diel,LS,WK
Diell,WK
Dielmann,WK
Diendorf,LS
Diendorfer,WK
Diener,GL(382),
    HW(13),WK
Dienerin,WK
Dieno,HW(6 entries)
Dienst,WK
Diepolt,W#(1.77)
Diernboch,WK
Dierring,GS(12)
Dies,WK
Diesner,GS(14)
Dießler,WK
Diest,W#(7.39)
Diestel,MM
Dieterich,WK
Dieterle,WK
Dietler,WK
Dietlichen,LS
Dietmann,WK
Dietmar,LS
Dietmayer,LS,WK
Dietrich,HS(54),
    IE(94,96),LS,WK
Dietrichheim,WK
Dietrichin,WK
Diettenhofer,WK
Dietterin,WK
Diettrich,WK
Dietz,LS,WK
Dietzin,WK
Dietzl,WK
Dietzler,WK
Dieudon,WK

Donarski,K1(165B)
Donat,MM,WK
Donatier,WK
Donbeck,WK
Donellin,WK
Dones,LS
Donge,WK
Donges,WK
Dönig,LS
Donkeil,WK
Donkels,WK
Donling,WK
Donné,WK
Donner,HS(43,46,55,
    65),WK
Donninger,WK
Donu,WK
Donvein,WK
Dony,LS,WK
Döör,WK
Dopf,WK
Dopler,W#(5.95)
Doplinger,WK
Dor,WK
Dörcks,MM
Dordian,WK
Dorer,WK
Dorf,WK
Dorffer,WK
Dorffler,WK
Dörfisch,WK
Dörfler,LS
Dorflinger,W#(4.92)
Dörflinger,WK
Dorfner,WK
Doriat,WK
Dorien,LS
Dorin,WK
Doringer,WK
Döringer,LS,WK
Doringhof,WK
Dorinia,WK
Dorinn,WK
Doris,WK
Dörkes,WK
Dörksen,BU
Dörl,LS
Dorloting,WK
Dormayer,LS,WK
Dormutz,WK
Dorn,LS,WK
Dörn,LS
von Dorn,MM
Dornacher,WK
Dornauer,WK
Dornbach,LS,WK
Dörnbach,WK
Dornbusch,WK

Dorneker,WK
Dornen,WK
Dorner,LS,WK
Dörner,GF(130B),LS,
    WK
Dornerberger,WK
Dornes,WK
Dornfeld,GS(91B)
Dornin,WK
Dörninger,WK
Dorr,LS
Dörr,GL(192),IE(90),
    LS,MM,SW(14),WK
Dörrenbacher,WK
Dorrheimer,WK
Dorsch,WK
Dörschlag,MM
Dorst,WK
von Dorthesen,MM
Dortmayr,WK
Dörwaldt,MM
Dorwart,LS
Dose,MM
Dosedla,WK
Doser,WK
Dosing,WK
Doß,MM
Dosse,HS(65)
Dossein,WK
Dosta,WK
Doster,HW(13,54,81)
Doterkuh,WK
Dotermann,WK
Dotter,WK
Doubner,WK
Douen,WK
Dounellin,WK
Doxia,WK
Doyse,WK
Dozauer,WK
Dozauerin,WK
Dozenbacher,WK
Drach,WK
Drachmann,MM
Dragendorff,MM
Dräger,KL(18)
Dragesser,WK
Draheim,HS(31),
    KL(54)
Drahotsch,W#(8.96)
Drakle,LS
Draksel,BU
Drakur,WK
Draskopp,WK
Draun,WK
Dravnicsek,WK
Drawinczek,LS
Draxler,SW(24,27),WK

Dreba,WK
Dreber,WK
Drechmann,MM
Drechsel,WK
Drechsler,LS,MM,WK
Dreffinger,HW(81)
Drefte,GL(496)
Drege,MM
Dreger,WK
Drehen,WK
Dreher,GL(490),HW(12
    entries),LS,WK
Drehner,WK
Dreier,WK
Dreiling,SW(64)
Dreisisch,WK
Dreitt,WK
Dremblmeyer,WK
Dremel,WK
Drenkhahn,MM
Drensinger,LS
Drer,LS
Dreschel,LS
Drescher,LS,WK
Dresser,LS
Dreßl,WK
Dreßler,GS(18,55),
    LS,WK
Dretsch,MM
Dreuhausen,W#(8.6)
Drewing,MM
Drews,HS(44),
    K1(165B),KL(18),
    MM
Drexheimer,WK
Drexler,WK
Dreyborn,WK
Dreyer,MM
Dreymann,WK
Dreysigacker,WK
Dreyß,WK
von Driberg,MM
Dribu,WK
Dricht,WK
Drie,WK
Driedger,BU
Driediger,BU
Driegert,MM
Dries,WK
Drinquell,WK
Drisch,WK
Drithart,WK
Driwo,WK
Drobnik,WK
Drödel,WK
Dromer,LS
Drommer,LS,WK
Dronecker,LS

Dronen,WK	Dumasch,WK	Dutz,WK
Drönle,WK	Dumka,SW(17)	Duve,MM
Droscher,WK	Dumke,HS(43,48),	Duversche,WK
Drößler,WK	KL(54)	Duwahl,WK
Drost,MM	Dümke,K1(165B)	Düwel,MM
Drosten,WK	Dumm,WK	Duwig,WK
Drotziger,SW(21)	Dumon,WK	Duy,LS,WK
Drozd,LS	Dumont,WK	Dvoracsek,WK
Druck,SW(16)	Dump,MM	Dvorsak,WK
Druckmüller,W#(7.92)	Dumung,WK	Dvorssak,WK
Druedger,BU	Duncker,MM	Dwener,WK
Drum,WK	Düng,WK	Dworzak,LS
Drumerschäusser,WK	Dünges,WK	Dybry,WK
Drümler,WK	Dunhaubt,WK	Dyck,BU
Drummerschhausen,LS	Dunkel,WK	Dycks,BU
Drummershausen,LS	Dunkhelter,WK	Dyll,LS
Drümpelmann,MM	Dunkler,WK	Dymek,K1(165B)
Drunckwalter,LS	Düns,WK	Dyrsen,MM
Druonz,WK	Dunst,WK	Dzbankiewicz,
Dryps,K1(165B)	Düpenoi,WK	K1(165B)
Dryszkowski,K1(166A)	Duperron,MM	Dzikowski,K1(165B)
Dubal,WK	Dupont,WK	Ebald,WK
Dubaril,MM	Duppert,GL(108)	Ebarth,WK
Dubas,WK	Dups,GF(92A)	Ebe,WK
Dubner,WK	Dur,K1(165B)	Ebel,MM,WK
Dubois,WK	Durck,WK	Ebeling,MM
Dubrabin,W#(4.65)	Dürckel,WK	Ebensperger,WK
Dubran,WK	Durckh,WK	Eberard,WK
Dubs,GF(125B,127B,	Durckl,WK	Eberbein,WK
130B)	Dureczek,WK	Eberhard,GL(287,
Ducca,WK	Durieux,WK	498),LS,MM,WK
Dück,BU,GL(402),WK	Dürk,WK	Eberhardt,LS,WK
Ducke,SW(17)	Durkalec,LS	Eberhart,WK
Dücker,MM,WK	Durkes,WK	Eberle,GF(93A),
von Dücker,MM	Dürkop,MM	GL(296),W#(7.30,
Duckwitz,MM	Durm,WK	8.109),WK
Dudcarn,WK	Dürmann,LS	Eberlein,GF(130B)
Dudek,GL(228,495)	Durmeyer,WK	Eberling,WK
Düdeno,WK	Dürnbach,WK	Ebersbach,WK
Dueck,BU	Dürner,WK	Ebersberger,LS
Dueckgroeb,BU	Durny,K1(165B)	Ebersold,WK
Dueckmann,BU	Dürr,IE(90),	Ebert,HS(26),LS,MM,
Duerck,BU	K1(165B),LS,	WK
Duercksen,BU	SW(14),WK	Eberth,WK
Duesterhoeft,HS(26)	Durrn,LS	Eberwein,LS,WK
Düetmer,WK	Durst,WK	Ebinger,GL(416)
Düfel,MM	Durstin,WK	Eble,WK
Dufer,WK	Durt,WK	Ebling,WK
Duffner,WK	Dury,WK	Ebmer,WK
Duflo,WK	Dusberger,LS	Ebner,W#(3.7,3.14,
Dufner,WK	Dusch,LS,WK	4.54),WK
Dühring,MM	Duschek,W#(8.66)	Ebnerin,WK
Duins,WK	Duschin,WK	Ebrecht,WK
Dül,BU	Dusena,WK	Eby,W#(3.47)
Düll,LS,WK	Dußberger,LS,WK	Eccabe,WK
Dum,WK	Düsterhoeft,HS(26)	Echinger,LS
Duma,WK	Düsterhöft,K1(165B)	Echleb,WK
Duman,WK	Dütenoi,WK	Echstein,WK

Eisenbard,WK	Ellmann,WK	Engbarth,WK
Eisenbarth,GL(336),	Ellmauer,WK	Engbrecht,BU
LS	Elmer,WK	Engebrant,WK
Eisenber,LS	Elmus,LS	Engel,GL(342),GS(57,
Eisenberger,LS,WK	Elner,WK	91A),IE(89),LS,
Eisenhart,WK	Elsasser,WK	MM,SW(14),
Eisenhauer,WK	Elsässer,GL(447),WK	W#(2.44),WK
Eisenkirch,WK	Elsen,WK	Engelbrecht,MM,WK
Eisenlohr,WK	Elser,GL(316),WK	Engelhard,W#(7.22),
Eisenmann,GL(31	Elsner,MM	WK
entries)	Elßner,WK	Engelhardt,GL(492),
Eisenmüller,GL(40)	Elstermann,MM	MM
Eisenreich,WK	Elstner,WK	Engelhart,WK
Eiserle,WK	Elter,WK	Engelin,WK
Eisert,GS(19)	Elts,WK	Engelmajr,WK
Eisinger,WK	Eltz,LS,WK	Engelman,WK
Eiskirch,WK	Eltzer,WK	Engelmann,LS,WK
Eisler,LS	Eltzner,WK	Engelmayer,WK
Eiß,WK	Elwanger,W#(7.88)	Engelmeyer,WK
Eissig,WK	Elzer,WK	Engels,WK
Eissle,HW(29)	Eman,WK	Engelsohn,MM
Eißler,WK	Emath,WK	Engelstetter,WK
Eißlinger,LS	Embten,WK	Engerer,LS,WK
Eistmännin,WK	Emel,WK	Engerin,WK
Eiszenbeiss,HW(40)	Emele,GS(18)	Engers,WK
Eitel,LS,WK	Ement,WK	Engert,WK
Eitelmüller,WK	Emer,WK	Engertin,WK
Eitzen,BU	Emerich,LS,WK	Engeser,WK
Eixel,WK	Emerle,LS	Enghard,WK
Eizen,BU	Emich,IE(88),SW(4),	Engl,WK
Eizunger,WK	WK	Englart,LS
Ek,WK	Emler,WK	Englbieler,WK
Ekala,WK	Emme,MM	Engler,W#(5.91),WK
Ekard,WK	von Emme,MM	Englert,LS,WK
Ekefall,WK	Emmel,WK	Englerth,WK
Ekel,LS,WK	Emmerich,LS,MM	Englhart,WK
Ekelberg,MM	Emmerle,LS	Englin,WK
Ekenroth,WK	Emon,WK	Englköpfer,WK
Ekert,LS,WK	Emrich,LS	Engst,WK
Ekerth,LS,WK	Emser,WK	Engsteller,WK
Ekes,LS	Emt,WK	Engstin,WK
Eket,WK	Enard,WK	Engstler,WK
Ekhardt,WK	Encker,WK	Engwer,HS(65)
Ekhert,W#(3.16,3.48)	Enckerich,WK	Enich,WK
Elbing,WK	End,LS	Enk,WK
Elbl,WK	Endel,LS	Enkerich,WK
Elblin,WK	Ender,WK	Enklin,WK
Elert,MM	Enderle,GL(223)	Enners,WK
Elexhauser,WK	Enderlin,GL(229)	Enns,BU,GL(410)
Elf,LS	Enders,LS,WK	Ennss,BU
Elfling,WK	Enderus,WK	Ennz,BU
Eli,WK	Endes,WK	Ens,BU,GL(410),LS
Elias,BU,WK	Endl,LS,WK	Ense,GL(397)
Elkan v Elkansberg,	Endler,WK	Enselmann,IE(98)
LS	Endner,WK	Enser,WK
Elkeß,WK	Endres,WK	Ensinger,GL(439)
Ellenberger,WK	Endulski,GL(202)	Ensminger,WK
Eller,LS,WK		Enss,GL(397)

Enssens,BU
Ensslen,HW(207)
Enßler,WK
Ensz,BU
Enszen,BU
Entler,WK
Entner,WK
Entz,BU
Entzi,GF(95B)
Enz,BU,LS,SW(34),WK
von Enzenberg,SW(29)
Enzer,WK
Enzle,WK
Enzminger,HW(45),WK
Epl,WK
Epler,GF(130B),LS
Epling,WK
Epp,BU,WK
Eppelin,GL(413)
Eppler,GL(263),HW(11
    entries),WK
Eraßmus,WK
Erat,WK
Erb,GS(90A),LS,WK
Erbach,LS,WK
Erbbachen,WK
Erbele,GL(403,496,
    505),HW(13
    entries)
Erben,LS
Erbenbach,WK
Erbert,SW(17,38,63,
    64,65)
Erbes,LS,WK
Ercker,LS
Erckert,LS
Erd,WK
von Erdberg,MM
Erdmann,BU,HS(38),
    HW(52),K1(168B),
    KL(14),MM
Erdnerin,WK
Eres,WK
Erfle,HW(18 entries)
Erhard,LS,SW(29),WK
Erhardt,WK
Erich,WK
Ering,GF(91B)
Erker,LS,WK
Erle,WK
Erlebach,WK
Erlenbusch,GL(43
    entries)
Erm,MM
Ermann,LS,WK
Ermel,GF(91A,126,
    130B),LS,WK
Ermer,WK

Ermi,WK
Ermini,WK
Ermler,WK
Erne,WK
Ernerich,WK
Ernhold,WK
Ernn,WK
Ernst,GS(18),HW(15,
    19),LS,WK
Ernt,WK
Ersch,WK
Erschmann,WK
Erstein,WK
Ertell,WK
Ertl,WK
Ertmann,WK
Ertz,WK
von Ertzen-Glairon,
    MM
Erz,BU,WK
Erzin,BU
Esau,BU
Esbeschidin,WK
Esbeschitt,WK
Esch,GL(337),WK
Eschbach,WK
Eschbischied,WK
Eschenbach,MM,WK
Eschenbecker,LS,WK
Eschenlauer,WK
Escher,WK
Eslinger,WK
Esmeist,WK
Esner,LS
Espe,LS,WK
Espenschied,LS,WK
Eß,WK
Esselin,WK
von Essen,MM
Essenburg,MM
Esset,WK
Essig,GL(273)
Eßkelson,MM
Eßler,WK
Eßling,WK
Esslinger,GL(337),
    HW(81)
Eßlinger,WK
Estadt,WK
Ester,WK
Esterlein,WK
Esterling,WK
Esto,WK
Etien,WK
Etinger,WK
Etrach,WK
Ettinger,LS,WK
Etzel,WK

Etzl,WK
Euhner,HW(13)
Eulen,WK
Euler,MM,WK
Eules,WK
Eusinger,GL(439)
Eva,WK
Even,WK
Everle,WK
Evers,WK
Evert,LS,MM,WK
Everth,GS(27,28,59)
Ewald,GS(91B),MM
Eweradt,WK
Ewerlein,WK
Ewert,BU,MM,WK
Ewerwein,WK
Ewrar,WK
Ewy,LS
Exle,WK
Exner,SW(31,66)
Ey,HW(67)
Eybach,W#(7.3)
Eybeck,WK
Eyber,GL(466)
Eych,WK
Eychhorn,WK
Eychkhorn,WK
Eyd,WK
Eyerd,LS
Eyler,WK
Eyloff,WK
Eyrich,WK
Eyring,WK
Eysel,WK
Eysen,WK
Eysler,LS
Eyß,WK
Eyßbach,WK
Eyssert,WK
von Eytzen,BU
Eyzig,W#(7.119)
Faas,GL(5 entries),
    HW(23,170)
Faass,HW(14 entries)
Faaß,GL(196),WK
Faasz,HW(125-A)
Faber,LS,MM,WK
Fäber,WK
Fabian,GL(368),LS,
    MM,WK
Fabing,WK
Fabri,WK
Fabricy,GF(114)
Fabrik,WK
Fabritzi,LS
Fabry,GF(122A),WK
Fachbach,WK

Fachet,LS	Fasl,WK	Federmann,WK
Fad,WK	Fasler,WK	Federolf,WK
Faderle,WK	Fasold,WK	Federspiel,WK
Fagt,MM	Faß,Kl(166B)	Federspill,WK
Fahbach,WK	Fassel,WK	Federspinn,WK
Fähder,Kl(167A)	Fassenacht,WK	Fedier,GL(408)
Fahey,GL(403,505)	Fassius,WK	Fedorow,MM
Fahrenholtz,MM	Faßler,WK	Feek,LS
Fährle,HW(6 entries)	Fast,BU,WK	Fegele,WK
Faidner,LS	Fastel,WK	Feger,LS,W#(1.70),WK
Faig,SW(27)	Fastnacht,LS,WK	Fęglerski,Kl(166A)
Faigle,WK	Fat,WK	Fehdow,MM
Faihe,WK	Fath,GL(459),WK	Feherváry,WK
Faist,W#(5.74)	Fatinger,LS	Fehinger,WK
Faistammel,WK	Fatteicher,SW(2)	Fehl,HW(50),WK
Faith,LS	Fatum,WK	Fehler,LS,WK
Faix,GF(125A)	Faude,LS,WK	Fehr,LS,WK
Fälchle,HW(12	Faul,WK	de Fehr,BU
entries)	Faulhaber,W#(7.24)	Fehrenbach,WK
Falcin,WK	Faullhaber,WK	Fehrle,HW(30)
Falick,WK	Fauner,WK	Fehrmann,GL(340)
Falk,BU,LS,WK	Faunhalder,WK	Fei,WK
Falkenburger,	Faus,WK	Feichner,WK
GF(122A)	Fauser,HW(7 entries)	Feicht,WK
Falkenhahn,KL(18)	Faussie,WK	Feichtenberger,WK
von Falkenhahn,	Faust,GF(92B),SW(17,	Feichtenbergerin,WK
KL(32)	18),W#(5.72,5.73,	Feichterer,WK
Falkenstein,WK	5.83),WK	Feichterin,WK
Fall,WK	Faustier,WK	Feichtinger,WK
Faller,W#(6.12),WK	Faustin,WK	Feidt,WK
Fallwasser,WK	Fauth,WK	Feif,WK
Falrian,WK	Fautsch,WK	Feifer,WK
Fälschet,WK	Fay,LS,WK	Feifhof,WK
Fälschle,HW(88,123)	Fayand,WK	Feifrod,WK
Falter,WK	Fayfer,LS	Feigel,SW(12)
Faltyński,Kl(165B)	Febel,WK	Feiger,WK
Faltz,WK	Feber,WK	Feigert,GL(494)
Fames,WK	Febre,WK	Feigle,WK
Famler,GF(120,130B)	Fecher,WK	Feiglin,WK
Fancka,Kl(165B)	Fecherin,WK	Feik,WK
Fanckusser,WK	Fechinger,WK	Feikert,GL(494)
Fandl,WK	Fechsner,WK	Feiks,GF(130B)
Fandrey,HS(37)	Fechter,WK	Feil,WK
Fandrich,GL(510),	Fechtig,WK	Feilen,WK
HW(208)	Feck,WK	Feiler,W#(1.67),WK
Fanghauserin,WK	Fecker,WK	Fein,HW(14)
Fanner,GL(275)	Fedder,HS(35)	Feineis,WK
Fanselow,HS(26)	Feddersen,MM	Feiner,MM
Fanta,WK	Feder,HS(35,37),	Feiser,WK
Fanter,MM	Kl(167A),WK	Feiserle,LS
Faoli,WK	Federau,BU	Feissende,WK
Faranzon,WK	Federchen,LS	Feißt,WK
Färber,WK	Federhehn,WK	Feist,WK
Faro,Kl(165B)	Federhin,WK	Feistel,WK
Faroniecki,Kl(165B)	Federich,WK	Feistenauer,WK
Farth,LS	Federkeil,WK	Feisthammel,WK
Fartleutnerin,WK	Federkiehl,WK	Feisthuber,WK
Faser,WK	Federkihl,WK	Feisty,LS

Feit,LS,WK
Feith,WK
Feitz,WK
Feitzelmayer,WK
Feitzinger,WK
Feix,WK
Fek,WK
Felbel,GF(126)
Felcher,WK
Feld,LS,WK
Felda,WK
Feldbausch,LS
Feldhaus,WK
Feldigel,SW(16)
Feldinger,WK
Feldl,WK
Feldmann,LS,MM,
   W#(8.30),WK
Feldmannin,WK
Feldmayer,WK
Feldpausch,LS
Feldstrauch,MM
Felgel,WK
Felger,GL(212,373),
   WK
Felgyes,WK
Feliger,WK
Feliks,WK
Feling,WK
Felite,WK
Felix,LS,WK
Felker,WK
Fell,WK
Felleitner,WK
Feller,GF(91A,104A),
   WK
Fellerin,WK
Fellermann,MM
Felleuthner,WK
Fellhase,MM
Fellinger,LS
Fellmann,MM
Fellmeth,WK
Fellner,WK
Felm,GL(280)
Felmayer,WK
Felner,WK
Fels,LS,WK
Felsch,GS(18),KL(33)
Felsenmayer,WK
Felsenmeyer,WK
Felten,MM,WK
Feltes,WK
Felwert,WK
Felz,WK
Femer,MM
Fendrik,WK
Fendt,WK

Fenger,MM
Feninger,WK
Fennig,MM
Fenske,K1(165B)
Fent,WK
Fentz,WK
Fenz,WK
Fenzke,MM
Ferber,WK
Ferdinand,LS
Ferenpach,WK
Ferenz,LS,WK
Ferich,WK
Ferie,WK
Ferkert,GL(486)
Ferlach,LS,WK
Ferling,WK
Ferme,WK
Fernau,WK
Fernbach,WK
Fernbacher,WK
Ferner,WK
Fernikin,WK
Ferniß,WK
Ferpach,WK
Ferré,WK
Ferres,WK
Ferry,WK
Fersch,WK
von Fersen,MM
Ferst,WK
Ferstler,WK
Fertig,WK
Fesburg,WK
Fesenmayer,WK
Feßl,WK
Feßler,WK
Fest,LS,WK
Festat,LS
Fester,LS
Festerkiewicz,
   K1(166A)
Festin,WK
Fet,WK
Feterowski,K1(166A)
Fetes,WK
Fett,LS,WK
Fetter,LS,WK
Fettich,WK
Fettler,WK
Fetzer,GF(127A),
   GL(446),LS,WK
Fetzler,WK
Feu,LS
Feuchhauser,WK
Feuereisen,MM
Feuerer,WK
Feuerle,WK

Feuerstein,WK
Feuler,GF(122A)
Feut,WK
Feuth,WK
Fex,HW(23)
Fey,LS,WK
Feyder,WK
Feyer,LS,WK
Feyerstein,WK
Feyl,WK
Feylisch,WK
Feysede,WK
Feysette,LS
Fezer,WK
Fezman,WK
Fiack,WK
Fiantia,WK
Fibich,WK
Fichtel,LS
Fichter,WK
Fichtl,WK
Fichtler,WK
Fichtner,GL(40
   entries),WK
Fick,LS,WK
von Fick,MM
Ficker,WK
Fickert,MM,WK
Fideke,HS(26)
Fidler,WK
Fidrich,WK
Fiechter,WK
Fiechtner,GL(74
   entries)
Fieck,WK
Fieckert,MM
Fiedler,GS(19,55),
   LS,WK
Fiege,GL(68)
Fieger,HW(30)
Fiekh,MM
Fielitz,MM
Fierling,WK
Fierneis,WK
Fiersiet,WK
Fiesing,MM
Fiet,WK
Fiffelt,WK
Figge,SW(57)
Figler,WK
Figurski,GL(112,346)
Fikert,LS,WK
Fikus,LS,WK
Filan,WK
Filbig,WK
Filcker,WK
Filebar,WK
Filer,LS

Folkierski,K1(166A)
Fölkl,W#(7.109)
Fölkle,LS
Foll,LS
Föll,GL(358)
Follmauer,LS,WK
Folmar,WK
Folmeher,WK
Folmer,WK
Folner,WK
Foltz,WK
Folz,LS,WK
Fonau,WK
Fonderbeck,WK
Fonne,MM
Fontain,WK
Fontanelli,WK
Fontenberger,WK
Fonyo,WK
Förenbach,WK
Forfein,WK
Forheim,LS
Forke,WK
Formann,WK
Formes,WK
Förnbach,WK
Förnebach,WK
Fornwald,WK
Forran,WK
Forst,WK
Forstein,LS
Forster,WK
Förster,LS,MM,
    W#(8.117),WK
Forstingerin,WK
Forstner,WK
Fort,WK
Förth,WK
Forthofer,WK
Fortier,WK
Förtig,WK
Fortinner,WK
Fortler,WK
Förtschjunger,WK
Fosse,WK
Fosy,WK
Foth,BU,MM
Föttinger,WK
Föttingerin,WK
Fourier,WK
Frach,WK
Fradl,WK
Fraehn,MM
von Fraenckel,MM
Fragenad,WK
Fragenath,WK
Fraintz,WK
Frambach,WK

Franciscus,WK
Franck,MM,WK
Franckbaumer,WK
Francke,MM
François,WK
Francz,WK
Frangot,WK
Franity,WK
Frank,GF(91A),
    GL(221),HS(26,
    33),HW(30),LS,WK
Franka,WK
Franke,KL(22),LS,WK
Frankenberger,LS
Franker,WK
Frankh,WK
Frankin,WK
Frankmann,MM
Frankois,WK
Frankord,WK
von Fransche,MM
Franss,BU
Franssen,BU
Franßen,LS
Frantz,BU,MM,WK
Frantzke,GS(89B)
Franz,BU,GL(311),LS,
    SW(24),WK
Franzen,BU,WK
Franzischkinell,WK
Franzmann,LS
Franzwa,WK
Frasch,WK
Fräser,MM
Fräß,WK
Fratovschi,SW(3)
Fraub,WK
Fräudig,WK
Frauendorfer,WK
Fraulen,WK
Frauß,WK
Fray,WK
Frech,WK
Frecher,WK
Fredrich,GL(399)
Frehse,MM
Frei,GF(91A,131A),
    GL(443),LS,WK
Freiberger,WK
Freid,WK
Freidich,WK
Freidinger,WK
Freienberger,WK
Freier,LS,WK
Freihait,WK
Freimarck,HW(88)
Freinberger,WK
Freind,WK

Freis,WK
Freisinger,WK
Freitag,GF(131A),
    HW(47,63),
    K1(167A)
Frek,WK
Frelich,WK
Frembdling,WK
Fremery,WK
Fremis,WK
Fremry,WK
Frencks,WK
Frencz,WK
Frenger,WK
Frengs,WK
Frenner,WK
Frenß,WK
Frentz,MM,WK
Frenzer,LS,WK
Frepson,WK
Frese,BU
Fresens,LS
Fresneker,W#(6.77)
Fressel,WK
Freßt,LS
Freth,WK
Freudemann,WK
Freudenberg,GL(80)
Freudenmann,WK
Freudt,WK
Freuger,LS
Freund,GS(19),LS,WK
Frewel,W#(2.89)
Frey,GF(95A),
    GL(200),HW(8
    entries),LS,
    W#(4.18,5.37,
    5.47,5.104),WK
Freyberger,WK
Freyburg,MM
Freyer,LS,WK
Freyermuth,W#(4.50),
    WK
Freyhalter,WK
Freyhaut,WK
Freyherr,WK
Freyin,WK
Freyl,WK
Freyman,WK
Freymann,MM,WK
Freymarck,KL(41)
Freymark,HS(44),
    KL(24)
Freymauer,WK
Freymuth,LS,MM
Freymuthin,WK
Freysach,WK
Freysthal,WK

Freystrober,WK
Freytag,LS,MM,WK
Freythöfer,WK
Friba,WK
Frichl,LS
Frick,GL(11 entries),LS,MM,WK
Fricke,IE(90)
Fricker,GL(293)
Frickert,GL(293)
Fricko,WK
Fricz,WK
Frid,WK
Fridel,WK
Friden,WK
Friderich,WK
Friderici,WK
Fridke,LS
Fridl,WK
Fridrich,WK
Fridrichberger,WK
Fridrik,WK
Frieberth,WK
Friebusch,HS(38)
Fried,LS
Friedel,WK
Friedenberg,GS(89B)
Friedenthal,LS
Friederich,WK
Friederika,HW(14)
Friedge,IE(90), SW(19),WK
Friedhof,WK
Friedl,WK
Friedländer,KL(34)
Friedlein,WK
Friedmann,LS,WK
Friedrich,GF(131A), GL(5 entries),LS, SW(24),WK
Friedrichin,WK
Friehe,GL(334)
Friel,MM
Fries,IE(92,96,97), LS,WK
Friesch,WK
Friese,GS(91B),MM
Friesel,MM,WK
Friesen,BU
Frieske,K1(166A)
Frieß,LS,WK
Frig,LS
Friger,HW(26)
Frigilla,WK
Frik,GL(215,233),WK
Frimer,WK
Fringer,LS
Frint,GF(119B)

Friol,WK
Frisan,WK
Frisch,WK
Frischauer,WK
Frischer,WK
Frischin,GF(96B),WK
Frischke,GS(89B)
Frischmann,WK
Frisics,WK
Frisiger,LS
Friß,LS,WK
Frith,LS
Fritsch,MM,W#(7.79), WK
Fritsche,MM
Fritz,GL(58 entries),HW(5 entries),IE(88, 94),LS,MM,SW(4), W#(5.2),WK
Friz,GL(263),WK
Frochmann,WK
Froelig,WK
Froerath,WK
Froese,BU
Froh,LS
Fröhlich,K1(167B), LS,WK
Fröhlicher,WK
Fröhlingen,WK
Frohn,WK
Frölich,LS,WK
From,LS,WK
Fromang,WK
Fromann,LS
Frombach,LS
Frömbter,MM
Fromhold,MM
von Fromhold,MM
Fromm,HW(16,17),MM
Fron,WK
Fronius,SW(41)
Frör,WK
Froschauer,WK
Froschin,WK
Froschmann,WK
Frösle,WK
Froson,WK
Froß,LS
Frost,GS(17,18), K1(166B),LS,WK
Frostorfer,WK
Fruar,WK
Fruber,WK
Fruck,HW(179,208)
Früh,GL(112,150,356)
Früher,WK
Frühstund,WK

Fründel,WK
Frydrychowski, K1(166A)
Frys,MM
Fuchs,GF(92B), GL(254),IE(89), K1(166B),LS,MM, SW(14,16,29,63, 64),WK
Fuchsberger,LS
Fuchsener,WK
Fuchshuber,WK
Fuchsin,WK
Fuchß,WK
Fuehrer,GL(351,501)
Fues,WK
Fugel,LS
Fugels,WK
Fugl,WK
Fuhler,WK
Fuhr,LS,WK
Führ,WK
Fuhrbeck,WK
Führer,MM,WK
Fuhrerin,WK
Führher,WK
Fuhrmann,LS,MM,WK
Fulding,WK
Fulersch,WK
Füll,WK
Füller,WK
Fulman,WK
Fülmann,WK
Fulmer,WK
Fulny,WK
Fulz,WK
Funck,BU,WK
Funcken,WK
Fünfstück,MM
Fung,WK
Funk,BU,LS,MM,WK
Funke,WK
Funker,LS
Furkatt,WK
Furkiewicz,K1(166A)
Furman,K1(166A)
Furmañski,K1(166A)
Fürmbach,WK
Furnand,WK
Fürnhofer,WK
Furscht,WK
Fürst,HW(7 entries), LS,WK
Fürstenau,MM
Fürstenberg,MM
Fürstenberger,WK
Fürster,MM
Fürtnerin,WK

Fuschka,WK
Fusenmayer,WK
Fuß,LS,WK
Fussin,WK
Fust,WK
Füst,WK
Futerer,WK
Futter,WK
Futterer,W#(5.5),WK
Futterleib,GS(91B)
Fuwegger,WK
Fux,LS,WK
Fuxhuber,WK
Fuxin,WK
Gaal,WK
Gaaß,W#(4.90)
Gab,WK
Gabel,GF(91A,131A),
 LS,WK
Gäbel,WK
Gabell,WK
Gabellin,WK
Gabelmann,WK
Gabergel,LS,WK
Gaberth,WK
Gabetter,WK
Gabirady,WK
Gabl,WK
Gablentz,MM
Gabony,LS
Gabriel,LS,MM,
 SW(17),WK
Gacke,WK
Gadelmayerin,WK
Gadewoldt,MM
Gadin,GL(397)
Gaede,BU
Gaedt,MM
Gaenger,WK
Gaenzle,GL(272,497)
Gafga,WK
Gafka,LS
Gahlnbaeck,MM
Gähring,W#(8.103),WK
Gaib,LS,WK
Gaie,KL(37)
Gaier,HW(31),WK
Gaiger,WK
Gailing,WK
Gaiser,GL(324),HW(12
 entries)
Gaiß,LS
Gaisser,HW(18)
Gaister,W#(6.10)
Gajet,WK
Gajewska,MM
Gajewski,HS(44)
Galander,MM

Galion,WK
Galischtschuk,
 HW(208)
Gall,GL(7 entries),
 WK
Gallasch,MM
Gallaß,WK
Gallert,WK
Gallinen,MM
Gallingerin,WK
Gallison,IE(98)
Galow,HS(34)
Galschnid,WK
Gambor,WK
Gambracher,WK
Gamelin,MM
Gamp,W#(3.12),WK
Gamper,MM
Gampner,LS
Gand,BU
Gandarme,WK
Gandel,GL(416,489)
Gander,WK
Gandoin,WK
Gäng,W#(3.17),WK
Gängenbahrer,
 W#(5.99)
Gangermeier,WK
Ganghammer,WK
Ganglin,WK
Ganglof,LS,WK
Gangloff,WK
Gangluff,WK
Gangwesch,W#(4.84)
Gans,LS,WK
Ganselmayer,WK
Ganser,LS,WK
Ganske,HS(75)
Gänsler,K1(166A)
Gansloser,WK
Ganß,LS,WK
GänßHirt,WK
Ganter,WK
Gantert,GL(448),WK
Ganther,GL(448),
 IE(88)
Gantner,SW(4),
 W#(5.66),WK
Gantnerin,WK
Gantz,MM
Gantzschow,MM
Ganz,LS,WK
Ganzemer,WK
Ganzke,GS(91B)
Ganzken,MM
Ganzloser,WK
Ganzmann,WK
Garber,WK

Gärber,LS,WK
Garcia,GL(340)
Garder,BU
de la Gardie,MM
Gardon,HS(44)
Garestorfer,WK
Gargamann,WK
Garie,WK
Garke,HS(44)
Garnerin,WK
Garnstorfer,WK
Garon,WK
Garrey,WK
Gartel,LS
Gärtel,SW(12)
Gartier,WK
Gärtig,HW(13
 entries)
Gärtler,WK
Gartner,LS
Gärtner,LS,SW(21),WK
Gärtnerin,WK
Gartzke,HS(44,45,46)
Gary,WK
Gasain,WK
Gaschler,SW(24)
Gaschna,WK
Gaschno,WK
Gascon,WK
Gąsiorowski,K1(166A)
Gaspar,WK
Gaß,LS,WK
Gaßauer,SW(44)
Gassenbauer,WK
Gassenmayer,WK
Gasser,WK
Gassinger,WK
Gäßle,WK
Gaßmann,WK
Gassner,IE(98),WK
Gaßner,LS,SW(19)
Gast,HW(16 entries),
 LS,WK
Gasteiner,WK
Gastenhuberin,WK
Gaster,W#(5.11)
Gastingerin,WK
Gastingin,WK
Gastmann,LS
Gatler,HS(65)
Gatschuff,WK
Gatter,WK
Gattering,WK
Gattermeyer,SW(24)
Gattinger,SW(12)
Gatto,WK
Gattringerin,WK
Gattung,WK

Gerens,WK
Gerentz,WK
Geres,LS,WK
Gergen,LS,WK
Gerhard,LS,MM,SW(7),
    WK
Gerhardt,GF(95A),
    GS(89A),WK
Gerhart,LS,WK
Gerhinz,WK
Gerhold,LS
Gerien,WK
Geriken,MM
Gering,LS,WK
Geringer,WK
Gerini,GS(89A)
Gerishofer,WK
Gerk,WK
Gerke,MM
Gerken,IE(94),MM
Gerlach,K1(166A),LS,
    WK
Gerle,LS
Gerlen,LS
Gerlib,WK
Gerlich,LS,WK
Gerlieb,LS,SW(36)
Gerling,MM
Gerlitz,WK
Gerloff,MM
Gerlsdorf,LS
German,GL(375),
    SW(44),WK
Germann,GL(375),LS,
    MM,SW(14,19,31),
    WK
Germans,WK
Gernand,WK
Gerndorf,LS,WK
Gerne,MM
Gernert,WK
Gernet,WK
Gernik,WK
Gerold,WK
Gerono,WK
Gerpacher,WK
Gerrach,HS(44)
Gersabek,W#(7.14)
Gersbach,WK
Gersch,K1(166A)
Gersdorff vel
    Gerstner,LS
Gersler,LS
Gerson,WK
Gerspach,WK
Gerspacher,W#(4.101)
Gerstel,LS,WK
Gerstenecker,GL(263)

Gerstermüller,WK
Gerstler,HS(65)
Gerstner,WK
Gerstorf,WK
Gert,WK
Gerteisen,WK
Gertel,SW(12)
Gerth,GS(89A),WK
Gerthen,WK
Gertig,GL(452)
Gertner,LS
Gertsen,BU
Gertzen,BU
Gerz,LS
Gerzen,BU
Geschler,SW(16)
Geschwendtner,SW(16)
Geschwentner,SW(64,
    65)
Gesebrecht,BU
Gesell,WK
Gesellius,MM
Geser,WK
Gesgen,WK
Gesin,LS
Geske,HS(44)
Gesner,LS,WK
Gessert,WK
Gessler,BU
Geßler,LS
Geßner,WK
Gestädner,WK
Gestat,LS
Gestättinger,WK
Gester,WK
Gestholt,WK
Gestholz,WK
Gesün,WK
Geth,LS,WK
Gethen,WK
Getkin,MM
Getschtow,HS(65)
Getter,LS
Getterst,LS
Gettler,LS
Getz,BU,WK
Getzel,MM
Geudemann,LS
Geuder,MM
Geya,WK
Geyer,GF(91B),
    GL(421),GS(19,
    22),IE(95,98),LS,
    SW(18),WK
Geyger,LS,WK
Geyo,WK
Geysler,LS
Gez,WK

Gezelius,MM
Gezen,WK
Gharlir,WK
Ghele,WK
Gibert,BU
Gibl,WK
Gibrich,WK
Gideibek,LS
Giebartowski,
    K1(166A)
Giebner,MM
Giebsche,HS(38)
Gieck,GL(280,497),
    HW(12 entries)
Gieda,K1(166A)
Gielmann,LS
Gielsdorf,LS,WK
Gienger,GL(5
    entries)
Gier,WK
Giering,WK
Gierre,WK
Giers,WK
von Giers,MM
Gierski,K1(166A)
Gierszewski,K1(166A)
Giese,K1(166A),MM,WK
Giesing,WK
Giesk,GL(284,289)
Gieske,LS
Giesler,MM
Gieß,GL(289),LS,
    W#(4.35),WK
Gieße,WK
Gießler,GL(305)
Giezen,WK
Gigmayer,WK
Gigy,WK
Gilberg,MM
Gilbert,WK
Gilberth,WK
Gilbertus,W#(2.23)
Gilbrandt,BU
Gilbrich,LS
Gild,WK
Gildner,LS
Gilen,WK
Gilert,WK
Gilger,GL(410)
Gilgert,GL(410)
Gilgin,WK
Giliaum,WK
Giling,LS
Gill,WK
Gillen,WK
Gillenberg,WK
Gillert,WK
Gilliaume,WK

Gillich,WK
Gilling,WK
Gillion,WK
Gillman,WK
Gillmann,LS,WK
Gillshoffer,LS
Gilmy,WK
Gilruth,GL(507)
Gilsdorf,WK
Gilson,WK
Gilten,LS
Giltner,WK
Giltzer,WK
Gily,WK
Gimbel,GL(334,476),
WK
Gimblaim,LS
Giml,WK
Gimpel,WK
Gimpl,WK
Gindermisch,WK
Gindling,WK
Ginger,GL(5 entries)
Gink,LS
Gino,WK
Ginon,WK
Gins,WK
Ginter,BU,LS,WK
Gintermann,LS
Ginther,WK
Gintzel,WK
Gion,WK
Gir,WK
Gira,WK
Girad,WK
Girard,WK
Girat,WK
Giretz,WK
Girge,WK
Girgen,WK
Girrich,WK
Girs,WK
Gisberg,WK
Gisbrecht,BU
Gischka,WK
Gisler,WK
Giß,WK
Gißheimer,WK
Gissi,WK
Gißler,WK
Gitere,WK
Giterle,WK
Gittinger,WK
Gittler,LS
Gitzhofer,LS
Gitzing,WK
Giuß,WK
Giza,K1(166A)

Gizhofer,WK
Gizinger,WK
Glaab,WK
Glad,WK
Gladt,WK
Glaeser,WK
Glaevecke,MM
Glaisle,WK
Glaissener,WK
Glans,WK
Glantz,LS
Glantzer,WK
Glantzerin,WK
Glanz,LS
Glas,WK
Glaser,HS(43),LS,
SW(24),W#(8.19),
WK
Glaserin,W#(7.8)
Glasert,WK
Glass,IE(89,94,97,
98)
Glaß,LS,MM,SW(4,14,
40),WK
Gläß,WK
Glasser,GF(96B)
Glässer,W#(4.66)
Glatt,WK
Glatte,WK
Glatz,LS,WK
Glatzin,WK
Glau,WK
Glaub,WK
Glaucke,WK
Glauert,MM
Glauß,WK
Glaussin,WK
Glebieka,MM
Gleck,WK
Gleckler,WK
von Glehn,MM
Gleich,WK
Gleisner,SW(21),WK
Gleiß,LS,WK
Glentsch,WK
Gleser,WK
Glesl,WK
Gleß,WK
Gleßner,WK
Gletzel,WK
Glezel,WK
Glidner,WK
Glimer,WK
Glinger,WK
Glisbitz,WK
Glober,LS
Glockner,W#(4.104)
Glode,WK

Glodin,WK
Glodis,WK
Gloede,MM
Glogau,MM
Glöggler,WK
Gloisner,WK
Glomann,LS,WK
Glomayer,WK
Glombin,HS(59)
Glose,LS,WK
Gloß,WK
Glotau,WK
Glotzbucher,WK
Głowacki,K1(166A)
Glück,GL(393),WK
Gluth,HS(75)
Gnab,WK
Gnad,SW(16)
Gnadenberger,WK
Gnadental,GL(76)
Gnamm,WK
Gnann,WK
Gnap,WK
Gnedig,WK
Gneissel,WK
Gobel,WK
Göbel,LS,WK
Gobelet,WK
Gobelius,WK
Göckel,WK
Goddel,WK
Göddel,WK
Göde,K1(166A)
Gödelmann,MM
Gödert,LS,WK
Goebel,LS
Göebel,WK
Goedke,MM
Göehlen,WK
Goeldner,WK
Goellner,GL(493)
Goeltl,GL(337)
Goercken,MM
Goergen,LS
Goerke,BU
Goerlitz,MM
Goerts,BU
Goertz,BU
Goertzen,BU
Goet,LS,WK
Goettel,LS
Goffin,WK
Göfry,LS
Gohl,LS,WK
Gohr,WK
Göhring,WK
Goi,WK
Gokell,WK

Gramnig,WK
Grams,HS(26)
Gramsched,WK
Gran,HW(30)
Granacher,WK
Grand,WK
le Grand,WK
Grandsiere,WK
Granies,WK
Granschan,WK
Grantz,WK
Granz,WK
Granzow,MM
Grapen,MM
Gras,WK
Grasen,WK
Gräser,GF(93B)
Grasmann,LS
Gräsmann,WK
Graß,LS,MM
Grassenau,WK
Grasser,WK
Grässer,WK
Grassinger,WK
Grassingerin,WK
Graßmann,LS,WK
Graßnickel,MM
Gräther,WK
Gratidie,WK
Gratis,WK
Gratschew,MM
Gratz,WK
Grau,GL(189),WK
Graube,WK
Grauber,LS
Grauer,LS,WK
Grauf,GL(215),WK
Graul,WK
Graule,LS
Graumann,MM
Graupner,LS,WK
Grausam,WK
Grauser,WK
Grausgruberin,WK
Grauß,W#(5.94),WK
Grauvogel,WK
Gray,WK
Graymannin,WK
Greb,LS,WK
Grebe,WK
Greber,LS,WK
Grebldinger,WK
Grebner,WK
Grech,WK
Gredinger,WK
Gredler,WK
Green,GL(388,505)
Gref,LS,WK

Greff,WK
Greger,LS,MM
Gregler,WK
Gregor,WK
Gregorie,WK
Gregorius,LS,WK
Grehenbild,LS
Grehn,MM
Greidenweiß,WK
Greif,WK
Greifenstein,LS
Greiffenstein,WK
Greil,WK
Greiling,LS,WK
Greim,MM
Greimb,WK
Greindl,WK
Greiner,WK
Greiß,WK
Grem,WK
Gremayer,WK
Greme,WK
Gremer,WK
Gremerin,WK
Gremgel,WK
Greming,WK
Gremisch,WK
Gremmer,WK
Grenauer,WK
Grener,WK
Grengor,WK
Grenz,GL(432,502)
Greschl,WK
Greser,WK
Gresing,WK
Gresl,WK
Greß,WK
Gressin,WK
Greßl,WK
Gressler,GF(119B)
Grethmann,MM
Gretien,WK
Gretz,WK
Gretzer,WK
Greulich,WK
Greve,MM
Grevratte,WK
Greyenbühl,WK
Greyne,GS(18)
Griber,WK
Griblin,WK
Gribnitz,MM
Grieb,WK
Griebe,K1(166A)
Griebnitz,MM
Grien,WK
Grienwald,WK
Griesbekin,WK

Griese,MM
Grieser,WK
Griesfelder,WK
Grieshaber,WK
Griesheimer,LS
Grieshober,WK
Griess,GL(457,460,
 509),HW(81)
Grieß,MM,WK
Grießbaum,WK
Grießmann,LS,WK
Grifaten,WK
Griffadon,WK
Griffat,WK
Griffaton,WK
Griffel,WK
Grikk,WK
Grill,BU,LS,WK
Grilling,WK
Grillmann,LS
Grim,WK
Grimath,WK
Grimbett,WK
Grimelmayer,WK
Grimer,WK
Griming,WK
Griminn,WK
Grimm,MM,WK
Grimmanns,MM
Grimmer,WK
Grimminger,WK
Grimmingerin,WK
Grin,LS
Gringure,WK
Grinn,WK
Grinsteiner,WK
Grisch,WK
Grischau,MM
Grischel,WK
Grischko,MM
Grisenbruch,WK
Grismann,LS
Grißbeck,WK
Griter,WK
Gritz,WK
Grivallon,WK
Grob,GF(91B),LS,WK
Grober,WK
Gröber,WK
Grobfinger,WK
Grodlock,WK
Grodt,MM
Groehl,BU
Groening,BU
Groeßmann,LS
Groganz,WK
Grögel,LS
Groh,WK

Grohmann,GS(90A)
Grohn,WK
Groiß,WK
Grökel,WK
Grokenberger,GL(235)
Groll,W#(5.43),WK
Gröll,WK
Gröller,WK
Grolowski,K1(166A)
Gröly,LS,WK
Grömling,WK
Gromowa,MM
Gronau,MM
Groner,WK
Gröner,LS,WK
Groniar,WK
Gronlen,WK
Gropholz,WK
Gros,WK
Grosch,GL(496,497),
    WK
Groschan,WK
Gröschel,WK
Groschl,WK
Gröschl,WK
Gröschle,LS
Grosglos,WK
Grosgurth,WK
Grosin,WK
Grösmann,LS
Groß,GS(14),LS,MM,
    SW(2),W#(1.48,
    5.33),WK
Grossart,WK
Großdidier,WK
Grosse,WK
Großend,LS
Größer,LS
Großhantz,WK
Großkopf,WK
Großkreutz,MM
Großman,WK
Grossmann,HW(28,31,
    48,90)
Großmann,GL(5
    entries),LS,MM,WK
Großmayer,LS,WK
Großmüller,LS
Grote,LS,MM,WK
Groth,MM,WK
Grottendorfer,WK
Growalet,WK
Groz,WK
Grub,LS,WK
Grüb,GL(296)
Grube,MM
Grubeit,LS
Grübele,GL(332)

Grubelt,WK
Gruber,IE(89),LS,WK
Grüber,WK
Grubert,GS(19,22,
    89B)
Grüder,MM
Grueber,W#(3.30),WK
Gruenther,BU
Gruger,LS
Grül,LS
Grum,WK
Grüm,WK
Grumacker,WK
Grümm,WK
Grummenacker,WK
Grummer,LS
Grun,K1(168A,168B),
    WK
Grün,HW(11 entries),
    LS,WK
Grunanger,WK
Grunau,BU
Grünberg,MM
Grünberger,WK
Grundhausen,WK
Gründl,WK
Grundler,GL(324)
Gründler,WK
Grundt,LS
Gruneberger,WK
Grunel,WK
Grünewald,LS
Grünke,K1(168B)
Grünn,LS,WK
Grunner,WK
Grunnwald,WK
Grünwald,LS,MM
Grünwalt,WK
Grupp,WK
Gruschke,MM
Grusling,WK
Gruß,WK
Grüss,HW(15)
Grussamayer,WK
Grüßler,LS
Gruton,WK
Grützmacher,KL(18)
Gruyer,WK
Gryb,K1(166A)
Gryons,WK
Grzyziński,K1(166A)
Gscheidle,GL(456)
Gscheidler,GL(371)
Gschrey,WK
Gschwendner,WK
Gschwind,GL(479),WK
Gsell,GL(296),LS,WK
Guber,GL(82),LS

Gubinger,WK
Gucher,WK
Guck,WK
Guckenbach,GL(206)
Gückenmuß,WK
Guckert,WK
Gude,MM
Güdemann,WK
Gudenkauf,WK
Gudiens,LS
Guedjes,MM
Guenter,BU
Gugacher,WK
Gugacherin,WK
Gugel,GL(438)
Gugenmaß,LS
Gugert,WK
Guhl,MM
Gühlstorff,MM
Gühr,WK
Guilaum,WK
Guillaume,WK
Guinot,WK
Guk,LS
Gukell,WK
Gülcher,WK
Gulden,LS
Gülden,LS,WK
Güldner,MM
Gulitz,MM
Gullis,MM
Güllmantel,LS
Guman,WK
Gumbel,WK
Gumpelin,WK
Gumpenseder,WK
Gundelmann,W#(1.38)
Günderin,WK
Gundermann,LS,WK
Gündermann,LS
Gundheimer,WK
Gundlach,GS(60,63,
    89A),MM
Gunert,WK
Günge,WK
Gungel,WK
Gungernaß,WK
Gunkel,WK
Gunneley,LS
Gunringer,WK
Gunt,WK
Günter,WK
Gunterman,WK
Güntert,WK
Günther,LS,WK
Günthner,SW(7)
Güntner,LS,WK
Guntolff,WK

Güntter,WK
Guntze,WK
Güntzel,WK
Guntzen,WK
Guntzer,WK
Guntzin,WK
Gunz,WK
Gurger,WK
Gurgerin,WK
Gurst,WK
Gürtler,LS
Gusch,WK
Guschel,WK
Guse,GS(91A),
  K1(166A)
Gusel,WK
Guß,WK
Güß,WK
Gussen,GL(303)
Gust,HS(44)
Gustav,WK
Gut,GL(413),WK
Güt,WK
Gutberl,WK
Gutbrod,WK
Gutendorf,WK
Gutenkunst,WK
Gutenthaler,LS,WK
Guterwill,WK
Gutfreund,WK
Gutfreundin,WK
Guth,MM,WK
Guthan,MM
Guthau,MM
Guthenthaler,LS
Guthier,WK
Guthines,WK
Guthrie,GL(389)
Guti,WK
Gutiens,LS
Gutier,WK
Gutikunst,WK
Gutjahr,WK
Gutleber,WK
Gutler,WK
Gutlinger,WK
Gutmann,WK
Gutmännin,WK
Gutnagl,WK
de Gutry,WK
Gutschar,WK
Gutsche,WK
Gutschmidt,MM
Gütschow,MM
Gutt,LS,W#(4.24),WK
Guttbrod,WK
Güttel,WK
Guttenacker,LS

Guttenberg,LS
Guttenberger,LS,WK
Gutterwill,LS
Guttmann,W#(4.36),WK
Guttsel,WK
Gutwein,WK
Gutwiński,K1(166A)
Gutwirt,LS
Gutzleff,MM
Gutzmann,KL(18,37,
  38)
Guza,K1(166A)
Gwand,LS
Gwinner,LS,WK
Gy,WK
Gyllienstack,MM
Gylow,MM
Gyr,WK
Gyssin,LS
Gzyk,K1(167B)
Haab,WK
Haabe,WK
Haaber,W#(3.39)
Haaberer,W#(5.61)
Haacke,WK
Haag,WK
Haager,LS,WK
Haak,LS,MM
Haam,LS
Haan,LS,WK
Haann,WK
Haar,W#(8.41),WK
Haas,GL(232,318),
  HW(14 entries),
  IE(89,96),LS,
  SW(7,16,52,57,59,
  64),W#(1.42,8.5),
  WK
Haase,LS,MM
Haaser,WK
Haaß,LS,WK
Hab,LS
Habe,WK
Haber,LS,WK
Haberauer,WK
Haberdiestl,WK
Haberger,LS
Haberkohrn,W#(2.78,
  4.19)
Haberkorrn,W#(1.39)
Haberland,MM
Haberle,WK
Häberlen,WK
Habermann,GL(381)
Habermeyer,WK
Habermüller,WK
Haberpusch,WK
Habersak,WK

Haberstock,LS,WK
Haberstok,WK
Haberstrau,WK
Haberstroh,WK
Habet,WK
Habich,WK
Habicht,MM
Habik,WK
Habisch,LS
Hable,SW(38)
Habner,WK
Hacbeyl,WK
Hacht,WK
Hack,LS,WK
Hacka,WK
Hackel,WK
Häckel,GL(461)
Hackemer,WK
Hackenmüller,LS,WK
Hackenschmied,LS
Hackenthal,MM
Hacker,LS,WK
Häcker,GL(360)
Hackert,MM
Hackisa,WK
Hackl,WK
Hackmann,MM
Hackmer,LS
Hackschmied,LS
Hadatsch,WK
Hadbawnik,SW(27)
Hadel,LS
Hadenberger,WK
Haderer,WK
Haderle,WK
Häderle,WK
Hadinger,LS,WK
Hadler,WK
Hadrawa,W#(6.42)
Hadrian,GS(89A)
Haecker,WK
Haeckert,MM
Haedge,MM
Haefke,GS(89A),MM
Haefner,LS
Haeger,GL(496)
Hael,LS
Haen,WK
Hafel,WK
Hafenbratl,WK
Hafendeber,WK
Haferzettel,GF(131A)
Häfferle,WK
Haffner,GL(43,44),WK
Haffstein,MM
Hafner,GL(407),WK
Häfner,HW(13
  entries),WK

Hag,GL(221)
Hage,BU
Hagedorn,MM
Hägele,GL(279,403, 476)
Hägelen,GL(28,29)
Hageloch,GL(385)
Hagemann,LS,WK
Hagemayer,WK
Hagemeister,MM
von Hagemeister,MM
Hagen,MM
Hagenbach,GL(40)
Hagenloch,GL(8 entries)
Hagenlock,GL(276)
Hagenmayer,WK
von Hagenow,MM
Hagenschmid,WK
Hager,LS,WK
Hagerstaedt,MM
Hägg,WK
Hagh,WK
Häglin,WK
Hagmann,WK
Hagmayer,WK
Haher,LS
Hahn,GL(456),HW(207, 208),K1(166B),LS, MM,SW(35,36),WK
von Hahn,GL(60),MM
Hahne,MM
Hahner,WK
Hahnisch,K1(166A)
Haibl,WK
Haid,GL(277,320), SW(29),W#(7.15), WK
Haideker,WK
Haidekerin,WK
Haiden,SW(16),WK
Haidenfelder,WK
Haidt,GL(277)
Haier,WK
Haigner,WK
Hailer,WK
Hailmayer,WK
Haim,GL(465),WK
Haimbucher,WK
Haimbuchinger,WK
Hain,WK
Hainer,WK
Hainisch,LS
Hainz,LS,WK
Hainzelmann,WK
Hainzmann,WK
Haipp,WK
Hairy,WK

Haisch,HW(14 entries)
Haische,LS
Haist,W#(5.49)
Haiter,WK
Haitz,WK
Hajnóczy,GF(115)
Hak,LS
Hake,WK
Hakenschmied,LS
Hakert,WK
Hakius,LS
Halang,GS(27,90A)
Halauer,WK
Halbach,MM
Halbher,WK
Halbherr,WK
Halbich,WK
Halbig,LS
Halboth,LS
Halder,WK
Haldmann,WK
Halibart,LS
Haliczek,WK
Haljall,MM
Halle,MM
Haller,GL(229),MM,WK
von Haller,MM
Hallerin,WK
Halli,WK
Hallinger,WK
Hallmann,WK
Hallung,LS,WK
Halm,WK
Halmbretl,WK
Halßbach,WK
Haltemann,MM
Haltenwanger,WK
Halter,WK
Haltmayer,WK
Ham,LS,WK
Hama,WK
Haman,WK
Hamang,WK
Hamann,HW(207), IE(89),LS,MM,WK
Hamb,LS
Hamburg,IE(94,96)
Hamel,GF(123,131A), WK
Hämel,WK
Hamele,WK
Hamelmann,LS
Hamen,WK
Hamengen,WK
Hamenschi,WK
Hamer,WK
Hamerl,WK

Hamermüller,WK
Hames,WK
Hameß,WK
Hamilton,WK
Hamlin,WK
Hamm,BU,GS(19,55), LS,WK
von Hamm,GL(65)
Hamman,WK
Hammas,WK
Hamme,WK
Hammel,HW(67),WK
Hammelmann,LS
Hammen,WK
Hammer,GL(360),LS,WK
Hammerling,LS
Hämmerling,HW(51)
Hammerschmid, W#(8.15)
Hammerschmidt,MM
Hammes,LS,WK
Hamon,WK
Hampe,MM
Hampel,LS
Hampf,MM
Hampl,LS
Hampp,GL(231)
Hamrich,WK
Han,LS,WK
Hanak,LS
Hanauer,WK
Hanck,WK
Hanckel,WK
Hancz,WK
Hanczlman,WK
Handel,GL(40,223), HW(20 entries), LS,SW(26)
Handkammer,LS
Handke,GS(26)
Handkramer,WK
Handl,WK
Händle,GL(40)
Handlowski,K1(166A)
Handrich,GS(19)
Handwich,MM
Handwig,MM
Handzlik,LS
Hane,MM
Hanekker,WK
Hanel,WK
Hänel,WK
Hanerkurt,WK
Hanewaldt,MM
Hanff,WK
Hangheiser,WK
Hanich,LS
Hank,GL(195)

Hanka,LS
Hanke,GL(468),LS
Hankes,WK
Hanl,WK
Hann,LS,WK
Hänn,LS
Hannauer,WK
Hannebach,LS
Hanneker,WK
Hannes,WK
Hannich,WK
Hannß,WK
Hanntze,WK
Hanosius,WK
Hans,LS,WK
Hänschke,GL(122,123, 134)
Hansel,LS,WK
Hanselmann,WK
Hansen,MM,WK
Hanses,WK
Hansge,LS,WK
Hänsle,WK
Hansman,WK
Hanß,LS,WK
Hanßelmann,WK
Hanster,GL(212)
Hanstull,WK
Hantes,WK
Hantsch,LS,WK
Hantz,WK
Hantzl,LS
Hanuś,K1(166A)
Hanx,GL(195)
Hanzel,LS
Hanzelmann,LS
Hanzl,WK
Happel,MM,WK
von Hapsburg,SW(24)
Haratin,WK
Harbach,LS
Hardenacke,WK
Harder,BU
von Harder,MM
Harders,BU
Hardi,WK
Härdle,GL(425)
Hardon,WK
Hardy,WK
Harferden,MM
Harg,WK
Hargard,WK
Hargart,WK
Hargesheimer,LS, SW(18,36,44),WK
Harich,GF(96A),WK
Harig,GF(93A),WK
Harik,WK

Harin,WK
Haring,WK
Häring,WK
Harion,WK
Harisch,WK
Harle,WK
Harlfinger,LS
Harling,WK
Harlos,LS
Harmes,MM
Harms,BU
Harn,WK
Harnischfäger,WK
Harpus,WK
Harr,GL(341)
Harra,WK
von Harrach,MM
Harri,WK
Harrison,MM
Harry,WK
Hars,MM
Harsch,GL(129 entries)
Harsche,LS,WK
Harschel,WK
Harschon,GL(371)
Hart,LS,SW(2),WK
Hartas,WK
Hartbusch,WK
Hartel,LS
Hartenbach,WK
Hartenstein,WK
Harter,GL(458,509), HW(19 entries),WK
Härter,HW(181),WK
Hartert,WK
Hartfelder,LS,WK
Hartfiel,HS(33)
Hartfuß,WK
Harth,LS,W#(8.107), WK
Harti,WK
Hartig,WK
Hartinger,SW(24,38)
Hartknoch,MM
Hartl,SW(17,68),WK
Härtle,GL(186)
Hartleb,LS,WK
Härtlein,WK
Hartlieb,LS
Hartman,WK
Hartmanin,WK
Hartmann,GF(91B, 92A),GL(356),LS, MM,SW(18),WK
Hartmannin,WK
Hartmanns,WK
Hartsch,LS

Hartschenko,GL(68)
Hartstein,WK
Hartung,LS,MM,WK
Hartwein,LS,WK
Harundin,WK
Hary,WK
Harz,LS,WK
Harzer,WK
Has,LS,WK
Hascher,WK
Haschler,SW(44)
Hase,K1(167B),MM
Haselbach,GF(92A),LS
Haselbacher,LS
Haselberger,WK
Hasen,WK
Hasenfuß,GL(261)
Haser,WK
Hasis,LS
Haslacher,WK
Haslerin,WK
Hasmann,LS
Haspach,WK
Haspel,LS
Haspeler,WK
Hass,GL(407)
Haß,LS,WK
Häß,WK
Haßdenteufel,WK
Hasse,MM,WK
Hässe,MM
Hassel,IE(90),LS, SW(19)
Hasselbecher,LS,WK
Hasselbergerin,WK
Hasselmann,WK
Hassenkuhr,WK
Hassenteibel,WK
Hasser,W#(4.95),WK
Hassewicz,K1(166A)
Häßgen,WK
Hassinger,LS,WK
Haßl,WK
Haßlauert,WK
Hassur,WK
Hast,MM,WK
Hastermann,WK
Hatamar,WK
Hatschenreiter,LS
Hatter,WK
Hattich,WK
Hättich,WK
Hättig,WK
Hau,WK
Haubach,LS
Haubeil,LS,WK
Hauber,LS,WK

Haubert,LS,W#(1.4,
  1.72),WK
Haubner,LS,WK
Haubrich,LS,WK
Haubscheid,WK
Haubt,WK
Hauch,WK
Hauck,LS,WK
Hauckin,WK
Hauer,GF(92B,131A),
  LS,W#(7.34),WK
Hauert,WK
Hauerwas,LS
Haues,WK
Hauff,GL(341),WK
Haufler,GL(138)
Haufner,WK
Hauft,HS(35)
Haug,GL(233,357),
  HW(26,82),LS,WK
Hauger,WK
Haugk,WK
Hauk,HW(15),LS,MM,
  W#(6.102),WK
Haumburg,WK
Haumesek,WK
Hauprich,WK
Haupt,GL(78),IE(90),
  LS,SW(19),WK
Hauptmann,GS(91B),WK
Hauranek,WK
Haurwas,WK
Haus,LS,WK
Hausauer,GL(508)
Hausbüchler,WK
Hauschild,WK
Hausel,WK
Hauser,GL(246,341),
  LS,W#(7.27),WK
Häuser,GL(40,233,
  273,274),LS
Hausild,WK
Hausknecht,WK
Hausleitscher,GS(11)
Häusler,HW(5
  entries),LS,WK
Hausman,WK
Hausmann,LS,WK
Hausner,LS
Hauß,WK
Haussauer,GL(433)
Hausse,LS
Hausser,LS,WK
Haußler,WK
Häußler,WK
Haußlung,WK
Haußner,WK
Haußnerin,WK

Haustadl,WK
Hausten,WK
Hausterer,WK
Hauter,WK
Hautz,LS
Hauwe,WK
Haux,GL(491)
Hauz,WK
Havemann,MM
Havenick,MM
Hävernick,MM
Havité,WK
Hawele,WK
Hawlica,LS
Hawlik,SW(38),WK
Hayd,WK
Hayden,SW(38)
Hayder,LS
Hayen,MM
Haym,HS(43),LS
Hayn,WK
Haynen,WK
Hayspringer,LS
Haytner,LS
Hazung,WK
Heaps,GL(191)
Heb,WK
Hebelt,MM
Heber,WK
Heberger,WK
Hebergerin,WK
Heberle,WK
Heberlein,WK
Heberlen,WK
Heberth,WK
Hebich,WK
Hebler,WK
Heblmeyer,WK
Hebner,WK
Hech,WK
Hechinger,WK
Hecht,MM
Hechtor,WK
Heck,LS,WK
Heckel,WK
Heckels,WK
Hecker,MM,WK
Heckl,WK
Heckler,WK
Heckmann,WK
Hecktor,LS,WK
Hector,WK
Hederich,WK
Hederl,WK
Hederle,GF(96A)
Hedig,WK
Hedrich,GF(91B),HW(9
  entries)

Hee,WK
Heeb,WK
Heed,WK
Heeg,WK
Heen,WK
Heensch,MM
Heer,GL(7 entries),
  HW(14,20,21,30),
  LS,WK
v. Heering,MM
Heese,BU
Hefele,LS
Hefelen,WK
Heffner,GL(40),WK
Hefler,WK
Hefner,LS
Heft,GS(19),HW(29)
Hefter,WK
Hegel,WK
Hegele,GL(205),LS,WK
Hegelman,WK
Hegen,MM
Heger,WK
Hegert,WK
Hegesch,WK
Hegg,WK
Heggen,WK
Heggerspacher,
  W#(3.54)
Hegst,WK
Hegster,WK
Hehn,LS,SW(14,19)
Heib,WK
Heibach,WK
Heiberger,WK
Heibling,WK
Heichert,LS,WK
Heichin,WK
Heiczman,WK
Heid,BU,GL(277,301,
  424),WK
Heide,BU,WK
Heidebrecht,BU
Heidelberger,HW(21)
Heidelmann,WK
Heidelspeck,WK
Heidemann,GS(19)
Heiden,MM
Heidenberger,WK
Heidenreich,MM,WK
Heider,WK
Heiderbrun,WK
Heiderich,LS,WK
Heidinger,LS,WK
Heidl,LS,WK
Heidmann,MM
Heidnisch,WK
Heidorfer,WK

Heidrichin,WK
Heidtmann,MM
Heiduk,WK
Heidwinckel,MM
Heifer,WK
Heigeth,WK
Heigis,LS
Heil,GF(92A,125B,
 127B,131A),LS,WK
Heiland,LS,WK
Heiler,LS,WK
Heiles,WK
Heilig,WK
Heiliger,WK
Heiling,LS,WK
Heillig,WK
Heillman,WK
Heilmann,WK
Heilus,WK
Heim,GL(204,465),
 HS(33),LS,MM,
 SW(29),W#(1.26),
 WK
Heimann,LS,WK
Heimbach,GL(397)
Heimberger,LS,WK
Heimbuch,GF(95B)
Heimburg,WK
Heimerdingen,WK
Heimerle,WK
Heimes,WK
Heiminger,LS
Heimke,WK
Heimling,LS
Heimösch,WK
Heimthal,WK
Hein,BU,GL(205),
 HS(65),KL(18),LS,
 MM,WK
Heinbrych,LS
Heinbuch,GL(397)
Heinchen,WK
Heincke,MM
Heincz,WK
Heindorfer,WK
Heine,MM,WK
Heinemann,LS
Heinen,WK
Heinerig,WK
Heines,WK
Heinig,W#(2.22)
Heiniger,LS
Heinisch,LS,WK
Heiniz,WK
Heink,WK
Heinke,MM
Heinle,GL(479)
Heinlein,WK

Heinne,WK
Heinnert,WK
Heinrich,HW(90),LS,
 MM,WK
Heinrichin,WK
Heinrichs,BU,MM
Heinrichsen,MM
Heinriks,BU
Heins,LS,WK
Heinsel,LS
Heinß,WK
Heintz,WK
Heintzmann,WK
Heinz,LS,WK
Heinze,LS,WK
Heinzel,WK
Heinzelmann,WK
Heinzgen,WK
Heinzmann,WK
Heis,WK
Heischer,WK
Heischle,LS
Heise,K1(166A),MM
Heiser,GL(273,274,
 498)
Heisinger,WK
Heisler,LS,WK
Heislinger,LS
Heismann,MM
Heisner,WK
Heiß,WK
Heisser,WK
Heissin,WK
Heißler,LS,WK
Heißmann,WK
Heister,WK
Heitmann,IE(94)
Heitmüller,GL(257)
Heitrich,WK
Heitz,LS,WK
Heitzer,LS
Heitzin,WK
Heitzmann,WK
Heiz,WK
Heizelmann,W#(8.87)
Heizle,WK
Heizmänin,WK
Heizmann,LS
Hejkow,GL(182)
Hek,LS,WK
Hekenberger,WK
Hekiger,LS
Hektor,LS
Hel,WK
Helbauer,WK
Helber,HW(16,19)
Helbich,LS,WK
Helbig,LS,WK

Helbing,LS
Held,LS,WK
Helderich,WK
Heldin,WK
Heldström,MM
Heldt,WK
Helefi,WK
Heleisen,WK
Helfenstein,GL(410)
Helfer,LS,WK
Helferich,LS,WK
Helferstein,WK
Helfert,MM
Helffen,WK
Helffenstein,WK
Helffer,WK
Helfferigs,WK
Helffert,WK
Helfig,WK
Helfigin,WK
Helfinger,HW(19)
Helfreich,WK
Helfrich,WK
Helfried,LS
Helinger,WK
Hell,LS,WK
Hellebrand,LS
Hellenblut,WK
Heller,GS(91B),
 HW(67),LS,WK
Helleringen,WK
Helli,WK
Hellinger,SW(7)
Hellmann,WK
Hellmer,WK
Hellmuth,LS
Hellreiter,LS
Hellwingerin,WK
Helm,GL(284,350,
 409),LS,MM,WK
Helman,WK
Helmann,MM
Helmayer,WK
Helme,WK
Helmer,WK
von Helmersen,MM
Helmesin,WK
Helmich,WK
Helms,MM
Helmschrat,WK
Helsen,WK
Helß,WK
Helstruber,WK
Heltenz,WK
Heltzner,WK
Helzel,WK
Hem,WK
Hemb,LS

Hemen,WK
Hemerlung,WK
Hemetsberger,GF(103)
Heminger,WK
Heml,WK
Hemm,WK
Hemmer,WK
Hemmerich,WK
Hemmerling,HS(54),LS
Hemmes,WK
Hemminger,WK
Hempel,MM
Hemsberg,WK
Hemse,WK
Hemstl,WK
Hemsuß,WK
Hen,WK
Henche,LS
Henchen,LS
Henck,MM
Hencke,MM,WK
Henckel,WK
Henckern,WK
Hencz,WK
Henczl,WK
Henders,WK
Henderscher,WK
Hendes,WK
Hendzelewski,
    K1(166A)
Henecke,WK
Heneke,IE(98)
Henekn,WK
Heneku,WK
Henes,WK
Heng,WK
Hengen,WK
Henger,WK
Henges,WK
Hengl,WK
Hengst,WK
Hengstenberg,WK
Heniger,LS
Heniko,WK
Heninger,HW(19),WK
Henk,LS,WK
Henke,GL(404),
    GS(19),KL(55),MM
Henkel,GF(131A),MM,
    WK
Henkelman,WK
Henkes,W#(1.12)
Henle,LS
Henn,LS,WK
Henne,GL(261),WK
Hennecker,WK
Henneken,MM,WK
Hennel,WK

Hennemann,LS
Hennenberger,WK
Henner,LS,WK
Hennes,WK
Hennet,WK
Hennich,WK
Hennicki,WK
Hennig,LS,MM
Henning,HW(30),MM,WK
Hennrizin,WK
Henns,WK
Henoy,WK
Henpacher,WK
Henri,WK
Henrich,WK
Henrichs,WK
Henrici,MM
Henriges,WK
Henring,WK
Henrion,WK
Henry,WK
Henschlewski,
    K1(166A)
Hensel,HS(65),LS,WK
Hensen,WK
Hensky,MM
Hensler,GL(212),WK
Henßler,WK
Henster,GL(212)
Hentge,LS
Hentges,WK
Hentschel,HS(70)
Hentschl,WK
Hentze,LS
Hentzien,WK
Hentzl,WK
Hentzöß,WK
Heny,LS,WK
Henz,LS,WK
Henzel,LS
Henzl,LS
Hepner,BU
Hepp,LS,WK
Heppe,LS
Hepting,LS
Her,WK
Herad,LS
Herall,LS
Herb,W#(2.77)
Herbach,WK
Herber,WK
Herberg,HS(75)
Herberger,LS
Herberholt,WK
Herbern,WK
Herbert,WK
Herberth,WK
Herbi,WK

Herbibo,WK
Herbiwo,WK
Herbold,WK
Herbst,LS,MM,WK
Herby,WK
Herck,WK
Herczeg,WK
Herd,WK
Herdeger,WK
Herder,MM,WK
Herdi,GF(93B),WK
Herdle,GL(425)
Herdt,WK
Herell,WK
Hereth,GL(496)
Herg,WK
Hergel,WK
Hergelt,WK
Hergert,WK
Herich,WK
Herinam,WK
Hering,GL(365),LS,WK
Heringer,WK
Heriot,WK
Herkommer,GL(371)
Herle,WK
Herling,GF(122)
Herman,GL(496),
    HW(82),WK
Hermang,WK
Hermani,WK
Hermanin,WK
Hermann,GL(5
    entries),HW(13
    entries),IE(89),
    K1(166A,167A),LS,
    MM,SW(31),WK
Hermannin,WK
Hermanowski,K1(166A)
Hermenucz,WK
Hermerstarf,WK
Hermes,MM,WK
Hermon,WK
Hernbarth,WK
Hernberger,WK
Herner,WK
Hernig,WK
Hernpach,WK
Hernstel,WK
Herold,LS,MM,WK
Heroth,LS,WK
Herr,GL(189),LS,
    W#(5.41),WK
Herre,WK
Herrmann,GF(92B,
    131B),GL(257),
    HW(7 entries),LS,
    WK

Hilgert,WK
Hilk,LS
Hilkene,WK
Hill,GL(337),LS,WK
Hillar,WK
Hillbroner,WK
Hillbrunner,LS
Hillebrand,LS,
  W#(8.114),WK
Hillenbrand,WK
Hiller,GL(286),
  HW(179,208),WK
Hillig,LS
Hilligert,WK
Hillmann,IE(98),MM
Hilmes,WK
Hilmeyer,WK
Hilmuth,WK
Hilser,WK
Hilserin,WK
Hilß,WK
Hilt,GL(26 entries)
Hilth,WK
Hiltig,GL(415)
Hiltner,IE(99)
Hilzer,LS,WK
Himber,WK
Himelken,WK
Himespach,WK
Himler,WK
Himmelheber,MM
Himmelreich,MM
Himmer,WK
Himmerich,GL(237)
Himsel,MM
Hinckel,WK
Hinderer,GL(180)
Hindersehr,WK
Hingel,WK
Hingelmann,MM
Hinger,GL(224)
Hingkelmann,MM
Hingot,WK
Hingst,MM
Hinkel,LS
Hinrichsohn,MM
Hinteregger,WK
Hinterhauser,WK
Hinterholz,WK
Hinterhölzel,WK
Hinterleutner,WK
Hintermann,LS
Hintz,KL(18,32)
Hintze,MM,WK
Hintzenstern,MM
Hintzke,MM
Hintzmann,MM
Hinz,GL(251),MM

Hinze,HW(31)
Hip,WK
Hipf,WK
Hipik,WK
Hipp,LS,WK
Hippach,WK
Hipper,WK
Hipperger,WK
Hippier,WK
Hippius,MM
Hippler,WK
Hipsch,WK
Hipsenberger,WK
Hirlinger,WK
Hirman,WK
Hirnigl,WK
Hirsch,GL(296),LS,
  MM,WK
Hirschabek,WK
Hirschbein,LS
Hirschfeld,LS,WK
Hirschl,WK
Hirschmann,GL(293),
  WK
Hirschmännin,WK
Hirschmüller,LS,WK
Hirschner,WK
Hirsekorn,GL(339)
Hirsterin,WK
Hirszowski,K1(166A)
Hirt,HS(33),WK
Hirtes,LS,WK
Hirth,WK
Hirtz,WK
Hirz,WK
Hirzel,GL(351)
Hischl,WK
Hissin,WK
Hissinger,LS
Hißl,WK
Hissung,WK
Hitelman,WK
Hitner,WK
Hittel,LS,WK
Hittenberger,
  GF(131B)
Hittentit,LS
Hittmayer,WK
Hittmayr,WK
Hittrich,WK
Hitz,W#(4.80)
Hix,WK
Hlaki,WK
Hlatki,WK
Hobay,WK
von Hobe,MM
Hobeck,MM
Hobel,LS

Hoberg,MM
Hoberin,WK
Hoberstro,WK
Höbl,WK
Hobler,LS,WK
Höblin,WK
Hobscheid,WK
Hobstein,WK
Hoch,GF(91A),
  GL(407),LS,MM,WK
Hochan,MM
Hochbacher,WK
Hochbein,WK
Hochbeinin,WK
Hochberger,LS
Hochegger,WK
Hochenberger,WK
Hochfleisch,WK
Hochgrindel,WK
Hochin,WK
Hochleithner,WK
Hochmajer,WK
Hochman,WK
Hochreiter,WK
Hochreither,WK
Hochreitherin,WK
Hochreuter,WK
Hochroiter,WK
Hochstädterin,WK
Hochstartzer,WK
Hochstein,WK
Hochvald,WK
Hochvarterin,WK
Hochvimerin,WK
Hochwärder,WK
Hochwerter,LS
Hochwörter,LS
Hock,HW(11 entries),
  WK
Hockauf,HS(31)
Hocke,WK
Hockenberger,WK
Hocker,WK
Hod,WK
Hodaczewski,LS
Hodel,IE(89),SW(31,
  44)
Hodenmayer,WK
Hoditschka,W#(7.103)
Hodkowslaja,MM
Hodler,WK
Hoentz,MM
Hoeppener,MM
Hoeppner,MM
Hoeschele,HW(68)
Hoevet,MM
Hof,WK
Hofacker,WK

Hofbauer,WK
Hofe,MM
Hofele,WK
Höfele,WK
Höfelein,WK
Hofeneder,WK
Hofer,GL(201,441),WK
Höfer,GL(226)
Hoferin,WK
Höferling,WK
Hoff,GL(508),MM,WK
Höffeln,MM
Hoffer,GL(496),
    HW(18,21,66),WK
Höffer,WK
Hoffert,WK
Höffert,MM
Hoffinger,WK
Hoffkoffler,WK
Hoffkofflerin,WK
Höffler,WK
Hoffman,GL(329),
    IE(94,97,98),WK
Hoffmanin,WK
Hoffmann,GF(91A,91B,
    93A,122B),GL(17
    entries),GS(18,
    22,26,89B,91A),
    HW(208),LS,MM,
    SW(7,16,17,21,24,
    38,58),WK
Hoffmannin,WK
Hofle,WK
Hofler,WK
Höflinger,WK
Hofman,IE(94),WK
Hofmann,GL(7
    entries),IE(93),
    LS,SW(62),
    W#(7.44,8.9),WK
Hofmayer,WK
Hofmeister,WK
Hofmon,WK
Hofner,WK
Höfner,WK
Hofsäß,GL(299)
Hofstädter,LS,WK
Hofstädterin,WK
Hofstaeter,LS
Hofstätter,LS
Hofstätterin,WK
Hofstetter,WK
Hofstetterin,WK
Hofstrasser,WK
Hofwald,WK
Hogar,WK
Hoge,BU
Högebeck,WK

Hoger,WK
Höger,HW(88),
    W#(8.29)
Höh,WK
Hohebuch,WK
Hohenacken,GL(240)
Hohenberger,WK
Hohenburger,WK
Hohendajski,K1(166A)
Höhendorf,HS(44)
Hohenmüller,WK
Hohensee,HS(44)
Hohensteln,GL(277)
Hohlen,MM
Hohlm,MM
Hohloch,GL(133,134,
    317),HW(31
    entries)
Hohlweck,WK
Hohn,LS,WK
Höhn,GL(192,309,
    414),LS,WK
Höhner,WK
Hohnmüller,WK
Höhr,GL(402)
Hokell,WK
Hökkel,GL(273)
Hokschari,WK
Hol,WK
Holänder,WK
Holbereiter,WK
Hölblinger,WK
Holbveiß,WK
Holch,WK
Holcz,WK
Höld,W#(3.31)
Holdemajer,LS
Holdenmeyer,LS
Holder,WK
Holderbaum,LS,
    SW(40),WK
Holderblum,LS
Holdernek,WK
Holdernekin,WK
Holdmann,WK
Holdnik,GL(450)
Holdt,WK
Holerin,WK
Holf,WK
Hölger,WK
Holik,GL(312)
Holinger,LS
Holitzer,LS
Holl,LS,WK
Hollaczek,SW(7,17)
Hollander,MM
Holländer,HS(35)
von Hollander,MM

von Hollau,MM
Hollbereiter,LS
Holldorf,MM
Holle,WK
Hollemdorfer,
    W#(8.77)
Hollender,HS(37)
Holler,LS,WK
Hollermayer,WK
Höllig,WK
Hollinger,WK
Hollis,WK
Höllrigel,WK
Höllwarth,GL(317)
Hollwegg,WK
Holmblatt,GL(81)
Holoch,MM
Holocher,LS
Holowitz,WK
Holpach,WK
Hölpel,WK
Holreiter,LS
Holser,WK
Holsio,MM
Holst,MM
von Holst,MM
Holstein,LS
von
    Holstein-Gottorp,
    MM
Holterhof,WK
Holterhoff,WK
Holthen,MM
Holtz,LS,MM,WK
Holtzer,LS
Holtzerer,WK
Holtzinger,WK
Holtzingerin,WK
Holtzkamp,MM
Holtzmayer,LS
Holub,LS
Holupp,W#(8.58)
Holz,LS,WK
Holzberger,IE(99)
Holzderber,WK
Holzdörfer,GF(93B)
Hölzel,W#(7.67),WK
Holzer,LS,WK
Holzhauer,WK
Holzhauser,LS,WK
Holzkam,LS
Holzkan,WK
Hölzlein,WK
Holzleuthner,WK
Holzleuthnerin,WK
Holzleutner,WK
Holzman,WK
Holzmeister,LS

Hubschwärel,WK	Humpach,WK	Hutmacher,WK
Huc,WK	Hun,WK	Hutmann,MM,WK
Huch,WK	Hunczovßky,WK	Hütner,WK
Huck,IE(96),WK	Hund,WK	Hutschenko,GL(288)
Hückel,WK	Hundt,MM	Hutschenreiter,LS,WK
Huckh,WK	Hundtemann,MM	Hutt,GL(424),WK
Hucs,WK	Hunerlach,MM	Hüttenberger,
Hudak,SW(27)	Hünerwartel,WK	GF(104B,127A)
Hudde,MM	Hung,W#(5.38)	Huttenlocher,GL(341)
Huder,WK	Hunger,IE(90),WK	Hutter,LS,WK
Huderich,WK	Huniar,WK	Hütter,LS,WK
Hudri,WK	Hunkel,WK	v Hütter,WK
Hudy,WK	Hunker,IE(90),SW(19)	Hutterer,WK
Huebauer,WK	Hunn,WK	Hutti,WK
Hueber,W#(3.50),WK	Hunni,WK	Hüttinger,WK
Huemer,GL(243)	Hünrich,WK	Hüttl,WK
Huet,WK	Hunsinger,WK	Huttmann,WK
Hueter,GL(396)	Huntz,WK	Hüttmayer,WK
Huether,GL(493)	Huntzsinger,WK	Hüttmayr,WK
Huett,WK	Hup,LS	Hüttner,WK
Huf,WK	Hupenthal,LS	Hutto,WK
Hufeland,MM	Hupert,LS,WK	Huttsperger,LS
Hufenus,WK	Huperth,WK	Hutty,LS
Hufing,WK	Hupp,WK	Hutwelker,SW(57)
Hufnagel,LS,MM,WK	Hüpper,WK	Hutz,WK
Hufnagl,WK	Huprich,WK	Hutzel,WK
Hufnaglin,WK	Huracsek,WK	Huwer,WK
Huft,GL(424)	Hurbin,WK	Huy,LS,WK
Hug,WK	Hurdt,W#(4.14),WK	Huza,KI(166A)
Hugel,WK	Hurenberg,MM	Hytzler,LS,WK
Hügel,WK	Hurmet,WK	Iba,WK
Hugenberger,MM	Hürth,WK	Ibbl,WK
Huget,LS	Husch,WK	Ibczer,WK
Hugeth,LS,WK	Huß,LS,WK	Ibel,LS
Hugg,WK	Hussar,W#(6.22)	Iber,WK
Hügl,WK	Hüßgens,WK	Iberschanboi,WK
Hügle,WK	Hußl,WK	Ibisics,WK
Hugler,WK	Hußli,W#(4.109)	Icde,GL(407)
Hugly,WK	Hußlin,WK	Ichters,WK
Hügner,W#(2.13)	Husson,WK	Idat,WK
Hugo,WK	Hussong,WK	von Ifflingen,MM
Huhn,IE(99),WK	Hußwald,WK	Igel,LS,WK
Hukler,LS	Hust,GL(318,511)	Igelin,LS,WK
Hüll,WK	Hüst,GL(424)	Igill,WK
Hulmann,LS	Huster,WK	Ignat,WK
Hulmer,WK	Hüstner,WK	Ignatius,MM
Hulnthal,WK	Hut,WK	Ignatowiec,MM
Hülsenbeck,MM	Hutab,WK	Ihlen,WK
Humal,WK	Hutensberger,LS	Ihrering,MM
Humann,WK	Huter,GL(396,505)	Ilg,WK
Humbel,WK	Huterer,WK	Ilgner,LS
Humbert,WK	Hutfiß,WK	Illa,WK
Humel,WK	Huth,LS,WK	Illecska,WK
Humerich,LS	Hüther,WK	Illgen,GF(122,122B)
Huml,WK	Hutinger,WK	Illgenn,GF(131B)
Hummel,GL(306,446),	Hutka,LS	Illi,GL(208,407),WK
W#(4.76),WK	Hütl,WK	Illich,W#(4.113)
Hummer,LS	Hütler,LS	Illier,WK

Illik,WK
Illin,WK
Illschund,LS
Illy,GL(407)
Ilson,WK
Imb,WK
Imbach,W#(4.94)
Imbern,WK
Imbs,WK
Imele,WK
Imesspeyer,WK
Imgrund,WK
Imhof,GL(187),WK
Imhoff,WK
Imlinger,WK
Imlingerin,WK
Imm,HS(46),WK
Imme,HS(48,65)
Immerling,WK
Immhof,WK
Imrech,LS
Imrich,WK
Imsel,SW(24)
Imsinger,WK
Ind,WK
Ingenwald,WK
d'Ingle,WK
Inglkoffer,W#(4.48)
Ingram,LS,WK
Inhof,WK
Inn,HS(43),WK
Innervinklerin,WK
Innhoff,WK
Insberg,LS
Insperger,WK
Intelmann,MM
Interwiß,WK
Intze,MM
Iprich,WK
Irdenkauf,WK
Irgart,WK
Irion,IE(90,93,97),
  LS,SW(19)
Irle,WK
Irrgang,GS(19),MM
Irsch,WK
Isaak,BU,GL(401,506)
Isakow,MM
Ische,LS
Ischen,LS
Isebrecht,BU
Isel,LS
Isemann,WK
Isernhagen,GL(511)
Ises,WK
Isile,WK
Iska,GL(197)
Isler,WK

Issa,WK
Issel,LS,WK
Ißmerth,WK
Istele,WK
Istemann,WK
Istenmann,W#(5.27)
Iversohn,MM
Iwanow,MM
Iwanowski,K1(166A)
Jaach,WK
Jaake,MM
Jablonowski,GL(305)
Jablonski,SW(38)
Jablowa,HW(208)
Jachin,W#(6.60)
Jäck,WK
Jacke,MM,WK
Jäckh,WK
Jäckle,SW(4),WK
Jäcklein,WK
Jacko,SW(31)
Jacob,HS(44),LS,MM,
  WK
Jacober,GL(415,508),
  WK
Jacobi,WK
Jacobs,MM,WK
Jacobsen,MM
Jacquart,WK
Jacquot,WK
Jada,K1(166A)
Jader,WK
Jadkovsky,W#(7.53)
Jaeger,WK
Jafrath,LS
Jagber,WK
Jage,LS
Jagel,WK
Jager,WK
Jäger,GL(203),LS,MM,
  WK
Jägerhorn,MM
Jagicza,WK
Jagiello,SW(42)
Jagodziński,K1(166A)
Jahn,GF(91A,92A),LS,
  MM,WK
Jahnenz,MM
Jahner,GL(313)
Jahnke,BU,MM
Jahnle,HW(28,89)
Jahnschmidt,WK
Jahnson,LS
Jahresschutz,GL(311)
Jainig,WK
Jak,LS,WK
Jakob,GL(481,489),
  LS,WK

Jakobczyc,LS
Jakober,GL(310,387,
  505)
Jakobi,LS,WK
Jakobs,MM,WK
Jakowleff,GL(305)
Jaksa,WK
Jakubowski,GL(411)
Jaky,WK
Jambach,WK
Jamine,WK
Janant,WK
von Janau,MM
Jancz,WK
Janda,WK
Janeck,WK
Janens,MM
Janenz,MM
Janer,WK
Janetzki,K1(166A)
Jäng,WK
Janhauser,LS
Janikovics,WK
Janisch,LS
Janke,K1(166A),WK
Janko,WK
Jankovics,WK
Jankowski,K1(166A)
Jannes,WK
Janoscheck,WK
Janowsky,LS
Janpach,WK
Jans,KL(14),LS
Jansa,WK
Jansch,GS(18)
Jansche,BU
Jansen,BU,GL(285),
  LS,WK
Janson,LS,WK
Janß,WK
Janssen,BU
Jantaßin,GF(95B)
Jantsch,LS
Janty,WK
Jantz,BU,LS
Jantzen,BU
Janutowa,GL(219)
Janz,BU,IE(97),LS
Janzen,BU,WK
Janzer,WK
Janzin,BU
Janzon,BU
Japes,WK
Jaque,WK
Jaquenin,WK
Jaques,WK
Jaquin,WK
Jarding,LS,WK

Jarlach,K1(166A)
Jarmatz,MM
Jarmer,MM
von Jarmer,MM
Jarmersted,MM
von Jarmersted,MM
Jarno,LS
Jaroszewicz,HS(26)
Jasevil,WK
Jasinski,MM
Jasko,K1(166A)
Jasper,WK
Jatsch,BU
Jauch,WK
Javorik,WK
Jaworek,LS
Jayß,WK
Jean,WK
Jeancles,WK
Jeaneolla,WK
Jean-Jaques,WK
Jeckl,WK
Jed,WK
Jedele,WK
Jeden,WK
Jedinger,WK
Jeditsch,LS
Jedlunger,WK
Jeg,WK
Jegele,W#(4.100)
Jeger,WK
Jeglitsch,WK
Jehl,WK
Jehring,HS(65)
Jeisli,WK
Jeja,WK
Jeklin,W#(6.83)
Jelagin,MM
Jele,WK
Jeli,W#(3.10)
Jelik,WK
Jell,SW(29)
Jely,WK
Jenal,LS
Jeneth,WK
Jenkner,LS
Jenne,LS,WK
Jenner,GL(412),LS
Jenowein,WK
Jens,WK
Jenßen,MM
Jepe,GS(18)
Jerch,WK
Jeremias,WK
Jerg,WK
Jerich,WK
Jerik,WK
Jerke,GS(18)

Jermis,WK
Jerni,WK
Jesalniks,GL(289, 498)
Jesch,WK
Jeschke,GS(91A)
Jesel,WK
Jeske,K1(166A)
Jeß,WK
Jesse,GL(80,81), HW(31,211,212)
Jessel,SW(34)
Jeßensky,GF(119B)
Jesser,GL(398)
Jeten,WK
Jethon,LS,SW(34),WK
Jett,WK
Jetter,LS
Jidlij,LS
Jirgel,WK
Jiro,WK
Joachim,GL(492),WK
Joachimski,LS
Joan,WK
Joann,W#(7.86)
Job,GL(311,313,499), LS,WK
Jobin,WK
Jobst,WK
Jochengantner,WK
Jocher,LS,WK
Jochum,LS,WK
Jöckel,GF(122A)
Jöde,K1(166A)
Joerg,WK
Joersch,MM
Johanken,MM
Johann,LS,WK
Johannes,WK
Johannides,LS
Johansen,MM
Johler,GF(131B)
John,GL(407,430)
Johner,WK
Johns,GL(492)
Johnson,GL(334,506), LS
Jokel,WK
Joker,WK
Jokesch,WK
Joky,WK
Jonas,WK
Jonasch,W#(7.85)
Jonathan,MM
Jonczer,WK
Jonk,WK
Joost,BU
Jopa,WK

Joppes,WK
Jörck,MM
Jordan,GL(200), HS(65),MM,WK
Jörg,LS,WK
Jörge,W#(7.68),WK
Jorgebarth,WK
Jörgens,LS
Jorgow,MM
Jörig,LS
Jörke,HW(227)
Jörn,MM
Jörß,MM
Jorßky,WK
Jos,WK
Jose,GL(206,270),WK
Joseph,WK
Josi,LS
Josik,WK
Josin,WK
Joß,WK
Jossik,WK
JÖßken,MM
Joßt,GL(383)
Jost,BU,GL(360),LS, W#(1.5),WK
Jostes,WK
Jostheim,WK
Josts,WK
Josua,LS,MM
Joswakowsky,IE(94, 95)
Jott,WK
Jouanne,KL(34)
Jouschka,WK
Jozity,WK
Juchen,WK
Juhn,GF(93A,131B)
Jukund,WK
Julgen,WK
Juli,LS,WK
Julig,WK
Julik,WK
Julkard,WK
Juls,HS(44)
Jun,WK
Junck,WK
Juncker,MM,WK
Jundt,HW(208)
Junes,WK
Jung,GF(91A,91B,92B, 93A,95B,131B), GL(108,245), K1(166A),LS, W#(2.7,2.26, 4.20),WK
Jungblat,WK
Jungblut,WK

Jungbluth,WK
Jungen,WK
Junger,WK
Jungermann,HS(65)
Jungers,WK
Jungfleisch,WK
Jungin,WK
Junginger,WK
Jüngk,WK
Jungker,WK
Jüngling,MM
Jungmann,WK
Jungnuk,LS
Jungowski,K1(166A)
Jungplut,WK
Jungwirth,WK
Junk,WK
Junka,K1(166A)
Junker,GL(313),LS,WK
Junkert,GL(313)
Junkes,WK
Jupiter,LS
Juratschek,WK
Jurgens,WK
Jürgens,GL(196),MM,
    WK
von Jürgensburg,MM
Jürß,MM
Jury,WK
Just,LS,MM
Justen,WK
Jute,WK
Juz,WK
Kaa,WK
Kaaß,LS,WK
Kabe,WK
Kabel,GF(96B),GL(26)
Kabesader,W#(3.63)
Kader,LS
Kaderle,GF(125B,
    131B),WK
Kadit,WK
Kaduk,LS
Kaegler,MM
Kaehler,BU,MM
Kaempf,BU
Kaempfe,BU
Kaeplerin,WK
Kaer,WK
Kaerker,MM
Kaes,LS,WK
Kaesner,LS
Kaethler,BU
Kaetow,MM
Kaffmeister,MM
Kafka,LS
Kaft,LS
Kahl,LS,MM,WK

Kahlbrenner,WK
Kahlen,MM
Kählen,BU
Kahm,WK
Kahrbohn,WK
Kahrn,WK
Kaidel,WK
Kailing,SW(27)
Kaim,LS
Kaip,WK
Kaiper,LS
Kaiser,GL(334),LS,WK
Kajetan,LS
Kalaturski,GL(197)
Kalb,WK
Kalbach,WK
Kalbel,WK
Kalbi,LS
Kalch,WK
Kalchgruber,WK
Kaldeyssen,WK
Kale,WK
Kalenbach,WK
Kalerth,W#(8.95)
Kalich,WK
Kalinski,HS(44)
Kalis,WK
Kalk,LS
Kall,WK
Kallachin,WK
Kallbruner,WK
Kalle,WK
Kaller,WK
Kallner,WK
Kallschall,WK
Kalmaß,WK
Kalmeß,WK
Kalnbach,GF(92B)
Kalo,WK
Kalt,WK
Kaltenbach,WK
Kaltenbrunner,WK
Kaltenbrunnerin,WK
Kaltenhuber,
    W#(7.113)
Kaltenstein,LS
Kalting,WK
Kaltschmid,WK
Kalvoda,WK
Kalwa,HS(31)
Kamann,WK
Kamenski,MM
Kamenskiy,MM
Kamer,WK
Kamerer,WK
Kamerl,WK
Kamesch,WK
Kamien,MM

Kaminski,KL(25)
Kamiński,K1(166A)
Kamla,GL(389,504)
Kammer,LS,WK
Kammerer,GL(286,404,
    492),GS(90B)
Kämmerer,MM,WK
Kämmeritz,MM
Kämmerle,HW(12,15,
    17)
Kammerlocherin,WK
Kammler,HW(67)
Kämmler,HW(21
    entries)
Kammy,WK
Kamp,W#(7.2),WK
Kampa,WK
Kampelmeyer,WK
v Kampen,BU
van Kampen,BU
Kampf,WK
Kampfin,WK
Kandel,LS,WK
Kandl,WK
Kandler,MM
Kanegießer,WK
Kanegisser,WK
Kanich,WK
Kanigl,WK
Kankler,LS
Kann,WK
Kannegießerin,WK
Kannel,WK
Kanner,LS
Kanning,MM
Kanslenger,WK
Kant,MM
Kantak,K1(166A)
Kantar,WK
Kanter,GF(131B)
Kanthack,K1(166A)
Kantou,WK
Kantz,WK
Kanz,WK
Kanzelmann,LS
Kanzer,WK
Kanzler,LS
Kap,WK
Kapel,LS
Kapfenberger,WK
Kaphengst,MM
Kapke,MM
Kapp,GL(202,243,
    416),HW(30),WK
Kappel,HW(208,213),
    WK
Kappus,WK
Kaps,WK

Kislering,WK
Kiss,GL(409)
Kiß,WK
Kisser,GL(404)
Kissinger,IE(88)
Kißinger,SW(4)
Kißlar,WK
Kißler,WK
Kisslinger,SW(52)
Kißlinger,SW(17,29)
Kißner,WK
Kiste,WK
Kistenfeger,WK
Kistler,GL(389),WK
Kistner,WK
Kitle,WK
Kitsch,LS,SW(2),WK
Kittel,LS,WK
Kittendorf,MM
Kittinger,WK
Kittl,WK
Kittlberger,WK
Kitz,LS,WK
Kitzel,LS
Kitzinger,WK
Kivilie,WK
Klaas,MM
Klaassen,BU
Klafner,WK
Klager,WK
Klahr,WK
Klai,LS
Klaiber,WK
Klam,WK
Klament,WK
Klamnitz,WK
Klanen,WK
Klapp,WK
Klapper,LS
Klapprodt,GL(298)
Klapthor,WK
Klar,LS,WK
Klär,WK
Klarenbach,LS
Klarer,WK
Klarmann,LS,WK
Klarner,WK
Klaser,WK
Klason,BU
Klaspecher,WK
Klassen,BU
Klasson,BU
Klatin,WK
Klatt,HS(33,38,65),
    KL(37)
Klau,WK
Kläuber,WK
Klaudel,WK

Klaudy,LS
Klauer,LS
Klaumwalk,MM
Klaus,GF(92A),
    GL(259),LS,WK
Klause,WK
Klausek,WK
Klausin,GF(96B)
Klausinger,LS
Klauss,W#(6.26)
Klauß,WK
Klaussinger,WK
von Klebeck,MM
Klebel,WK
Klebert,LS
Klebes,WK
Klebrich,WK
Klebsattel,GS(12)
Klebsch,WK
Klecker,WK
Kleckler,GF(132A)
Klee,LS,MM,WK
Kleer,WK
Klees,WK
Kleeß,W#(1.47)
Klegh,LS
Klehmaier,WK
Kleiber,WK
Klein,BU,GF(91A,93B,
    95A,132A),GL(6
    entries),HW(8
    entries),LS,
    SW(17,21,29,30),
    W#(4.8,7.80),WK
Kleinberin,WK
Kleindienst,GS(89A),
    WK
Kleine,WK
Kleiner,W#(6.46),WK
Kleinfeld,MM
Kleinfelder,WK
Kleingütel,WK
Kleinhancz,WK
Kleinhofner,LS
Kleinin,WK
Kleininger,WK
Kleinlog,WK
Kleinman,WK
Kleinmann,LS
Kleinmeyer,WK
Kleinsasser,WK
Kleinschmidt,MM
Kleis,LS,WK
Kleisasser,WK
Kleisner,WK
Kleiß,WK
Kleist,MM,WK
Kleitsch,WK

Kleiz,LS,W#(2.49),WK
Klem,WK
Klemen,WK
Klemens,IE(90),LS,
    SW(19),WK
Klement,WK
Klemenz,WK
Klemingshaß,LS
Klemler,WK
Klemmer,LS,WK
Klen,WK
Klenck,WK
Klenn,MM
Klennert,MM
Kleps,LS
Klepsch,LS,WK
Kler,LS,WK
Klerer,WK
Kleres,GF(92A)
Klerin,WK
Klerner,LS
Klesky,WK
Klesner,WK
Kleß,WK
Klessen,WK
Kleßner,W#(2.84)
Kletcke,KL(30)
Kletsch,SW(21)
Klett,WK
Kletzel,WK
Kletzka,WK
Klevesadel,MM
Klevesahl,MM
Kley,LS,WK
Kleyn,WK
Klibert,WK
Kliebenspies,WK
Kliebenstein,WK
Kliem,GS(89A)
Kliewer,BU
Klim,W#(3.26)
Kliman,WK
Klimmer,WK
Klinar,WK
Klinckener,WK
Klincz,WK
Kline,WK
Kling,LS,WK
Klingel,MM
Klingelmajer,LS
Klingenberg,MM
Klingenfuß,LS
Klingenstein,WK
Klinger,HW(31),LS,
    W#(7.61),WK
Klinghamer,WK
Klingler,W#(4.116),
    WK

Klingsmeyer,SW(24)
Klingspor,MM
Klink,GL(316),LS
Klinke,WK
Klinner,MM
Klipenstein,BU
Klipfel,WK
Klipfele,WK
Klipl,WK
Klippe,MM
Klippel,GF(132A),LS
Klippenberg,LS
Klippenberger,LS
Klippenstein,BU
Klippl,WK
Klissing,MM
von Klitzing,KL(33)
Klix,MM
Klobassa,LS
Klober,WK
Klock,WK
Klöckner,WK
Klockow,MM
Kloepfer,LS
Kloesel,WK
Klogner,W#(2.86)
Klöhn,MM
Klomus,WK
Kloncz,WK
Kloner,WK
Klopf,WK
Klopfer,WK
Klöpfer,GL(302,490),
   LS
Klopfstein,WK
Klopp,WK
Klopper,WK
Klopstein,WK
Klor,WK
Klöres,WK
Klösbeck,WK
Klöser,LS,SW(29)
Klosius,WK
Kloß,LS,WK
Klosse,WK
Klostermann,SW(7,16)
Klotz,GL(23
   entries),HW(67,
   128,131,170),WK
Klotzbiger,WK
Kloz,GL(316)
Klozbücher,WK
Kluck,HS(43)
Kludt,GL(69,284),
   HW(67,179,207,
   208)
Klüe,MM
Kluf,WK

Klug,LS,WK
Kluge,MM
Klugesherz,WK
Klugtaler,LS
Klukas,GL(344),
   HS(31)
Klukow,GS(90A,90B,
   91A)
Klumb,WK
Klumk,WK
Klump,WK
Klung,WK
Klüpfel,WK
Klupstein,WK
Klüßendorff,MM
Knaack,MM
Knab,LS,WK
von Knaben,MM
Knaf,WK
Knaff,LS
Knaker,WK
Knap,LS,WK
Knapp,GL(187,192,
   416),LS,WK
Knapski,K1(166A)
Knaß,WK
Knauber,WK
Knaubert,WK
Knauer,GL(416),
   HW(13),LS,SW(44),
   WK
Knauf,WK
Knaup,WK
Knaupert,LS
Knaus,LS,WK
Knaut,LS
Knauth,WK
Kneb,WK
Knebel,SW(21)
Knebl,W#(5.92,5.111,
   5.114,5.118)
Knebusch,MM
Knechalsky,WK
Knecht,GL(18
   entries),LS,WK
Knedler,WK
Knefeli,WK
Knegendorf,MM
Kneib,WK
Kneicz,WK
Kneifel,GS(89B)
Kneip,WK
Kneipp,WK
Kneiß,WK
Kneller,LS
Knels,BU
Knentz,WK
Knep,WK

Kner,GF(95A)
Knesebeck,MM
Knet,WK
Knetl,WK
Kneuer,WK
Knichl,WK
Knieling,IE(94,96,
   98),SW(62)
Knielotter,LS
Kniep,MM,WK
Knieper,MM
Knieriem,MM
Knies,WK
Kniesböck,WK
Kniesel,GF(91A)
Kniessel,WK
Knipers,WK
Kniping,WK
Knipp,WK
Knippel,LS
Knippelberg,LS,
   SW(34)
Knirer,WK
Knirmüller,WK
Knitl,WK
Knitschky,MM
Knittel,WK
Knoblauch,LS,SW(21),
   WK
Knobloch,GF(93A),LS,
   MM,WK
Knoch,WK
Knoche,WK
Knodel,HW(6
   entries),LS
Knodl,LS
Knödl,WK
Knödler,GL(245),WK
Knödlin,WK
Knok,GL(233)
Knol,WK
Knoll,LS,WK
Knöll,GL(21
   entries),HW(17
   entries)
Knoodt,WK
Knoop,MM
Knop,LS
Knopf,LS,MM,WK
Knopius,MM
Knöpke,MM
Knopp,HW(17),WK
Knopper,WK
Knor,WK
Knorczin,WK
Knorr,GL(423,487,
   499,511)
Knörr,GF(91A)

von Knorring,MM
Knörzer,GL(233)
KnoschinBky,WK
Knosp,WK
Knot,LS,WK
Knoth,LS,WK
Knott,LS
Knovsky,WK
Knüpfer,WK
Knuppenberg,WK
Knüttlin,WK
Kob,BU,WK
Kobber,LS
Kobbs,MM
Kobe,WK
Kobel,LS
Köbele,WK
Kobelin,WK
Kobelster,WK
Kobenik,HS(33)
Kober,LS,WK
Kobets,WK
Kobing,WK
Koblenzer,WK
Kobraß,WK
Koch,GF(119B),GL(8
  entries),GS(14),
  HW(29),LS,MM,
  W#(5.24,5.31,
  5.35),WK
Kochanowski,LS
Kochem,WK
Kochenburger,WK
Kocher,WK
Köcher,LS
Kochin,WK
Kochius,MM
Kochlefl,WK
Kock,LS,WK
Kocke,MM
Kocsiß,WK
Koczarowsky,LS
Koczenberger,WK
Kodelka,SW(24)
Koeffler,GL(184)
Koehler,LS
Koehn,BU
Koehne,MM
Koeling,WK
Koelner,WK
Koenemann,MM
Koenig,IE(95),WK
Koeppe,K1(166A)
Koeppen,MM
Koerber,WK
Koerner,GS(18)
Koert,LS
Koesler,GS(19)

Koestel,LS
Koeve,MM
Kofer,WK
Köffer,WK
Koffin,WK
Koffke,HS(38)
Koffler,WK
Köffler,WK
Kofflerin,WK
Koffnerin,W#(3.69)
Kofler,WK
Kögel,LS
Kögler,LS
Köglerin,WK
Kögn,LS
Kogut,LS
Kögy,WK
Kohl,K1(166B),LS,WK
Köhl,K1(166A),WK
Köhle,LS
Kohler,HW(52),
  IE(89),MM,WK
Köhler,BU,LS,MM,
  SW(33),WK
Kohlgruber,WK
Kohlhaas,LS
Kohlhase,MM
Kohlhep,WK
Kohlmann,LS
Kohlmayer,WK
Kohlmetz,MM
Kohlmos,SW(16)
Kohlruß,SW(12,16)
Köhn,MM
Kohrer,W#(5.58)
Kohrtz,MM
Kohsow,MM
Kohut,WK
Koichert,MM
Kokocińska,K1(166B)
Kokron,WK
Kol,K1(166B)
Kolar,LS
Kolb,GL(180,318),
  HW(9 entries),
  IE(99),LS,
  W#(7.12),WK
Kolbe,GL(269),MM,WK
Kolberg,MM
Kolberger,LS
Kolberth,W#(7.111),
  WK
Kölbing,WK
Kolbow,MM
Kold,WK
Kolde,WK
Kolényi,GF(119A)
Köler,WK

Kolerus,MM
Kolet,WK
Kolhas,LS
Kolhoff,MM
Köli,LS
Kolignion,WK
Kolin,WK
Koll,LS,WK
Kolla,W#(8.10)
Kollacki,LS
Kollan,WK
Kollar,LS
Kollardi,WK
Kolle,WK
Köllen,WK
Kollenbach,WK
Koller,IE(89),LS,
  SW(7,16),W#(1.41,
  1.76,5.36),WK
Köller,LS,WK
Kollerth,W#(8.4)
Kollet,WK
Kollhaus,WK
Kollin,WK
Kolline,WK
Kollinet,WK
Kolling,WK
Kollmann,WK
Köllner,HW(28),LS,WK
Kollon,WK
Kollweg,WK
Kolly,WK
Kolm,WK
Kolmann,LS
Kolmeyer,WK
Koloch,WK
Kołodzi,K1(166B)
Kolpet,WK
Kolprenner,WK
Kolsch,WK
Kölsch,WK
Kölser,WK
Koltermann,HS(26)
Kölz,WK
Kolzer,WK
Kölzer,LS,WK
Kölzow,MM
Kömer,WK
Komeringer,WK
Komeß,WK
Kömlinger,WK
Komment,GS(19)
Konasek,WK
Kondermann,LS
Kondrat,LS
Kondurake,HW(87)
Konfens,WK
Konig,WK

König,IE(92,94,96, 97,98),LS,SW(18, 19),WK
Königin,W#(3.66)
Königsfeld,LS,WK
Königsmarck,KL(33)
Königund,WK
Königxknect,WK
Konitzer,HS(65)
Können,WK
Kononenko,GL(108)
Konopatzki,K1(166B)
Konrad,BU,GF(93A), GL(5 entries), HS(34),LS,WK
Konrat,LS
Konrath,LS
Kontenius,GL(39,64)
Konter,WK
Kontner,WK
Konusch,HW(152)
Konzelmann,LS,WK
Konzi,GL(40,326)
Konzka,W#(8.94)
Koob,WK
Koop,BU
Kooß,WK
Kop,WK
Kopatka,LS
Kopetka,WK
Kopf,LS,MM,WK.
Kopff,MM
Kopi,LS
Kopisch,GS(19)
Köpke,MM
Köpler,LS
Koplin,WK
Kopp,BU,K1(166A),LS, WK
Koppe,LS,MM
Koppel,MM
Köppellin,WK
Koppen,WK
Kopper,WK
Kopphamer,MM
Kopplow,MM
Koppmann,LS
Kopschitz,WK
Kopsicz,WK
Korb,WK
Korbach,WK
Korber,WK
Körber,LS,WK
Kordsen,MM
Koreck,WK
Korell,GF(93B,95B, 104B)
Koren,WK

Korffmann,WK
Korfmann,LS,WK
Korin,MM
Koringer,WK
Körkes,WK
Korn,LS,WK
Korndahl,MM
Kornelius,WK
Kornelson,IE(89), SW(31)
Korner,LS
Körner,HS(65),WK
Kornfeil,WK
Kornhumel,WK
Kornibe,WK
Korny,WK
Körper,LS,WK
Korry,WK
Korschl,W#(8.82)
Korss,MM
Kortie,WK
Kortzen,MM
Korz,LS
Körz,LS
Korzill,W#(8.53)
Kosara,LS
Koscher,WK
Koschitz,WK
Kosegarten,MM
Kosin,GL(80,81)
Kosl,WK
Kösler,W#(8.26),WK
Kosmowski,K1(166B)
Koß,WK
Köß,WK
Kossar,WK
Kossel,MM
Kössel,WK
Kossik,WK
Kost,WK
Koster,W#(1.64)
Köster,MM
Kostern,MM
Kostjal,LS
Köstler,LS,W#(7.7)
Kostrzelski,LS
Köszögy,WK
Kotasch,LS
Kotecki,K1(166B)
Kotillion,WK
Kotowitsch,GL(470)
Kotsutnik,WK
Kott,WK
Kottbauer,WK
Kottbauerin,WK
Kottel,WK
Köttel,WK
Köttelgruber,WK

Kottenhuber,WK
Kottich,WK
Kötting,WK
Kottke,K1(166B)
Kottlin,WK
Kottmann,WK
Kottmayr,WK
Kottmayrin,WK
Kounfeld,WK
Kovacs,WK
Kovacsics,WK
Kovalter,WK
Kovats,WK
Kövesdy,WK
Kowalewska,MM
Kowalski,K1(166B)
Kowarik,GL(305)
Kowas,LS
Kowatsch,LS
Kowengowen,BU
Kowol,HS(35)
Kowos,LS,WK
Kozel,WK
Kozka,LS,WK
Kozlowski,K1(166B), SW(15)
Kozner,WK
Kraale,LS
Krabat,WK
Krach,LS,WK
Krachfelsin,WK
Krachnauerin,WK
Kracht,WK
Krächter,WK
Krack,MM
Kracz,WK
Kraeer,LS
Kraemer,LS,WK
Kraemeyer,WK
Kräenbring,HW(208)
Kraf,WK
Kraff,WK
Krafft,WK
Kraft,GL(271,297), LS,WK
Kräft,MM
Krag,WK
Kräger,GF(93B)
Krahl,LS
Krahn,BU
Krai,WK
Kraicsi,WK
Krailach,GF(132A)
Krain,WK
Krainer,WK
Krainhofer,LS
Krall,LS
Krällen,WK

Kuharek,SW(38)
Kühbler,WK
Kuhe,WK
Kuhfeld,K1(166B),MM
Kuhl,HS(26),LS,MM,WK
Kühl,HS(26),MM,SW(4)
Kühle,IE(88)
Kuhler,WK
Kuhlhaber,WK
Kühling,LS
Kuhlmann,LS,MM
Kühlmeyer,WK
Kuhn,GF(95B),
  GL(322),HS(38),
  LS,WK
Kühn,GS(90B),HS(33),
  K1(166B),LS,WK
Kühne,HS(38)
Kühnemann,WK
Kuhner,WK
Kühner,GF(91B,127,
  127A,132A),LS,WK
Kühnesberger,WK
Kuhnle,HW(13,29,89),
  WK
Kuhnmann,WK
Kuhrmannin,WK
Kühry,LS
Kuhse,MM
Kuja,HS(26)
Kujat,GS(91B)
Kukacz,K1(166B)
Kukla,SW(41)
Kuks,LS
Kul,LS,WK
Kulak,LS
Külbi,LS,WK
Kulbus,WK
Küler,WK
Kull,WK
Küllen,LS
Kullmann,LS
Kulm,GL(297,348)
Kulmann,LS,WK
Kulow,MM
Kulsch,WK
Kultin,WK
Kultmann,WK
Kuman,WK
Kumann,WK
Kumb,WK
Kumbach,WK
Kumbenberger,WK
Kümel,WK
Kumenich,WK
Kumer,W#(3.49)
Kumin,WK
Kümmel,WK

Kummer,LS,WK
Kummerau,MM
Kumpf,WK
Kumph,WK
Kun,WK
Kuncewicz,K1(166B)
Kuncz,WK
Kunczer,WK
Kunczmann,LS
Kunder,WK
Kundermann,LS
Kunduchow,GL(197)
Küne,WK
Küner,LS
Kungel,WK
Küngel,LS
Kunitz,KL(37)
Kunitzer,GS(63,90A,
  90B),HS(65)
Kunkel,GS(18,19),
  KL(14),WK
Kunkl,WK
Kunle,LS
Kunn,WK
Künner,WK
Kunnig,WK
Kunst,MM
Kunster,WK
Künstler,GL(40),LS
Künstner,GL(442)
Kunstorferin,WK
Kunter,WK
Kuntinger,WK
Kuntner,WK
Kuntz,LS,MM,WK
Kuntze,WK
Küntzel,LS
Kuntzelmann,LS,WK
Kuntzinger,WK
Kuntzki,K1(166B)
Kuntzmann,WK
Kuny,LS
Kunz,GL(327),LS,WK
Kunzelmann,LS,WK
Kunzenhäuser,WK
Kunzi,GL(8 entries)
Kunzin,WK
Kunzman,WK
Kunzwald,LS
Kuper,WK
Kupfer,WK
Kupfersmidt,WK
Kupffer,MM
Kuppel,WK
Kuppetz,IE(95)
Kuprion,WK
Kurak,K1(166B)
Kuras,WK

Kürch,WK
Kurcz,WK
Kurd,WK
Kurenders,WK
Kuret,WK
Kuritschki,WK
Kuritschky,WK
Kurle,GL(351,451,
  501)
Kürn,WK
Kürner,WK
Kurpisz,KL(6,7,9,32)
Kurr,GL(308)
Kurrle,GL(351,451)
Kursar,WK
Kursky,WK
Kurtz,HW(9 entries),
  IE(88),LS,WK
Kury,WK
Kurz,GL(283,372,
  424),GS(14,58),
  HW(80),LS,SW(4),
  WK
Kürz,WK
Kurzhals,WK
Kurzmanowski,
  K1(166B)
Kurzweil,WK
Kuse,MM,WK
Kusik,LS
Kuß,GL(308),LS,WK
Küß,WK
Kussack,WK
Kußler,WK
Küßler,WK
Kußmann,WK
Kussmaul,HW(14
  entries)
Küster,GF(92B),MM,WK
Kustermann,WK
Kustner,WK
Küstner,GL(343),WK
Kütel,WK
Kutenberger,WK
Kutinger,LS
Kutler,WK
Kutman,WK
Kutruff,HW(26)
Kutschenreiter,LS
Kutschenreither,WK
Kutscher,LS,WK
Kutschera,SW(19,40)
Küttenhofer,WK
Kutter,WK
Kuttingerin,WK
Kuttler,LS
Kutyar,WK
Kutz,WK

Lehrmann,WK	Leins,WK	Lender,BU,WK
Lehrner,WK	Leinveber,WK	Lene,MM
Lehrs,LS	Leinweber,WK	Lenebach,WK
Lehwalder,LS	Leipold,WK	Lener,WK
Leib,IE(89),LS,WK	von Leipziger,KL(33)	Lenert,WK
Leibach,WK	Leirer,WK	Lenerts,WK
Leibbranden,GL(154)	Leischman,WK	Lenewebisch,WK
Leibbrandt,GL(63	Leiserin,WK	Lenges,WK
entries)	Leisgang,WK	Lenglin,WK
Leibbrandtin,GL(157,	Leising,WK	Lengner,GL(389)
158)	Leisinger,WK	Lenhard,GF(93B),LS
Leibbrrandt,GL(172)	Leißter,WK	Lenhart,LS,WK
Leibel,WK	Leist,WK	Lenhoff,WK
Leiber,WK	Leistenschneider,WK	Lenies,MM
Leiberz,WK	Leister,WK	Lenius,LS
Leibfrid,WK	Leitenberger,GL(286)	Lenn,WK
Leibfritz,LS	Leiter,WK	Lennert,WK
Leibl,LS,WK	Leitgeb,WK	Lenninger,WK
Leibling,W#(4.44)	Leitgebin,WK	Lenoer,WK
Leibold,WK	Leithamm,WK	Le Noire,WK
Leibrek,WK	Leitner,GL(396),WK	Lenschau,MM
Leibrock,WK	Leitnerin,WK	Lensendeker,WK
Leibrod,LS	Leitsch,WK	Lent,MM
Leichle,LS,WK	Leittner,WK	Lentz,GF(93A),LS,MM,
Leichnahm,WK	Leitwein,WK	WK
Leichner,LS	Leitzel,WK	Lenz,KL(9),LS,MM,WK
Leichs,WK	Leixner,LS,WK	Lenzner,GL(278,456)
Leicht,GL(187,351,	Lejeun,WK	Leonard,LS,WK
451),LS,WK	Lejeune,WK	Leonhard,WK
von Leicht,GL(443)	Lejlo,WK	Leonhart,GF(132A),
Leichtenberger,WK	Lekers,WK	LS,WK
Leichtmann,WK	Leleitner,WK	Leopold,MM,W#(8.27,
Leid,WK	Leli,WK	8.37),WK
Leidebruk,WK	Lelik,WK	Lepp,BU
Leidemann,GF(132A)	Lelkes,WK	Leppert,GS(91B)
Leiden,LS,WK	Lelle,WK	Ler,WK
Leidenthal,LS	Lellich,WK	Lerbach,WK
Leidig,WK	Lelling,WK	Lerch,SW(27),
Leidinger,WK	Lem,LS	W#(7.122),WK
Leiendecker,LS,WK	Le Mair,GL(276)	Lerche,GL(257)
Leikinger,WK	Lemaire,GL(276)	Lerchel,WK
Leimer,WK	Leman,WK	Lercherle,LS
Leimert,HW(31)	Lemański,K1(166B)	Lereder,WK
Leimgruber,WK	Lembcke,MM	Lerencz,WK
Lein,WK	Lembert,WK	Lermerin,WK
Leinauer,WK	Lembke,GS(23,89A)	Lernaciński,K1(166B)
Leinberger,LS,WK	Lemcke,GL(305)	Lerner,WK
Leindecker,LS,WK	Lemcken,MM	Lerval,WK
Leinebacher,LS	Lemel,WK	Lescher,WK
Leiner,WK	Lemke,BU,GL(68),MM	Leschert,WK
Leinerin,WK	Lemky,BU	Leschier,WK
Leingang,GL(258)	Lemlin,WK	Lesel,WK
Leinhard,WK	Lemm,LS,MM	Leser,WK
Leinholtz,WK	Lempert,LS	Leske,K1(166B)
Leininger,LS,WK	Lencewicz,K1(166B)	Lessing,HS(29,31,
Leinl,WK	Lenckart,WK	42),LS
Leinmeister,WK	Lencz,WK	Leßlen,WK
Leinne,WK	Lendenbach,WK	Letan,WK

Linnebach,LS	Lithar,WK	Löhel,GL(296)
Linnemann,WK	Litsch,WK	Löhlbach,WK
Linnenbacher,WK	Litter,WK	Lohm,WK
Linnvitz,WK	Littich,WK	Lohman,GL(508)
Linsboden,WK	Littke,GS(91A)	Lohmann,WK
Linscheid,LS	Litz,GF(104A,127B,	Lohmer,SW(17)
Linsler,WK	132A),WK	Lohn,WK
Linsmayer,W#(8.17)	Litzin,WK	Lohner,GF(132A),WK
Linß,WK	Litzinger,LS,WK	Löhner,WK
Linsser,WK	Litzler,WK	Lohnert,GF(132A)
Linßmayer,WK	Litzlschwab,W#(6.63)	Lohnfing,LS
Linstner,W#(3.28)	Livi,WK	Lohr,LS,WK
von Linstow,MM	Livonius,MM	Löhr,WK
Linter,LS	Lix,WK	Lohrentz,BU
Lintner,WK	Lizinger,LS	Lohrfink,WK
Lintscher,WK	Lob,LS,WK	Lohrin,WK
Lintzinger,LS	Löb,GF(92B),WK	Lohrmann,WK
Linz,WK	Lobemeyer,WK	Loibel,WK
Linzhauer,LS	Lobenmayer,WK	Loirsohn,WK
Linzler,WK	Loberer,WK	Lois,LS
Linzmaier,LS	Lobneger,WK	Loj,WK
Linzner,WK	Lobner,LS	Lojoier,WK
Lipert,WK	Loch,LS,WK	Lolauer,WK
Liperth,WK	Lochem,LS	Lomei,WK
Lipietz,LS	Locher,LS,WK	Lomerer,WK
Lipińska,K1(166B)	Lochmann,K1(166B)	Lomert,WK
Lipold,WK	Lochmanowicz,	Lomprecht,HS(33)
Lipp,WK	K1(166B)	Londrecht,HS(33)
von der Lippe,MM	Lochner,LS,WK	Lonée,WK
Lippert,LS,MM,WK	Löchner,LS	Longeberger,WK
Lippinger,MM	Lockenbiel,WK	Longl,WK
Lippmann,GL(452)	von Lockum,MM	Longo,WK
Lipps,WK	Locler de	Lönnbeck,MM
Lipsen,WK	l'Andrinon,WK	Lonner,GF(93B),WK
Lipsmayer,WK	Lodelmayer,WK	Lonzer,WK
Lirau,WK	Loder,MM	Loos,LS
Liro,WK	Loderer,WK	Looser,WK
Lis,K1(166B)	Löding,MM	Looß,WK
Lisch,MM	Lodmann,WK	Lör,WK
Lischer,WK	Loefler,WK	Loran,WK
Lischke,MM	Loel,K1(166B)	Lorbach,WK
Lischy,WK	Loepcke,BU	Lorch,LS,MM,WK
Lisefeld,WK	Loeper,MM	Lorcher,SW(4)
Liseleer,WK	Loepp,BU	Lorck,MM
Lisenfeld,WK	Loew,LS	Lorein,WK
Liser,WK	Loewens,BU	Lorencz,WK
Lisicki,K1(166B)	Löfel,WK	Lorenß,WK
Liske,WK	Lofert,MM	Lorentz,BU,WK
Lisker,GL(276)	Löffel,WK	Lorentzen,MM
Liskoplin,WK	Löffelmann,SW(24)	Lorenz,GL(184,215),
Liso,WK	Loffi,WK	LS,MM,W#(1.25),WK
Lisowski,K1(166B)	Löffler,GL(30,341),	Lorenzin,WK
Liß,WK	WK	Loresserin,WK
Lissen,WK	Löfflerin,WK	Lorez,LS
Lissi,WK	Lofink,WK	Lorfing,LS
Lissius,WK	Löfler,WK	Lorger,IE(88)
Listenederin,WK	Loge,LS	Lorich,WK
Lister,WK	Login,WK	Lorin,WK

Machse,WK
Machwirth,WK
Mack,LS,SW(16),WK
Mäck,LS
Macken,WK
Macker,WK
Macklot,WK
Macz,WK
Made,WK
Madega,SW(12)
Mader,LS
Mäder,WK
Madfeld,MM
Maeder,WK
Maennle,WK
Maertens,BU
Maeserer,LS
Maevius,WK
Mag,WK
Magare,W#(1.54)
Magbar,WK
Mägel,WK
Magemer,LS
Magenheim,LS
Magenheimer,LS,WK
Magenwirt,LS
Mager,WK
Mägle,WK
Magling,WK
Magnette,WK
Magnina,LS
Magnus,MM
von Magnus,MM
Magonet,WK
Magrie,WK
Magsam,WK
Magzer,WK
Mahala,WK
Mahalin,WK
Mahl,MM
Mahlenner,WK
Mahler,HW(10
    entries),LS,
    W#(7.35),WK
Mähler,WK
Mahlert,WK
Mählmann,MM
Mahner,LS
Mahnke,MM
Mahr,MM
Mähr,WK
Mahrend,WK
Mahringer,WK
Mai,IE(93,97,98),
    K1(166B),SW(19)
Maichle,WK
Maidatschenko,
    HW(208)

Maier,GL(21
    entries),HW(23),
    IE(99),LS,WK
Maierhauser,SW(44)
Maigner,WK
Mair,WK
Maiser,WK
Maith,LS,WK
Majer,GF(115),
    GL(361,362,363),
    LS,WK
Majerer,LS,WK
Majerski,K1(166B)
Majerus,WK
Majery,WK
Majett,WK
Majewski,K1(166B)
Majus,WK
Mak,W#(7.16),WK
Makamull,WK
Makamulla,WK
Makar,WK
Maker,WK
Maki,WK
Makle,WK
Makoviz,WK
Makowsky,MM
Makus,HW(88)
Malach,WK
Malakowitz,HS(43)
von Malama,MM
Malch,WK
Malchau,MM
Malchow,MM
Malczyński,LS
Maldaner,WK
Maldine,WK
Maldinier,WK
Maleck,WK
Maledyk,LS
Malemen,LS
Maler,WK
Malerich,LS,WK
Maleschinski,LS
Malhion,WK
Malian,WK
Malin,MM
Maling,WK
Malingis,WK
Maliyn,MM
Maljean,WK
Malkamus,WK
Mallaber,WK
Mallak,LS
Malledick,LS,WK
Malledik,LS
Maller,WK
Mallesy,WK

Mallet,WK
Mallgra,WK
Mallin,WK
Mallinger,WK
Mallison,MM
Mally,WK
Malmann,WK
Malthaner,LS
Malton,WK
Maltz,HS(38)
von Maltzahn,MM
Malzacher,WK
Malzon,WK
Man,WK
Manantz,WK
Mandel,WK
Mandelt,KL(18)
Mander,WK
Manderscheid,WK
Mandtler,BU
Mandy,WK
Mane,MM
Maneber,WK
Manever,WK
Mang,IE(89),LS,
    SW(12,14),WK
Mangenheimer,LS
Manger,WK
Mangerig,WK
Mangers,WK
Mangie,WK
Mängl,WK
Mangold,LS,WK
Mangoldtin,WK
Mangolt,LS,WK
Manhem,WK
Manichfeldt,WK
Maniet,WK
Manigel,GS(91B)
Maninger,WK
Maniß,WK
Manitius,GS(23,24,
    26,57,58,89A,
    89B),MM
Manjeanjean,WK
Manjer,WK
Mank,LS,SW(14)
Mänlein,WK
Mann,LS,MM,WK
Manner,WK
von Mannerheim,MM
Mannhalter,WK
Mannhardt,WK
Manninger,WK
Manns,WK
Mannsky,GL(354,355)
Mannweiler,HS(26),
    LS,WK

Matern,LS,WK
Materna,LS,WK
Materni,WK
Maternus,WK
Matez,WK
Matgen,LS,WK
Math,LS
Mathaei,WK
Matheile,WK
Matheis,IE(89),LS,WK
Matheiß,WK
Mathes,IE(89),LS,WK
Mathesin,WK
Matheus,LS
Mathews,HS(31)
Mathge,LS
Mathi,WK
Mathias,LS,WK
Mathie,LS,WK
Mathies,BU,HS(44)
Mathiesen,MM
Mathieu,LS,WK
Mathiku,WK
Mathil,WK
Mathis,WK
Mathiu,WK
Mathreu,WK
Maths,WK
Matlitsch,WK
Matner,WK
Matot,WK
Matschell,WK
Matt,LS,WK
Matter,GF(91B,104B,
   127A,132A,132B),
   WK
Mattern,LS,WK
Mattheis,GL(250),WK
Matthes,SW(36),WK
Matthias,BU
Matthies,BU
Matthiesen,MM
Matthus,MM
Mattis,BU
Mattlin,WK
Matuschka,K1(166B)
Matuschkin,MM
Matuska,WK
Matz,GS(19),WK
Matze,WK
Mau,MM
Maubach,GL(269),WK
Mauch,GL(14
   entries),GS(18),
   HW(208)
Mauder,WK
Mauer,LS,WK
Mauerbacher,WK

Maul,WK
Maulbach,WK
Mäule,GL(281,345,
   445,448)
Mauls,WK
Maulz,WK
Maurer,GF(91B,92B),
   LS,WK
Maurerin,WK
Maurus,WK
Maus,WK
Mauser,GL(27
   entries)
Maushut,WK
Mausler,WK
Mauß,WK
Maut,LS
Mauternacht,WK
Mauthe,LS
Mautner,WK
Mautschen,WK
Mautter,WK
Mautz,LS
Mauz,HW(16)
Mavländer,WK
Maximilian,W#(7.71)
Maximin,LS
Maximini,LS,WK
Maxy,WK
May,GS(89A),LS,WK
von Maydell,MM
Mayer,GF(93A,96A),
   GL(22 entries),
   HW(179,208),LS,
   MM,SW(13),
   W#(3.52,4.43,
   4.78,4.82,4.86,
   4.103,5.42,5.75,
   5.76,5.84,6.6,
   6.14,8.97),WK
von Mayer,GL(72)
Mayerhofer,WK
Mayerhöfer,WK
Mayerin,WK
Mayerrus,WK
Mayers,WK
Mayerus,WK
Mayes,LS
Mayeurs,LS
Mayfurth,LS
Mayländer,WK
Maylender,WK
Maynzer,WK
Mayr,WK
Mayrhofer,WK
Mayrhoferin,WK
Mayrhoffer,WK
Mayrin,WK

Mayringer,WK
Mayschneider,WK
Maywurm,WK
Mazak,W#(8.54),WK
Mazekof,WK
Mazetta,W#(8.111)
Mazur,LS
Mecher,WK
Mechinner,LS
Mechler,WK
Mechtel,WK
Meck,LS
von Meck,MM
Meckart,MM
Meckel,WK
Mecklein,WK
von Mecklenburg,MM
Meckling,LS
Mecsár,WK
Meczker,WK
Meczler,WK
Medek,WK
Medel,GF(92B,132B)
Meder,LS,WK
Mederle,WK
Medern,WK
Medernach,WK
Medich,WK
Medicus,LS
Mediger,HS(48)
Medl,WK
Meecat,MM
Meeß,WK
Mefert,WK
Megel,WK
Meggler,WK
Mehl,GL(446)
Mehlhaf,GL(339,388)
Mehlhaff,GL(242,397,
   447,450)
Mehlhorn,MM
Mehner,LS
Mehr,WK
Mehrer,WK
Mehrmacher,WK
Mehrmann,MM
Meichsner,WK
Meickel,WK
Meidl,SW(6,7)
Meidlein,WK
Meier,GL(68,69,406),
   K1(166B),LS,MM,WK
Meiershauser,LS
Meiher,LS
Meile,GL(82)
Meilke,HW(87)
Meinard,MM
Meincke,MM

Meßer,W#(4.51)
Messerschmid,WK
Messerschmidt,
    K1(167A)
Messerschmied,LS
Messing,LS,WK
Messinger,GF(104A,
    127B,132B),WK
Meßler,WK
Meßmar,WK
Meßmer,WK
Meßner,LS,WK
Mester,MM,WK
Mestle,LS
von Mestmacher,
    GL(65)
Mészáros,WK
Metelmann,MM
Meter,WK
Metgen,WK
Methner,GS(90B,91A)
Metie,WK
Metler,WK
Metrich,WK
Metschang,WK
Metschberger,WK
Metschung,WK
Mettauer,WK
Metter,WK
Mettler,LS
Mettling,WK
Metvesel,MM
Metz,LS,WK
Metzel,WK
Metzen,WK
Metzer,W#(5.82),WK
Metzger,GF(91B),
    GL(34 entries),
    LS,WK
Metzgerin,GF(96B)
Metzinger,WK
Metzke,MM
Metzl,W#(4.85)
Metzler,IE(98),LS,WK
Metzmacher,MM
Metzner,GF(132B),
    GS(14,15,16,17,
    22,23,89A)
Meunier,WK
Meurer,WK
Mewes,MM
Mey,WK
Meybehr,WK
Meyenn,MM
Meyer,GF(91A),
    GL(361,362,363),
    GS(14,19,90A,
    90B),HS(26),HW(5

entries),IE(89),
    LS,MM,WK
von Meyer,GL(72),MM
Meyereber,WK
Meyerin,WK
Meyers,WK
Meymann,MM
Meyrer,LS
Meyres,WK
Meythers,WK
Mez,W#(1.22)
Mezer,WK
Mezger,WK
Mezier,WK
Mezinger,WK
Mezker,WK
Mezler,WK
Mich,LS,WK
Michael,LS,WK
Michaelcz,WK
Michaelis,MM
Michäli,GF(93B)
Michel,GF(92A),
    GL(492),GS(27,
    89B,90A,91B),LS,
    MM,W#(3.76),WK
Michelich,WK
Michels,WK
Michelsen,MM
Michelz,WK
Michetz,WK
Michitz,WK
Michl,W#(4.99),WK
Michlecz,WK
Michler,WK
Michlewski,K1(166B)
Michls,WK
Michoel,WK
Micholz,WK
Michwitz,MM
Mick,WK
Micke,WK
Mickely,WK
Mickow,MM
Micz,WK
Midinger,WK
Miecznik,K1(166B)
Mięczny,K1(166B)
Mielentz,MM
Mielke,GL(406)
Miell,WK
Mierau,BU
Miersch,WK
Mies,WK
Miesbach,HS(26)
Mieß,WK
Mießman,WK
Mieth,WK

Mietzer,MM
Mietzner,HS(65)
Migin,WK
Miglitz,WK
Mihalovics,WK
Mihitz,WK
Mihl,WK
Mik,LS,WK
Mikecz,WK
Mikert,WK
Mikin,WK
Mikl,WK
Mikla,WK
Mila,WK
Milbach,WK
Milbradt,KL(18)
Mildner,LS
Miler,GL(391)
Milhauser,WK
Milher,WK
Milich,WK
Milinkovich,WK
Militzki,BU
Milke,LS
Milla,WK
Miller,GL(491,505),
    LS,W#(1.24,1.32,
    3.75),WK
Millerin,WK
Millerley,W#(6.3)
Millgruber,WK
Millhaus,WK
Millich,LS
Millies,MM
Millifahrli,
    W#(5.100)
Millou,WK
Milner,WK
Milot,WK
Miloth,WK
Milrod,WK
Milve,W#(6.35)
Minars,WK
Minaß,WK
Minch,WK
Minchheimer,WK
Mindel,WK
von Minden,MM
Minder,WK
Minderer,MM
Minderle,GL(459)
Minenko,GL(108)
Minges,WK
Minia,WK
Minich,WK
Minie,WK
Minigerode,LS
Minikus,WK

Minil,WK	Mitternacht,WK	Monbusin,WK
Minion,WK	Mittlestaedt,GL(383)	Mönch,WK
Mink,WK	Mittnacht,WK	Monhard,WK
Minnerath,WK	Mittoff,GL(196)	Monir,WK
Minnich,WK	Mizler,WK	Monition,WK
Minrad,W#(6.9)	Möberth,WK	Mönke,KL(54)
Minut,WK	Moch,WK	Monn,WK
Miran,WK	Mock,SW(19)	Monper,WK
Mirgon,WK	Möck,LS,WK	Monpere,WK
Mirisch,WK	Möckel,LS	Monse,LS,WK
Mirleng,WK	Mockenhaupt,WK	Monsering,WK
Miron,GL(338)	Moder,WK	Montag,WK
Mirsa,GL(196)	Moderau,GL(286)	Montaniol,LS,WK
Mirten,WK	Modl,GS(16,22,26,55,	Montfort,WK
Mirwald,SW(38)	89A)	Monti,LS,WK
Misbach,WK	Moeck,LS	Montoniol,LS
Mischel,WK	Moedbeck,MM	Monzert,WK
Mischler,WK	Moehle,GL(280)	Moor,LS,WK
Mischlerin,WK	Moehn,WK	Moore,GL(337)
Mischo,WK	Moennig,HS(26)	Moos,GL(500),LS,WK
Mischung,WK	Mögel,WK	Moosmann,LS
Misdorfer,WK	Mögers,KL(14)	Mooß,WK
Miserey,WK	Mogk,HW(16)	Möple,HW(19)
Misinger,WK	Mögle,GL(280)	Mopmann,WK
Misjun,GL(198)	Möglich,MM	Moppel,WK
Misliwetz,WK	Mohk,WK	Möps,WK
Mißbrandner,WK	Mohl,LS	Mor,WK
Missel,WK	Möhner,LS	Morainville,WK
Misselberger,WK	Mohr,GL(438),IE(95),	Moran,GL(334),WK
Misselbergerin,WK	LS,SW(2,18,19),WK	Morath,WK
Mißler,WK	Möhr,WK	Moraths,WK
Misso,WK	Mohrin,W#(7.33)	Morber,WK
Mistat,LS	Möhring,MM	Morbiu,WK
Mistelbergerin,WK	Möhringius,MM	Morel,WK
Mith,WK	Mohrmann,MM	Morell,WK
Mitkewitsch,GL(446)	Mohs,LS	Morer,WK
Mitleider,GL(309)	Moich,WK	Moretz,WK
Mitlerin,WK	Mokry,GF(103)	Morgen,WK
Mitnacht,WK	Moldauer,LS	Morgenthaler,WK
Mitnerics,WK	Moldt,MM	Mori,WK
Mitsch,WK	Mölenbeck,MM	Morian,WK
Mitscham,WK	Molgenmecz,WK	Moricz,WK
Mitschele,WK	Molicz,WK	Moring,WK
Mitscherle,LS	Molitor,WK	Möring,MM
Mittel,WK	Moll,WK	Möringius,MM
Mittelmann,MM	Molle,WK	Moritz,GL(366),WK
Mittelslode,GL(506)	Moller,WK	Moriz,W#(7.41)
Mittelstad,GL(506)	Möller,MM,WK	Mörk,LS
Mittelstädt,HS(38)	Molnar,WK	Mörle,WK
Mittelstaedt,GL(383,	Molner,MM	Morlo,W#(1.52)
503)	Molter,LS	Morman,WK
Mitterampel,WK	von Moltke,MM	von Mörner,KL(34)
Mitterdorferin,WK	Moltrecht,MM	Moroltz,WK
Mitterebner,WK	Molz,WK	Morosiewicz,SW(67)
Mitterer,WK	Mölzner,W#(6.49)	Morovicz,WK
Mitterhuber,WK	Momber,WK	Mörsch,LS,WK
Mittermayer,WK	Mömersheim,WK	Mörscher,WK
Mittermiller,WK	Mompu,WK	Morß,WK

Morst,W#(4.16)
Morsy,WK
Morx,WK
Mörz,LS
Morzykowski,K1(166B)
Mos,LS,WK
Mosauer,WK
Mosbauer,WK
Mosch,WK
Moschberger,WK
Mösel,WK
Mosenheimer,LS
Moser,GL(236,467,
    485),LS,WK
Moserin,WK
Moses,HS(44),LS,WK
Mosger,LS
Moshamer,WK
Moshammer,WK
Mosinger,WK
Moskalenka,MM
Moskaliuk,SW(15)
Moskopp,HS(26)
Mosler,WK
Mosman,WK
Mosmann,LS
Mosner,WK
Mösner,LS
Moß,LS,WK
Möß,WK
Moßbach,LS,WK
Moßberger,WK
Moßbrugger,WK
Mosser,WK
Mößle,WK
Moßler,WK
Moßmann,WK
Moßner,WK
Mössner,GL(335)
Mößner,GL(357)
Mossoi,WK
Most,WK
Mösters,WK
Mosth,WK
Motard,W#(2.15)
Mote,WK
Motsch,WK
Motter,WK
Mottix,HW(31)
Motz,WK
von Motz,MM
Mougon,WK
Moular,WK
de Moulin,WK
Mouliné,WK
de la Mouline,WK
Moursch,WK
Mouschon,WK

Mousel,WK
Mousins,WK
Moussong,WK
Movius,MM
Mozer,WK
Mroziński,K1(166B)
Much,HS(74)
Muchin,GL(433)
Mück,LS
Muehr,WK
Mueller,IE(98)
Muff,WK
Mühl,WK
von der Mühl,GF(92A)
Mühlbach,LS
Mühlbacher,WK
Mühlbauer,LS
Mühle,GS(90B),WK
Mühleisen,HW(22,24),
    WK
von Mühlendahl,MM
Mühler,LS,WK
Mühlhauser,WK
Muhlheim,IE(95)
Mühlman,WK
Mühlmichel,WK
Muhm,LS,WK
Mühner,WK
Muhr,WK
Mührbach,WK
Mühring,MM
Muhsehl,MM
Muhsel,MM
Muhsehlius,MM
Muhselius,MM
Muhssehl,MM
Muhssehlius,MM
Muhssel,MM
Muhsselius,MM
Mukert,WK
Muklin,WK
Mulczner,WK
Mulen,WK
Mülheim,IE(94)
Mülich,WK
Mull,WK
Müll,WK
Mullbacher,WK
Muller,WK
Müller,GF(92B,132B),
    GL(10 entries),
    GS(60),HW(25
    entries),KL(33),
    LS,MM,SW(17,19,
    21,24,36,41,42),
    W#(5.40,5.45,
    5.68,5.106,
    8.106),WK

Müllerin,GF(92B),WK
Müllin,WK
Müllner,SW(24),WK
Müllnerin,W#(2.56)
Mülner,W#(8.20)
Multanowski,GS(89A)
Mumel,WK
Münch,GL(108,109),
    LS,WK
Münchin,WK
Munchow,MM
Muncz,WK
Mund,LS
Mundkowski,K1(166B)
Mündlein,LS
Mundloch,WK
Mundt,MM
Mundvein,WK
Muner,WK
Mungenheimer,WK
Munich,WK
Münich,LS
Munier,WK
Müninger,WK
Munk,LS
Münnich,KL(42),MM
Munsch,GL(349,501)
Münsch,WK
Münster,LS,WK
Munterfeld,WK
Müntz,W#(4.25),WK
Munz,GL(377)
Münz,WK
Münzel,MM
Münzenberg,MM
Munzin,WK
Murall,WK
Murat,WK
Mürb,WK
Muret,WK
Murget,WK
Muro,WK
Murphy,GL(349)
Murr,MM
Murschel,GL(9
    entries)
Mury,WK
Musa,WK
Muschat,SW(42)
Muschel,GL(370)
Müschel,WK
Muschig,SW(29)
Muschu,WK
Musehl,MM
Musehlius,MM
Museille,WK
Musel,MM
Museler,WK

Muselius,MM
Muselzeller,WK
Muser,WK
Müsig,GL(385)
Muskot,WK
Musler,WK
Muß,WK
Mussehl,MM
Mussehlius,MM
Mussel,MM
Musselius,MM
Musser,WK
Mußer,W#(4.72)
Mußmann,MM
Mustazza,SW(18)
Mustie,WK
Mutat,WK
Muth,LS,WK
Müthel,MM
Mutig,WK
Mutsch,WK
Mutschell,WK
Mutscheller,WK
Mutscher,WK
Mutte,WK
Mutter,WK
Muttersgleich,WK
Mützmann,MM
Muznerowski,K1(166B)
Myck,LS
Myres,GL(337)
Mystelkowski,
  K1(167A)
Mystkowski,K1(167A)
Naaß,WK
Naasz,GL(494),IE(98)
Naaz,MM
Nabinger,LS,WK
Nach,WK
Nachbron,WK
Nachet,LS
Nachmann,LS,WK
Nachrunfth,WK
Nacht,LS
Nachtigal,BU
Nachtigall,K1(167B)
Nachtmann,WK
Nackel,BU
Nädel,WK
Nadelstumpf,WK
Näder,WK
Nadich,GF(104A,104B)
Nadig,GF(93B),WK
Nadler,WK
Nadschew,HW(208)
Naegeler,WK
Naeher,LS
Naf,WK

Nafzger,GL(456)
Nagel,GL(248),HW(8
  entries),LS,WK
Nagele,GL(422),WK
Nägele,WK
Nägelen,WK
Nagengast,WK
Nagi,LS
Nagl,WK
Nagle,WK
Nagler,LS,WK
Nagu,WK
Nagy,WK
Näher,GL(8 entries),
  WK
Näherin,GL(371)
Nähr,GL(371,372),
  IE(89),SW(31)
Naigebauer,WK
Naimaier,WK
Najderski,K1(167A)
Najedel,WK
Nalbach,WK
Nalick,LS
Naling,WK
Namen,WK
Namo,WK
Nandt,MM
Nargang,LS,WK
Narrgang,LS
Narusni,WK
Naser,LS
Naski,WK
Naß,WK
Nath,GL(338,500)
Natzer,WK
Nau,WK
Nauert,WK
Naufack,MM
Naufaock,MM
Naumann,MM,WK
Naupersfeld,LS
Nauth,WK
Naver,WK
Naygebau,WK
Neb,WK
Nebe,MM
Nebel,WK
Nebke,MM
Nebl,WK
Nebling,WK
Nebuchna,WK
Nechwiller,LS
Neckel,BU,MM,WK
Neckermann,WK
Nedelt,GL(229)
Nederisch,WK
Nedin,WK

Neef,WK
von Neefe und
  Obischau,GL(338)
Neese,MM
Nef,WK
Neff,GF(92B),LS,WK
Neffin,WK
Negel,LS
Negeli,WK
Neher,GL(371,372),
  IE(89)
Nehlich,WK
Nehlig,WK
Nehr,IE(89)
Neiberger,WK
Neidel,MM,WK
Neider,WK
Neidhard,WK
Neidhardt,W#(6.27)
Neidorf,BU
Neiheislein,WK
Neils,LS
Neilson,GL(510)
Neimer,WK
Neises,WK
Neiß,LS,WK
Nelich,WK
Nelinger,WK
Nell,WK
Nellenbacher,WK
Nellius,WK
Nembsgern,WK
Nemburg,WK
Nemechek,SW(64)
Nemecz,WK
Nemeczek,SW(16)
Nemega,SW(12)
Nemeth,WK
Nemetz,SW(44)
Nenich,WK
Nenig,WK
von Nepomuk,SW(6)
Ner,WK
Nerbas,LS
Nerbes,WK
Nerlich,WK
Nerling,GL(81)
Nern,WK
Nernhausen,WK
Nero,WK
Nerola,W#(8.49)
Nesch,WK
Nescicius,WK
Nesemann,MM
Nesius,WK
Neskusil,W#(8.110)
Neslin,WK
Neß,WK

Nessel,LS	Neunkirchen,MM	Nieberle,LS
Nesselhhof,WK	Neurath,MM	Niebuhr,BU,IE(98)
Nesselhof,LS	Neurautner,WK	Niedenthal,LS,WK
Nester,WK	Neurohr,WK	Nieder,WK
Nesterer,WK	Neuschwandtner,WK	Niederdorff,WK
Nestor,MM	Neuser,WK	Niederkorn,WK
Neth,GL(318)	Neusserin,WK	Niederländer,WK
Netschen,WK	Neustaedter,BU	Niedermayer,WK
Nettelblad,MM	Neustaeter,BU	Niedermayr,WK
Netzer,WK	Neustaetter,LS	Niederst,WK
Neu,IE(89),LS,WK	Neustetter,BU	Niederstartzer,WK
Neubach,LS,WK	Neuwirth,SW(17),WK	Niederthal,LS
Neubauer,BU,GL(360),	Neven,WK	Niedrich,LS
LS,WK	Nevermann,MM	Niefer,HW(16,80,81,
Neubaumerin,WK	Nevfermann,MM	89)
Neubaur,MM	Newel,WK	Niehusen,MM
Neubecker,LS,WK	Newrkla,WK	Niekrantz,MM
Neuber,LS,WK	Ney,WK	Niel,WK
Neuberg,MM	Neybauer,WK	Niemand,WK
Neubert,K1(167A)	Neyberg,WK	Niemann,MM
Neubich,WK	Neyberger,WK	Niemetz,LS
Neubold,GF(92A)	Neydebach,WK	Niemser,WK
Neuburger,LS,SW(24,	Neyder,WK	Nieny,MM
64),WK	Neyen,WK	Nierstheimer,LS
Neudhoffer,WK	Neyhaus,WK	Nies,WK
Neudorf,BU,K1(167A)	Neyhäussel,WK	Niesen,WK
Neudorfer,WK	Neykam,WK	Nieß,GL(468),WK
Neudörfer,LS	Neyrohr,WK	Niessen,BU
Neudorff,BU	Neys,WK	v Niessen,BU
Neuenberger,WK	Neywurm,WK	Nießlein,WK
Neuendahl,MM	Nezer,WK	v Nieszen,BU
Neuendorff,MM	Niberle,LS	Niethan,MM
Neuer,WK	Nibes,LS	Nikel,LS,WK
Neuers,WK	Nick,WK	Nikitin,MM
Neufeld,BU	Nickel,BU,GF(92A),	Nikla,WK
Neufeldt,BU	HS(26),WK	Niklas,LS,WK
Neufert,WK	Nickelwarth,HW(48,	Niklou,WK
Neuffert,GL(201)	81,89,112)	Nikola,WK
Neuge,MM	Nickelworth,HW(19,	Nikolai,LS,WK
Neuhämmer,WK	25)	Nikolaus,LS
Neuhaus,WK	Nickl,WK	Nikomet,WK
Neuhauser,W#(7.93),	Nicklas,WK	Niles,LS,WK
WK	Nicl,WK	Nill,GL(453)
Neuheimer,LS	Niclas,WK	Nille,LS,WK
Neuhofer,WK	Niclaus,WK	Nilles,WK
Neuman,WK	Nicodemasser,WK	Nilowski,K1(167A)
Neumann,BU,GS(90B),	Nicodemus,WK	Nimbler,WK
HS(75),HW(23,39,	Nicola,WK	Nimbske,WK
81,208),K1(167A),	Nicolae,WK	Nimecz,WK
LS,MM,SW(29),	Nicolai,HS(29),LS,WK	Nimijean,IE(95)
W#(7.115),WK	Nicolas,WK	Nimsch,LS
Neumark,SW(24)	Nicolay,HS(26),WK	Nirstheimer,LS
Neumayer,SW(17),WK	Nicomet,WK	Nischler,WK
Neumiller,WK	Nicometh,WK	Nisen,WK
Neumüller,GL(401)	Niderlender,WK	Nisis,WK
Neundorfer,WK	Nieb,WK	Nisl,WK
Neuner,WK	Niebergaal,LS	Niso,WK
Neuneyer,WK	Niebergall,WK	Niß,WK

Ochß,WK
Ochstadt,WK
Odenat,WK
Odendahl,WK
Odl,WK
Odlo,WK
Oechsle,GL(235)
Oehland,MM
Oehlke,HS(26)
Oehme,GS(91B)
Oelgard,MM
Oenitsch,LS
Oertling,MM
Oeß,WK
Oesterle,LS,WK
Oesterling,WK
von Oettingen,MM
von Oettinger,GL(65)
Oexle,WK
Of,GL(373,374,480)
Off,GL(373,374)
Offenbächer,WK
Offenmüller,WK
Offenpecher,WK
Offin,WK
Öffinger,WK
Ofholz,WK
Ofner,WK
Ogenpech,WK
Ogl,WK
Ohl,WK
Ohlenschlager,WK
Ohler,WK
Öhler,WK
Öhleyer,WK
Ohli,LS
Ohliger,LS,WK
Ohlinger,LS,WK
Ohlschläger,WK
Ohly,LS,WK
Ohm,MM
Ohnverzagt,WK
Öhr,MM
Ohrenleitner,WK
Ohrmann,GL(69,502)
Ohster,KL(33)
Oilcher,LS
Okerman,WK
Oktave,WK
Okuniewski,K1(167A)
Oland,WK
Olbert,WK
Olbrecht,MM
Oldach,MM
Oldekop,MM
Oldenburg,MM
Oldendorf,MM
Olfert,BU

Oliar,WK
Olich,WK
Oliger,WK
Olinger,LS
Ölinger,WK
Olivus,MM
Olleshanczl,WK
Ollinger,WK
Ollmisch,WK
Ollnat,W#(7.6)
Olman,WK
Olmeß,WK
Olson,SW(64)
Ölßner,WK
Olszewski,SW(54)
Oly,WK
Omann,MM
Omayer,WK
Ombach,LS
Ombital,WK
Omeltschenko,GL(195)
Omer,WK
Omrei,WK
Onan,WK
Oneanxt,WK
Onkelbach,WK
Önnke,WK
Opach,LS
Opera,WK
von Operau,MM
Operman,WK
Opfer,WK
Opmann,MM
Opp,HW(5 entries),
   LS,WK
Oppenhauser,LS
Oppenheiser,WK
Oppenländer,GL(180,
   464)
Oppermann,MM,WK
Opter,WK
d'Or,WK
Orb,LS
Orban,WK
Ordenthal,WK
Ordes,WK
Ordner,WK
Ordt,WK
Oriol,LS,WK
Orlow,GL(220)
Ormann,GL(20
   entries)
Oroeng,WK
Orschau,WK
Orschit,GF(96A)
von Orssich de
   Slavetich,MM
Ort,WK

Ortal,WK
Ortel,MM
Ortemburg,WK
Orth,GF(104A),LS,WK
Orther,WK
Orthmann,SW(24)
Orthner,LS,WK
Orthnerin,WK
Ortle,WK
Ortlieb,WK
Ortman,WK
Ortmann,SW(16),WK
Ortner,HW(87)
Ortwein,HW(208)
Osborn,MM
Öschker,WK
Oseling,MM
Oser,WK
Osswald,GL(76)
Oßwald,WK
Ost,HW(50),LS,WK
Osten,WK
Oster,GL(5 entries),
   HW(41),WK
Osterhof,MM
Osterhoff,MM
Ostermann,WK
von Ostermann,MM
Ostermayer,WK
Österreich,WK
Österreicher,WK
Osterstock,MM
Ostert,WK
Ostertag,WK
Ostheimer,WK
Östreicher,WK
Ostrieder,WK
Ostrowski,GS(18),
   K1(167A)
Osvald,WK
Oswald,HW(31,88,227,
   237),LS,MM,WK
Oth,WK
Otschwald,W#(5.16)
Ott,LS,WK
Otte,LS,W#(7.57)
Ottembrey,LS
Ottenbacher,GL(15
   entries),WK
Ottenberger,LS
Ottenbreit,LS,WK
Otter,WK
Ottermat,WK
Ottermode,WK
Otth,W#(5.39)
Ottho,WK
Ottinger,WK
Ottmann,WK

Otto,BU,GL(68),
   GS(89B),LS,WK
Ötz,WK
Oument,WK
Owitsch,HW(23)
Ox,WK
Oxenius,WK
Paar,LS
Paarmann,MM
Pablaz,WK
Pabst,LS,WK
Pac,HS(35)
Pach,WK
Pacher,WK
Pacherin,WK
Pachhamer,WK
Pachhamerin,WK
Pachinger,WK
Pachman,WK
Pachmann,WK
Pachmayer,WK
Pachmayrin,WK
Pachmeyer,WK
Pachmeyrin,WK
Pachner,WK
Packin,WK
Packolt,WK
Packowski,K1(167A)
Paczkowski,K1(167A)
Pade,GL(405)
Paetow,MM
Paff,LS,WK
Page,MM,WK
Pagel,MM
Pagels,MM
Paget,LS
Pagrer,WK
Pahl,K1(167A),LS,MM,
   WK
Pahlau,MM
von Pahlen,MM
von der Pahlen,MM
Paidlstein,WK
Paier,WK
Pail,LS
Pailler,WK
Pairin,WK
Paisich,WK
Paitaß,WK
Pakert,WK
Pakes,LS
Pal,K1(167A)
Palamartschuk,
   GL(256)
Palasty,WK
Paldes,W#(2.45)
Paldinger,WK
Paldingerin,WK

Pales,WK
Palger,WK
Paling,WK
Palinger,WK
Pallas,MM
Pallasch,WK
Palli,WK
Palmer,LS
Palmerh,WK
Palmi,LS,WK
Palmowski,K1(167A)
Palmrich,LS
von Palmstrauch,MM
Palmy,LS
Palschensky,WK
Palter,WK
Pamgartner,WK
Pamp,WK
Pana,WK
Panetice,WK
Pangraz,WK
Panholczer,WK
Panie,WK
Pank,MM
Pankracy,K1(167A)
Pankratz,SW(16)
Pann,LS,WK
Pannek,WK
Panninger,WK
Panowicz,K1(167A)
Pansegrau,HS(75)
Panske,K1(167A)
Pant,WK
Pantschulidsew,MM
Pantzer,HS(44)
Panz,LS,WK
Panzer,WK
Pap,WK
Pape,WK
Papke,MM
Papst,WK
Papstin,WK
Paptist,WK
Paquay,WK
Paquet,W#(7.100),WK
Paqueta,WK
Paquin,WK
Par,LS
Paracher,WK
Paradis,MM,WK
Parb,WK
Parboth,WK
Pardon,WK
Pardua,LS
Pareck,WK
Parfahl,MM
Pari,WK
Paris,MM,WK

Park,WK
Parkany,WK
Parki,WK
Parling,WK
Paroisse,WK
Parr,LS
Parsau,MM
Part,WK
Partach,WK
Parten,WK
Partet,WK
Parth,WK
Parthel,WK
Parthenß,WK
Partheymüller,WK
Partmes,WK
Partos,WK
Partz,WK
Partzer,WK
Paruck,WK
Parzygroch,K1(167A)
Pasch,MM,WK
Paschal,WK
Paschale,WK
Paschlo,WK
Passel,LS
Passow,MM
Paßtorovics,WK
Pastenacy,GS(89A)
Pastian,GL(108)
Pastor,WK
Patay,WK
Paternik,LS
Pathe,WK
von Pathkull,MM
Patin,WK
Pätkau,BU
Patuch,HS(43)
Patzer,GS(89A),LS,MM
Patzke,K1(167A)
Patzner,WK
Patzum,WK
Pauczer,WK
Pauderer,WK
Pauer,W#(7.95),WK
Pauerin,WK
Paul,MM,W#(6.44),WK
Paule,WK
Pauli,LS,WK
Paulin,WK
Pauline,WK
Paulini,LS
Paulino,GL(336)
Paulmann,WK
Paulo,GL(336)
Pauls,BU
Paulus,LS,WK
Paum,W#(2.85)

Petermann,WK
Peternek,LS
Peterreins,GL(145)
Peters,BU,GL(495,
   497),GS(19),LS,
   MM,WK
Petersen,BU,MM
von Petersen,MM
Petersick,WK
Petersiller,WK
Petersohn,MM
Peterson,GL(392,504)
Peterssen,MM
von Peterssen,MM
Petersson,MM
Petesch,WK
Pethran,MM
Peti,WK
Petimange,WK
Petin,WK
Petischheimer,WK
Petit,WK
Petit-Jean,WK
Petkau,BU
Petnarsch,WK
Petri,GF(91B,93A,
   95A,119B),LS,WK
Petrich,GS(14)
Petrinath,WK
Petrofßsky,WK
Petrovitz,SW(24)
Petrowicz,SW(18)
Petrowitsch,SW(19)
Petrowski,GL(386),LS
Petrus,WK
Petry,LS,WK
Petsch,W#(2.51)
Petschel,GF(132B)
Petter,WK
Pettermann,WK
Petuger,WK
Pety,WK
Petz,LS,WK
Petzel,LS
Petzer,W#(7.11),WK
Peyerin,WK
Peyerlin,W#(3.66)
Peykert,WK
Peyskamer,WK
Pfabl,WK
Pfaf,WK
Pfaff,GF(93A,95B),
   GL(6 entries),LS,
   WK
Pfaffenhuber,WK
Pfaffin,WK
Pfaidl,WK
Pfal,WK

Pfals,WK
Pfänder,GL(380)
Pfändler,WK
Pfaner,WK
Pfau,GL(429)
Pfefermann,WK
Pfeffelmann,WK
Pfeffer,WK
Pfefferkorn,WK
Pfeifaust,WK
Pfeifel,LS
Pfeifeld,WK
Pfeifenroth,WK
Pfeifer,GL(269),
   IE(90),LS,SW(14,
   26,27),WK
Pfeiferin,WK
Pfeiff,MM
Pfeiffer,GS(91A,
   91B),LS,W#(6.86),
   WK
Pfeifle,GL(500)
Pfeil,LS,WK
Pfeilstücker,WK
Pfendler,WK
Pferd,LS,WK
Pferer,WK
Pfersch,WK
Pfeyffer,WK
Pfillip,WK
Pfisser,WK
Pfister,LS,WK
Pfisterer,WK
Pfistner,WK
Pfitzer,GL(431)
Pflätschinger,WK
Pfleider,GL(206)
Pfletschinger,WK
Pfliegler,WK
Pflug,MM,WK
Pflügel,WK
Pflum,WK
Pfohl,LS,WK
Pford,LS,WK
Pforten,MM
Pfortscheller,WK
Pfost,WK
Pfuderer,HW(14)
Pfuhl,LS,WK
Pfulmer,WK
Pfund,GL(373)
Pfünder,GL(204,205)
Pfundheller,MM
Pfundsteinin,WK
Pfüster,WK
Phal,WK
Phar,WK
Pheen,WK

Pheiffhoffer,WK
Phibel,LS
Phil,WK
Philipi,GF(92A),WK
Philipie,W#(2.39)
Philipp,LS,WK
Philippe,WK
Philippi,GF(93B,
   96A),LS,WK
Philipps,WK
Philippsen,BU
Philiproka,MM
Phillip,WK
Phillipet,WK
Phlanig,WK
Phost,WK
Phul,WK
Piątek,K1(167A)
Pibernig,WK
Pibernigin,WK
Pibl,WK
Pichert,MM
Pichl,LS
Pichler,LS,WK
Pick,LS,WK
Pickart,WK
Pickelberger,WK
Pickert,WK
Piczl,WK
Pidan,WK
Pidde,K1(167A)
Pidlbauer,WK
Pidopryhora,GL(108)
Pieck,SW(12)
Piekrich,WK
Pieller,WK
Pienkowski,K1(167A)
Pieper,KL(18),MM
Pieplow,MM
Piere,WK
Piergne,WK
Pieri,WK
Pieringer,WK
Pieringerin,WK
Pieroth,WK
Piersan,WK
Pierschon,WK
Pierson,MM,WK
Pieru,WK
Piesch,LS,WK
Pietz,HS(44),WK
Piewald,LS
Piez,LS
Pifortin,WK
Pihl,WK
Pikar,WK
Piko,WK
Piłatowski,K1(167A)

Pilatzki,KL(46)	Pistori,WK	Plet,WK
Pilch,LS	Pistorius,WK	Pletsch,WK
Pilger,LS,WK	Pithl,WK	Plett,BU
Pilgram,WK	Pitinger,WK	Pletz,WK
Pillenmayer,LS	Pitischan,WK	Plez,WK
Piller,LS,WK	Pitner,WK	Plinerd,WK
Pilli,WK	Pitsch,WK	Plinius,WK
Pillinger,WK	Pitschkowski,GS(90B)	Plitong,WK
Pilo,WK	Pittermann,WK	Plo,WK
Pilsner,SW(7)	Pittischan,WK	Ploch,WK
Pilsudski,MM	Pittmann,WK	Plöd,LS
Pilz,WK	Pittner,LS	Plonczyska,MM
Pinckel,WK	Pitz,LS,WK	Plonger,WK
Pinckman,WK	Piwer,WK	Ployer,WK
Pincz,WK	Piwko,GF(119A)	Ployerin,WK
Pinder,LS	Pix,LS,WK	Ployrin,WK
Pinell,WK	Plagemann,MM	Pluchin,WK
Pingeßt,WK	Plaha,WK	Plum,WK
Pinion,WK	Plaison,WK	Plumeredi,WK
Pins,WK	Planck,WK	Plumich,WK
Pinter,WK	Planckin,WK	Plunder,WK
Pinth,WK	Plank,LS	Plundi,WK
Pióro,K1(167A)	Plansche,WK	Plusch,WK
Piot,WK	Planzer,LS,WK	Pluskus,MM
Pioter,K1(167A)	Plaschke,LS	Plutschek,W#(6.90)
Pipauer,WK	Plasing,WK	Pluvi,WK
Piquo,WK	Plaskie,MM	Pob,WK
Pir,WK	Plasky,WK	Pöbel,WK
Pirckl,WK	Plaß,WK	Pobersacherin,WK
Piringer,WK	Plasser,LS,WK	Poch,WK
Piringerin,WK	Plate,MM	Pochlauer,W#(3.25)
Pirkenmayer,WK	von Platen,MM	Pochmann,WK
Pirker,WK	Plath,MM	Pock,W#(6.100),WK
Piroge,WK	Platner,WK	Pöcker,WK
Pirot,WK	Platteicher,LS,WK	Pocsák,WK
Piroth,WK	Plattet,WK	Podivin,LS,WK
Pirr,WK	Platz,LS,WK	Podnerin,WK
Pirt,WK	Plätz,WK	Poetkau,BU
Pisarski,GS(91A)	Platzer,WK	Poetker,BU
Pisbacher,WK	Platzerin,WK	Poff,WK
Pisch,LS	Plausch,WK	Pogar,LS
Pische,WK	Plaz,WK	Pogenmayer,WK
Pischenoth,LS	Plazer,WK	Pogge,MM
Pischl,WK	Plechinger,SW(24),	Pögl,WK
Pischnoth,LS	W#(7.20)	Poh,LS
Pisek,LS	Plecz,WK	Pohfeld,MM
Pisen,WK	Plehnert,BU	Pohl,GL(409),GS(61),
Pisinger,LS,WK	Plei,WK	LS,MM,W#(8.121),
Pismüller,WK	Pleif,WK	WK
Pisof,WK	Plein,WK	Pöhl,WK
Pisoff,WK	Pleiss,HW(51)	Pohle,WK
Pisport,WK	Pleli,WK	Pohleber,LS
Piß,WK	Plemling,WK	Pohler,WK
Pissek,LS	Plen,WK	Pöhler,LS,WK
Pissier,WK	Plenich,GF(127A,	Pohlian,WK
Pister,LS	132B)	Pohlmann,MM
Pisterer,WK	Ples,WK	Pohlmillner,WK
Pistor,WK	Pleß,WK	Pöhnlein,WK

Prechel,HS(53)	Preweisen,WK	Prokop,WK
Predi,LS	Preyerl,WK	Pröllin,WK
Prediger,LS	Preys,MM	Pronstein,WK
Preding,WK	Preyß,WK	Prophet,WK
Prefrid,LS	Preyßl,WK	Prosar,WK
Prefried,WK	Preytegl,WK	Prosch,LS
Prefur,WK	Priaude,MM	Prose,WK
Pregler,MM	Pribesnik,WK	Prosen,WK
Prehauser,WK	Pribill,LS	Proßer,SW(38)
Prehn,MM	Prichta,WK	Prove,WK
Preil,WK	Priebe,KL(18)	Prowe,MM
Preinersdorfer,WK	Priedöhl,K1(167A)	Pruch,WK
Preis,BU,LS	Priefert,MM	Pruchenow,MM
Preisen,WK	Pries,BU,LS	Pruck,WK
Preisendanz,LS	Priesin,WK	Prucker,WK
Preisler,LS	Priess,BU	Prückler,WK
Preiß,LS,WK	Prieß,MM	Pruczawski,LS
Preissig,WK	Priestersbach,WK	Pruditz,WK
Preissin,BU	Prill,W#(6.39),WK	Prüfer,LS
Preissing,BU	Prim,WK	Prug,LS
Preißler,WK	Primmer,WK	Prugyil,WK
Preisz,BU	Prims,WK	Pruker,LS,WK
Preiszin,GL(40)	Prince,MM	Prukerin,WK
Preit,LS	Prinsignon,WK	Prukler,WK
Preithoffer,WK	Printz,WK	Prüll,WK
Prelicz,SW(15)	Prinz,LS,MM,WK	Prunder,WK
Prell,WK	Prinzler,W#(8.38)	Prunerin,WK
Prem,W#(7.110),WK	Priron,WK	Prünewald,WK
Premer,LS,WK	Prischo,WK	Prunner,WK
Prencz,WK	Prislinger,WK	Prüß,MM
Preneßt,WK	Priß,WK	Prüssing,MM
Prening,WK	Prißl,WK	Prut,WK
Prenna,WK	Prißlinger,WK	Pryll,HS(58)
Prenner,WK	Prister,WK	Przehode,WK
Prentner,WK	Pritsch,LS	Przepiórka,K1(167A)
Prenzelin,MM	Pritzbuer,MM	Przihoda,LS
Prenzing,WK	Prizies,WK	Pub,WK
Presch,WK	Proaska,WK	Puber,WK
Preschell,LS	Prob,WK	Pubuk,LS
Prescher,LS	Probach,W#(5.28)	Püburger,WK
Preserl,WK	Probost,W#(6.41)	Puch,WK
von Pressentin,MM	Probst,SW(12,24),	Puchel,W#(8.85)
Presser,LS	W#(5.88,5.89),WK	Pucher,WK
Preßmann,WK	Pröbstl,WK	Puchinger,WK
Pressovay,WK	Prockert,WK	Puchingerin,WK
Pretemdorfsky,WK	Procomercy,WK	Püchler,WK
Preter,LS,WK	Prodisch,WK	Püchlerin,WK
Pretorius,LS	Prodl,W#(3.62)	Puchmüller,LS
Prêtre,MM	Prodvisser,WK	Puchner,WK
Pretsch,LS,WK	Profiet,LS	Puchnerin,WK
Pretung,LS	Progil,WK	Puel,WK
Pretz,W#(1.13),WK	Progle,WK	Pufeding,WK
Pretzinger,W#(5.14)	Proglia,WK	Puff,WK
Preunig,WK	Prohaczka,WK	Puffy,LS
Preuss,BU	Prohaska,WK	Pugge,MM
Preuß,LS	Prokaß,WK	Pühl,WK
Preussin,BU	Prokob,W#(6.85),WK	Puhrmann,WK
Prevost,MM	Prokoczka,WK	Puk,WK

Puknveiß,WK
Pulch,WK
Puljung,WK
Pull,WK
Pulleon,WK
Pullier,WK
Puls,MM
Pult,WK
Pum,WK
Pumplet,LS
Pundus,LS,WK
Punto,HS(43)
Puntzen,WK
Puntzin,WK
Punzen,WK
Puper,WK
Pupo,WK
Pur,WK
Purbus,WK
Purckert,WK
Purgartin,WK
Pürge,WK
Purger,WK
Purgert,WK
Purgiman,WK
Purgstaller,WK
Puri,WK
Purk,WK
Purker,WK
Purman,WK
Purner,WK
Purpes,WK
Purpur,LS
Pusch,LS,WK
Puschai,WK
Puschet,WK
Puspacher,WK
Pußlawsky,WK
Pusters,MM
Pustrich,MM
Püttner,WK
Putz,LS,WK
Putzer,WK
Pützinger,WK
Puver,WK
Puving,WK
Pux,WK
Puxbaum,WK
Pyk,LS
Quade,K1(166B)
Quallon,WK
Qualmann,MM
Quanz,WK
Quapp,BU
Quargen,WK
Quargl,WK
Quaßniczka,WK

Quat,WK
Quedjes,MM
Queisseck,WK
Queisser,WK
Quelle,K1(166B)
Quenker,WK
Quentin,WK
Quiling,WK
Quillian,WK
Quind,WK
Quint,WK
Quintus,WK
Quiot,WK
Quiram,HW(51)
Quiria,WK
Quirin,WK
Quiring,BU
Quistrop,MM
Quitinns,W#(2.73)
Quittenbaum,MM
Quitter,WK
Quitzow,MM
Quivillie,WK
Quoika,W#(8.83)
Raab,LS,W#(7.49),WK
Raaß,WK
Rab,WK
Rabeneck,MM
Raber,WK
Rabier,WK
Rabies,WK
Rabom,WK
Rabort,WK
Rabung,WK
Rache,WK
Rachersdorfer,WK
Rachesdorfer,WK
Rachmann,LS
Rachow,MM
Rack,LS
Raczkowski,K1(167A)
Rad,WK
Radanitsh,WK
Radeck,WK
Radel,MM
Rädelberger,WK
Rademacher,K1(166B),
WK
Rader,WK
Räder,MM
Radetz,SW(12)
Radinger,WK
Radius,WK
Radke,HW(67),
K1(167A)
Radkowski,K1(167A)
Radloff,MM
Radlow,MM

Radmacher,IE(88),
SW(4,14)
Radmann,LS,WK
Radoicsich,WK
Radu,WK
Radva,WK
Raff,GL(8 entries),
WK
Raffelsberger,WK
Rager,WK
Rägers,LS
Rahl,WK
Rahm,MM
Rahn,BU,MM,WK
Raidebach,WK
Raiffmesser,WK
Raikl,WK
Raile,GL(5 entries)
Rainammer,WK
Rainer,WK
Raisdorf,WK
Raiser,GL(212,284,
448),WK
Raitt,WK
Rakitsch,WK
Rakowicz,K1(167A)
Rakowski,K1(167A)
Rall,GL(358,490),WK
Rambach,MM,WK
Rambachin,WK
Rambicourt,WK
Rambow,MM
Rambur,WK
Rameil,WK
Ramer,WK
Rameschlaeger,LS
Ramich,WK
Ramin,MM,WK
Rammel,WK
Ramp,WK
Rampel,LS
Rampf,WK
Rams,LS
Ramsein,WK
Ramstädter,WK
Ramstein,WK
Ran,WK
Ranacher,WK
Ranerin,WK
Rang,WK
Rangemar,LS
Ranser,LS
Ransperger,WK
von Ranzow,MM
Rapedius,WK
Raphael,LS
Rapp,GL(5 entries),
HW(26),LS,WK

Rappig,WK
Rasch,HW(41),WK
Raschko,WK
Rascop,WK
Raser,WK
Raski,K1(167A)
Raskoph,WK
Rasmundt,MM
Raspe,MM
Raß,WK
Raßcob,WK
Raßweiler,WK
Rast,MM
Rastaedter,WK
Raster,WK
Rastner,WK
Rastweiller,WK
Rat,HS(45)
Rath,GL(12 entries),
  WK
Räth,GL(307)
Rathgeber,LS,WK
Rathlef,MM
Rathmacher,IE(95),WK
Ratlef,MM
Rätnerin,WK
Ratschke,WK
Ratta,LS
Rattmann,HS(33)
Ratz,WK
Ratzlaff,BU
Rau,IE(89),LS,SW(14,
  31),WK
Raubach,WK
Rauber,WK
Raubinger,WK
Rauch,K1(166B),LS,
  MM,WK
von Rauch,MM
Rauchin,WK
Rauecker,WK
Rauen,WK
Rauenschwinder,LS
Rauensweider,LS
Rauert,MM
Raugust,HW(67)
Rauh,GS(23)
Rauida,WK
Rauland,LS
Raumann,WK
Raumer,WK
Rauner,WK
Raunert,MM
Raunest,LS,WK
Rausch,WK
Rauschenberger,WK
Rauschendorfer,
  W#(7.104)

Rauschenschoeder,LS
Rauschenschwender,LS
Rauscher,HW(28),
  W#(6.25),WK
Rauscherin,W#(6.84)
Rauschert,MM
Rauß,LS
Rauter,WK
Rauterin,WK
Rauth,LS,WK
Rauther,WK
von Raven,MM
Rawer,WK
Raya,WK
Rayeur,WK
Reb,WK
Rebel,WK
Rebenschön,WK
Reber,WK
Rebin,WK
Reblin,WK
Rebmann,GF(95A),LS,
  WK
Rebstock,WK
Rech,GF(91A),LS,WK
Rechenberg,SW(22)
Recher,WK
Rechlin,MM
Rechner,WK
Rechtberger,WK
Rechtkämmer,HW(12,
  22,24)
Reck,WK
Reckentin,MM
Reckenwall,WK
Recker,WK
Reckewald,WK
Reckle,WK
Recklmayer,WK
Recktermann,W#(4.46)
Ręcz,K1(167A)
Reddelien,MM
Reddelin,MM
Redekop,BU
Redekopp,BU
Redenbach,LS,WK
Redentin,MM
Reder,MM,WK
Redern,WK
Redicher,WK
Reding,WK
Redinger,LS
Redl,WK
Redlhamer,WK
Redlich,GL(257),MM
Redlig,WK
Redlin,MM
Redlinger,WK

Redmann,GL(390,503),
  GS(14)
Reeb,GL(175,177,
  321),WK
Reeber,GL(382)
Reeh,WK
Reer,BU
Rees,LS,MM
Reeß,WK
Reffelt,MM
Reg,WK
Regehr,BU
Regele,LS
Regenbach,WK
Regenspurger,
  W#(6.32),WK
Reger,BU,WK
Regert,WK
Reget,WK
Regett,WK
Regg,WK
Regier,BU
Regner,WK
Regnie,WK
Regnier,WK
Regus,WK
Reh,IE(88),LS,SW(4),
  WK
Rehacsek,WK
Rehan,BU
Rehbein,HS(65),LS,WK
Rehbronn,KL(9)
Rehder,MM
Rehland,MM
Rehling,GF(132B)
Rehnert,HS(34)
Rehrich,WK
Rehse,MM
Rei,WK
Reibach,WK
Reibel,WK
Reiberger,LS
Reibholz,LS
Reibl,WK
Reibold,LS
Reich,GL(311),
  HS(26),HW(67),
  IE(97),K1(167B),
  WK
Reichard,LS,MM,WK
Reichardt,LS,WK
Reichart,WK
Reiche,MM
Reichel,MM,WK
Reichelt,WK
Reichenbach,LS,WK
Reicher,GF(132B),WK

Reichert,HW(179, 207),LS,WK
Reicherzd,WK
Reichhardt,SW(6,7, 17,53)
Reichhart,WK
Reichheimer,LS
Reichhert,WK
Reichlin,GL(465)
Reichsman,WK
Reidebach,WK
Reidenbach,WK
Reidinger,WK
Reier,GL(68,69,406)
Reif,LS,WK
Reifenkugl,WK
Reifer,WK
Reiff,WK
Reifferscheid,WK
Reiher,GL(503),WK
Reihl,LS
Reihnberger,LS,WK
Reihnehmer,LS
Reihoda,W#(7.74)
Reihott,WK
Reiker,GL(381,503)
Reil,LS
Reiland,WK
Reimann,GS(90A),MM, WK
Reimer,BU
Reimers,MM
Reimert,HW(22,39)
Reiminger,WK
Rein,HW(12 entries), IE(88),LS,SW(4, 19),WK
Reinbach,WK
Reinberger,LS
Reindl,SW(27)
Reinecke,MM
Reinegg,MM
Reinehemer,LS
Reineke,MM
Reinemer,LS
Reiner,GL(249,310, 337,495),MM,WK
Reinerds,WK
Reineri,WK
Reinerin,WK
Reiners,GL(337),MM
Reinert,GF(133A), GL(337),LS,WK
Reinerth,WK
Reinfahrt,HS(65)
Reinfuß,LS
Reinhalt,WK
Reinhard,LS,WK

Reinhardt,HW(15 entries),LS,WK
Reinhart,MM,WK
Reinheimer,LS,WK
Reinherr,WK
Reinhold,GS(90A),LS, WK
Reinholt,LS
Reinich,WK
Reininger,WK
Reinisch,LS
Reinke,GS(91B), HW(63),MM
Reinlein,WK
Reinold,LS
Reinowski,K1(167A)
Reinsbach,WK
Reinsfeld,LS
Reinspach,WK
Reinspitz,WK
Reipoldt,LS
Reir,BU
Reis,LS,WK
Reisch,LS,WK
Reischer,WK
Reischmann,LS,WK
Reisdorf,LS
Reiser,GF(132B), GL(194,237),HW(11 entries),WK
Reisert,WK
Reising,WK
Reisinger,WK
Reiske,K1(167A)
Reisman,WK
Reismiller,WK
Reiss,IE(95)
Reiß,LS,SW(14,27),WK
Reißdorf,LS
Reißenberger,WK
Reißenbergerin,WK
Reißendorf,WK
Reisser,HW(152)
Reißer,LS,WK
Reißhaufer,WK
Reissig,GL(133)
Reißinger,WK
Reißler,WK
Reißmann,LS
Reißmon,WK
Reißner,MM
Reiste,WK
Reister,WK
Reiszer,HW(41,42,44, 46)
Reit,WK
Reitarin,WK
Reitberger,WK

Reitenbach,GF(92A, 132B,133A),LS,WK
Reiter,LS,WK
Reitewald,WK
Reither,LS,WK
Reitherin,WK
Reitknecht,LS,WK
Reitmaier,SW(16)
Reitmann,WK
Reitmayer,SW(24),WK
Reitmon,WK
Reittenbach,WK
Reitter,WK
Reittermann,WK
Reitz,GF(92B,96A),WK
Reiz,WK
Reize,WK
Reizner,WK
Rekalow,HW(67)
Rekg,WK
Rekinger,WK
Rekow,HS(26)
Rekwald,MM
Relinger,WK
Rell,WK
Relli,WK
Relly,W#(1.36,2.71)
Rembler,WK
Remeling,WK
Remi,WK
Remillon,WK
Remler,LS,WK
Remli,WK
Remmer,WK
Rempagel,MM
Rempel,BU
Rempels,BU
Rempening,BU
Remto,W#(8.63)
Remy,WK
Renalter,WK
Renard,WK
Rendel,WK
Rendtl,WK
Renert,WK
Renger,WK
Renn,K1(166B)
Renne,WK
Renner,LS,MM,WK
Rennert,WK
Rennfeldt,MM
Reno,WK
Renodem,WK
Renon,WK
Renpening,BU
Rens,LS
Rensel,WK
Renter,WK

Riemer,WK	Rinner,GL(212)	Rodaucher,WK
Rienesbergerin,WK	Rinsger,WK	Rode,GS(11,18),
Rier,WK	Rip,WK	K1(165B),KL(16),
Ries,GF(95B),WK	Riper,WK	MM
Riesberg,MM	Ripp,GL(453),WK	Rodebücher,WK
Riesch,GL(490),WK	Rippel,LS,SW(7,24),	Rodel,GL(386,503)
Riesel,WK	WK	Rödel,GF(92A),GL(69,
von Riesen,BU	Ripson,WK	386,503)
Riesenkampf,MM	Risch,GL(233),WK	Roden,WK
Riesle,WK	Rischanek,LS	Rodenbach,WK
Rieß,GF(93B,133A),	Rischar,WK	Rodenbucher,WK
GL(490),LS,WK	Rischer,WK	Rodenbusch,WK
Rießenzek,WK	Rischscheid,WK	Röder,GL(64,386),LS,
Rießner,WK	Riser,WK	WK
Riesz,GL(40)	Rispeck,WK	Roderich,WK
Rieter,WK	Riß,WK	Roders,WK
Rieth,WK	Risser,WK	Rodi,WK
Riethaler,WK	Rissinger,WK	Rödig,WK
Riethmüller,GL(373)	Rissling,GL(313)	Roding,WK
Rietsch,LS,WK	Rist,LS,WK	Rödlich,LS
Riexinger,GL(436)	Ristow,MM	Rodmayer,WK
Riff,GL(453),WK	Ritiche,WK	Rodt,WK
Rifner,WK	Ritsch,WK	Rodzynka,K1(167A)
Rigel,WK	Ritscher,MM	Roeder,GL(503),WK
Rigelsen,MM	Ritt,WK	Roegel,LS
Rigill,WK	Rittaler,LS	Roehl,HS(26,44)
Rigl,WK	Rittberger,WK	Roen,HS(44)
Rihlin,WK	Ritte,WK	Roeper,LS
Riker,WK	Ritter,GL(390,504),	Roes,LS
Riley,GL(349,501)	HW(28),LS,MM,WK	Roessel,LS
Rill,LS	Ritthaler,LS	Roetschel,K1(167A)
Rillart,WK	Ritz,LS,WK	Rog,WK
Rilling,LS	Riu,WK	Róg,K1(167A)
Rimatzki,K1(167A)	Rixer,WK	Rogalewicz,MM
Rimbeck,WK	Rizar,WK	Rogalscky,BU
Rimes,WK	Rizer,WK	Rogalsckye,BU
Rimke,MM	Rjepin,MM	Rogenmosser,WK
Rimmel,WK	Roatsch,WK	Roger,WK
Rimping,WK	Rob,WK	Rogg,WK
Rimsinger,WK	Robb,WK	Rogge,MM
Rinck,GF(92B),MM	Robe,WK	Roggenbau,MM
Rind,LS	Robeck,HS(31)	Rogier,WK
Rinder,WK	Robenschon,WK	Rögier,BU
Rindvald,WK	Rober,WK	Rogler,GL(286)
Ring,LS,W#(5.57),WK	Robert,LS,WK	Rogowski,K1(167A)
Ringel,LS	Roberth,WK	Roh,WK
Ringfort,WK	Robey,WK	Rohatsch,WK
Ringk,WK	Robinet,WK	Rohde,BU
Ringler,WK	Roch,WK	Rohenschon,WK
Rings,MM	Rochert,MM	Rohl,WK
Ringschmidt,WK	Rock,WK	Rohlfs,IE(95)
Ringvald,WK	Rockel,LS	Rohlof,MM
Ringwald,LS,WK	Röcker,WK	Rohloff,K1(167B),MM
Ringwelski,K1(167A)	Rockh,WK	Rohm,SW(38)
Rinikel,WK	Röckl,WK	Röhm,WK
Rink,HW(51),LS	Rod,WK	Rohmann,K1(167A)
Rinkel,LS	Rodan,WK	Rohmer,WK
Rinne,MM	Rodauch,WK	Rohn,WK

Rothemberg,KL(9)
Rothenberger,GL(68)
Rothenbucher,WK
Rothenbücher,WK
Rothenöder,W#(3.32)
Röther,WK
Rothermel,WK
Rothgerber,WK
Rothhan,WK
Rothhäusler,WK
Röthig,WK
Rothin,WK
Rothister,LS
Rothländer,LS
Rothlechner,WK
Rothlehner,WK
Röthlein,WK
Rothmacher,LS,WK
Rothmann,GL(438)
Rothmüller,WK
Rotholz,WK
Rothschild,MM
Rothtag,WK
Rotinger,WK
Rötler,WK
Rotman,WK
Rotner,WK
Rott,GL(82,196,344),
  LS,WK
Rottenberger,WK
Rottenbücher,WK
Rottenburger,WK
Rotter,WK
Rottermann,LS
Rottgärber,WK
Rottin,WK
Rottinger,LS,WK
Röttinger,LS,WK
Rottler,WK
Röttler,GL(427),
  HW(17)
Rottmann,WK
Rötz,WK
Rötzer,WK
Roufosse,WK
Roujer,WK
Rouland,WK
Rouscher,WK
Rowatsch,WK
Röwe,MM
Rowohl,MM
Roy,WK
Różalski,K1(167A)
Rożcnas,MM
Rozinberger,WK
Rözler,WK
Rözlerin,WK
Rozwelt,K1(167A)

Rozyn,K1(167A)
Rub,LS,WK
Rüb,GL(51 entries),
  HW(17,25)
Rübel,GF(125,125A),
  WK
Ruber,WK
Rüber,WK
Ruberin,WK
Rubert,LS,WK
Ruberth,WK
Rubesan,WK
Rubint,WK
Rubitschum,WK
Rubner,WK
Rubricht,LS
Rubsamen,WK
Rucherd,GL(220)
Ruchert,BU
Ruck,K1(167A),WK
Rückemann,LS
Rückemuß,WK
Rücker,LS
Rückerich,LS
Rückert,LS
Rückl,SW(24,55)
Rückner,WK
Rudeklovics,WK
Rudel,WK
Ruden,WK
Rudenbach,WK
Rudicherin,WK
Rüdiger,MM
Rudinger,WK
Rudius,WK
Rudizina,MM
Rudloff,WK
Rudolf,LS,WK
Rudolph,GF(92A),LS,
  WK
Rudow,MM
Rüdt,WK
Rudzynski,K1(167A)
Rueb,GL(6 entries),
  WK
Ruef,WK
Rueger,GS(14)
Ruess,GL(490)
Rüetschi,WK
Ruf,LS,WK
Ruff,HW(87,88),LS,WK
Rufflin,WK
Rügers,WK
Ruh,WK
Ruhardt,WK
Ruhe,MM
Ruhl,WK
Rühl,WK

Rühlen,LS,WK
Rühling,IE(98),LS
Ruhm,WK
Rühtz,MM
Ruies,WK
Ruker,WK
Rukmichin,WK
Rulach,WK
Ruland,WK
Rulf,LS
Rulinger,WK
Rüll,WK
Rüllen,LS
Rum,WK
Ruman,WK
Rumele,WK
Rumeschottel,MM
Rumi,LS
Ruminger,WK
Ruml,WK
Rump,MM,WK
Rumpel,IE(93,95,97),
  LS
Rumpf,GL(198),WK
Rumpold,GL(371)
Runcka,WK
Rund,WK
Runde,WK
Rundio,WK
Rundt,WK
Rundwasser,WK
Rundzieher,GS(14,19,
  22,89B)
Rung,WK
Runge,LS,MM
Runk,WK
Runkel,WK
Runkwitz,WK
Runtzi,W#(4.98)
Rup,LS,WK
Rupert,WK
Rupf,WK
Rupp,LS,WK
Ruppana,WK
Ruppel,GL(408),WK
Ruppen,WK
Ruppenthal,LS,WK
Rupper,WK
Ruppert,WK
Ruprecht,GF(116),WK
Rurpacher,WK
Rus,MM,WK
Rusch,LS,WK
Ruschet,WK
Ruschizka,W#(8.50)
Rusen,WK
Rusizka,WK
Russ,MM,W#(7.112)

Ruß,LS,WK
Rüß,LS
Russel,WK
Rußle,WK
Rußmann,WK
Rußwurm,MM
Rust,WK
Ruthenberg,MM
Ruthz,WK
Rüting,MM
Rutkowski,GS(89A),
   K1(167A)
Rutowski,LS
Rutsch,WK
Rutscher,WK
Rutschli,W#(5.51)
Rutt,WK
Rutter,WK
Rütter,WK
Rüttger,WK
Rutz,WK
Rutze,MM
Ruy,W#(4.108)
Ruyer,WK
Rybe,WK
Ryczel,K1(167A)
Rydel,K1(167A)
Rygiert,LS
Ryk,K1(167B)
Rymaszewski,GS(18)
Rynner,GL(40)
Saaghy,WK
Saal,WK
Saall,WK
Saar,LS,WK
Sabel,WK
Sabelmann,MM
Sablotzki,GL(483)
Sablotzky,GL(483)
Sabluk,WK
Sabner,WK
Sacher,LS
Sachs,LS,WK
Sachß,WK
Sack,K1(168A)
Sackmann,GL(502),
   HW(31,63)
Sacz,WK
Sadecski,WK
Sadewater,MM
Sadler,WK
Sadowski,K1(167B)
Saedler,MM
Saenger,GS(19),
   KL(36)
Saffel,GL(371)
Safron,GL(112)
Sage,HS(74)

Sager,LS,MM
Sagillek,WK
Sahaunaja,GL(410)
Sahling,LS
Sahm,GF(125B,127A,
   133A)
Saier,WK
Saile,WK
Sailer,WK
Sak,WK
v. Sala,HS(29)
Saladin,WK
Salamon,WK
Salber,WK
Salemon,MM
Salfeld,MM
Salin,WK
Saling,WK
Salladin,WK
Saller,WK
Salling,LS
Sally,WK
Salm,WK
Salmon,WK
Salo,MM
Salome,GL(375)
Salomo,MM
Salomon,WK
Salzberger,WK
Salzenberger,LS
Salzer,WK
Salzgeber,WK
Salzwedel,MM
Salzwig,MM
Samer,WK
Samhuber,WK
Samie,WK
Samsel,WK
Samsell,LS
Samstach,WK
Samwerber,WK
Sand,WK
Sandau,GL(450)
Sandei,GL(450)
Sandel,LS
Sander,LS,MM,WK
Sandhas,WK
Sandhöfer,WK
Sandion,WK
Sandler,LS,WK
Sandmann,MM
Sandmayerin,WK
Sandmayr,WK
Sandmeyer,GL(247)
Sandner,LS
Sandrer,WK
Sandrock,MM
Sandschuster,WK

Sandt,MM
Sanftleben,MM
Sanheim,WK
Sanhem,LS
Sanhen,LS
Sanitz,HS(29)
Sann,WK
Sannders,GL(501)
Santer,WK
Santner,WK
Santnerin,WK
Sanzenbächer,GL(209,
   368)
Sapert,LS
Sapieha,MM
Sarger,WK
Sarie,WK
Sarner,WK
Sartor,WK
Sartorius,LS,WK
Sas,SW(11)
Sasanoff,MM
Sasmenko,HW(208)
Saß,MM
Sasse,HS(26),MM,WK
Sastawa,GL(197)
Satlberger,WK
Satler,LS,WK
Satow,MM
Sattelberger,WK
Sattler,WK
Sättler,WK
Säuberlich,GS(18)
Säuberlin,MM
von Saucken,MM
Sauder,LS
Sauer,GL(29
   entries),HS(43),
   IE(90,93,95,97),
   LS,SW(14,31,34),
   WK
Saueressig,WK
Sauerwein,LS
Säulle,WK
Saum,LS
Saumann,MM
Saumer,WK
Saunders,GL(349)
Saur,GL(172,209,393,
   394)
Saurbeyn,WK
Saurer,WK
Saurin,WK
Saurland,WK
Saurterelle,WK
Saurwald,WK
Saurwein,WK

Sauter,GL(462),
  GS(19),LS,WK
Sauterer,WK
Sauther,WK
Sautter,WK
Sawatzki,BU
Sawatzky,BU
Sawilla,SW(27)
Sax,WK
Saxe,WK
Saxemeyer,WK
Saxer,WK
Sayller,WK
Scabina,WK
Scarianz,WK
Scencz,WK
Schaad,LS
Schaaf,GL(258),MM
Schaal,GL(430,473),
  HW(35 entries),LS
Schaar,LS,WK
Schaat,WK
Schabe,WK
Schabel,WK
Schabenbauer,LS
Schaber,GL(370),LS
Schabert,LS,WK
Schabier,WK
Schabillie,WK
Schach,WK
Schachenreither,WK
Schacher,GL(212,475)
Schacherer,WK
Schachinger,WK
Schachingerin,WK
Schachner,WK
Schacht,MM
Schächterle,GL(332,
  334,500)
Schack,WK
Schackh,WK
Schackin,WK
Schackmein,WK
Schackmin,WK
Schacko,WK
Schackon,WK
Schad,GF(92A),LS,WK
Schade,K1(167B),WK
Schadeck,WK
Schadelbeber,LS
Schadenberg,MM
Schäderlein,WK
Schaderu,HW(15,29,
  39)
Schadeweber,LS
Schadl,LS,WK
Schädler,HW(29,31)
Schaeberlein,LS

Schaefenacker,WK
Schaefer,GL(464),LS,
  MM,WK
Schaeffer,GL(464),
  IE(95),MM,WK
Schaer,WK
Schaf,GL(258),WK
Schafaczek,SW(7)
Schafenberger,LS
Schafer,GL(511),
  IE(95),WK
Schäfer,GF(92A,93A,
  133A),GL(5
  entries),HS(33,
  38),HW(17,30,41),
  IE(88),LS,MM,
  SW(4),W#(8.98),WK
Schaff,WK
Schäff,HW(20)
Schaffer,GL(278,
  508),IE(94)
Schäffer,LS,MM,WK
Schäfferin,WK
Schaffert,GL(37
  entries)
Schaffhauser,SW(6,7,
  24,52,57)
Schaffner,GL(485),WK
Schaffot,WK
Schafheitlin,WK
Schafheltin,WK
Schäfler,WK
Schafner,WK
Schafrath,LS,WK
Schafro,WK
Schafstätter,LS,WK
Schaible,WK
Schak,WK
Schakma,WK
Schakmann,WK
Schakmin,WK
Schal,WK
Schalck,WK
Schalen,MM
Schalich,LS
Schalk,WK
Schalkin,WK
Schall,GL(380),WK
Schallardo,WK
Schaller,GF(92A,
  93B),LS,MM,
  SW(38),WK
Schäller,LS
Schallier,WK
Schallio,WK
Schallor,WK
Schalt,WK
Schaltes,WK

Scham,WK
Schamar,WK
Schamber,WK
Schamberger,LS,
  W#(5.122)
Schambre,WK
Schámosy,WK
Schamper,WK
Schamplon,WK
Schamul,GS(60)
Schanbeck,WK
Schande,LS
Schandl,WK
Schandlmayer,WK
Schandolly,W#(7.77)
Schanen,WK
Schang,WK
Schangon,WK
Schank,WK
Schankweiler,LS,WK
Schannal,WK
v Schannanberg,WK
Schanner,LS
Schanners,WK
Schannring,LS
Schanschack,WK
Schanter,W#(4.106)
Schanz,LS
Schaparn,WK
Schapenski,BU
Schapenskiy,BU
Schapert,WK
Schappert,LS
Schar,LS,WK
Scharbach,WK
Scharbannt,WK
Scharboug,WK
Scharburg,LS
Scharck,MM
Schardan,WK
Schardt,MM
Scharer,WK
Scharf,MM,WK
Scharff,GL(348,501),
  K1(167A),WK
Scharffbillig,WK
Schargon,WK
Scharier,WK
Scharl,WK
Scharmüllerin,WK
Scharn,WK
Scharnagl,WK
Scharnal,WK
Scharnel,WK
Scharping,HS(75)
Schärs,WK
Schart,WK
Scharwat,WK

Scharz,WK
Schasbier,WK
Schasni,WK
Schaton,WK
Schatt,WK
Schattie,WK
Schattman,WK
Schattner,WK
Schatz,GF(91B),
  GL(289),WK
Schätz,LS,SW(24),WK
Schätze,LS
Schatzin,WK
Schätzle,WK
Schaub,MM,WK
Schauber,IE(98)
Schäuble,HW(17)
Schauck,LS
Schaude,LS,WK
Schauer,GL(5
  entries),WK
Schauerte,WK
Schäufele,GL(430),
  HW(11 entries)
Schauff,WK
Schauffler,GL(56,57,
  59,117)
Schaufler,WK
Schaumberger,WK
Schaup,HW(40,67)
Schaupp,HW(63)
Schaus,IE(95,97),
  SW(61)
Schausman,WK
Schauss,IE(94,97)
Schauß,WK
Schauss-Ast,IE(97)
Schausse,WK
Schautz,WK
Schayer,WK
Schaz,WK
Schäzer,WK
Schecht,WK
Schechtele,W#(4.110)
Scheck,GL(508),
  HW(30),WK
Schectenz,WK
Sched,WK
Schedel,WK
Schedlberger,WK
Schedler,GS(89A,
  89B),WK
Scheel,HS(65),MM
Scheep,WK
Scheer,LS,MM,WK
Schefczuk,SW(17)
Schefer,LS,WK
Scheferin,WK

Scheff,WK
Scheffel,MM
Scheffer,HW(43),
  W#(1.30,1.50,
  5.53),WK
Scheffzschegg,WK
Schefner,WK
Scheib,LS,WK
Scheibel,LS,WK
Scheibin,WK
Scheibl,WK
Scheible,WK
Scheibler,GS(24,89B,
  90A),WK
Scheibli,WK
Scheid,LS,WK
Scheidecker,WK
Scheider,WK
von Scheiding,MM
Scheidl,WK
Scheidler,WK
Scheidlin,WK
Scheidt,WK
Scheier,LS
Scheiffelen,WK
Scheimer,WK
Schein,LS,WK
Scheiner,LS,WK
Scheinost,SW(36)
Scheiren,WK
Scheirich,WK
Scheirmann,WK
Scheit,WK
Scheitherin,WK
Scheitweller,WK
Schekin,WK
Schel,WK
Schelcke,WK
Scheld,WK
Schelenberger,WK
Schelkin,WK
Schell,GF(91A,95A,
  133A),GL(202,
  405),LS,WK
Schelle,MM,WK
Schelleberger,WK
Schellein,WK
Schellenberg,BU,LS
Schellenberger,
  GL(269,270),LS,WK
Scheller,LS,WK
Schellhamer,WK
Schellhammer,WK
Schellhorn,GL(450),
  WK
Schels,WK
Schemel,WK
Schemer,LS

Scheml,WK
Schemmer,WK
Schems,WK
Schenberger,WK
Schenbor,WK
Schenchen,WK
Schenck,WK
Schendel,HS(47),
  KL(18,24)
Schender,LS
Scheneider,WK
Schener,WK
Schenfeld,WK
Schenhardt,W#(5.10,
  6.55)
Schenini,WK
Schenk,K1(165B),LS,
  WK
Schenkel,WK
Schenkenbach,LS
Schenkenberger,WK
Schentzia,WK
Schepel,MM
Schepp,LS,WK
Scheppels,WK
Schepps,GL(69)
Scher,WK
Schera,WK
Scheraus,WK
Scherbaum,LS
Scherbe,WK
Scherbekour,WK
Scherber,WK
Scherbert,GL(370)
Scherchs,WK
Scherdt,HW(81)
Schere,WK
Scherer,GF(133A),
  GL(241),LS,
  W#(8.92),WK
Scherf,LS
Scherff,LS,WK
Scherg,WK
Scherkler,W#(6.11)
Scherl,LS,SW(24)
Scherlaub,WK
Scherle,IE(90,98),
  LS,SW(14),WK
Scherman,WK
Schermer,LS
Schermes,WK
Scherp,LS
Scherpfin,WK
Scherph,WK
Scherr,WK
Scherrar,WK
Scherrenbacher,WK
Scherrer,LS

Schoenthaler,SW(60, 61,62)
Schoertz,BU
Schoettle,LS
Schoettler,MM
Schofeler,LS
Schofer,LS,WK
Schöfer,LS,WK
Schoff,WK
Schöffel,WK
Schoffer,WK
Schöffer,LS
Schöffler,GL(360)
Schoffra,WK
Schöfle,WK
Schohm,WK
Schok,WK
Schöl,MM,WK
Scholberger,LS
Scholdes,WK
Scholemberger,LS
Scholer,WK
Schöler,MM
Scholk,WK
Scholl,GF(122A, 133B),LS, W#(5.13),WK
Schöll,GL(130,131)
Schollberg,LS
Scholle,WK
Schöllenberg,BU
Schollenberger,WK
Schöller,WK
Schöllheimer,WK
Scholling,WK
Schöllkopf,WK
Schollyon,WK
Scholt,WK
Scholte,WK
Scholtes,WK
Scholtus,WK
Scholtz,WK
Scholz,W#(6.92),WK
Schom,WK
Schomann,MM
Schomer,WK
Schommer,WK
Schomp,WK
Schon,WK
Schön,LS,MM,WK
Schonauer,WK
Schönauer,W#(6.91)
Schönbach,WK
Schönbeck,WK
Schönberg,LS,MM,WK
Schönberger,LS, W#(8.21),WK
Schönborn,LS,WK

Schöndorf,WK
Schöneburger,WK
Schöned,WK
Schönemann,LS,MM
Schönenberger,WK
Schonenwald,WK
Schöner,WK
Schönerin,WK
Schönermark,MM
Schönfeld,MM
Schönfelder,WK
Schönhals,WK
Schönheit,WK
Schönherr,WK
Schönhof,WK
Schönhofer,LS
Schonith,WK
Schönmann,WK
Schönn,WK
Schönnagel,WK
Schöntag,LS
Schönthal,WK
Schonthaler,IE(97)
Schönthaler,IE(92, 94,96,97,98),LS
Schönus,WK
Schönweiler,LS
Schoon,HW(16 entries)
Schoor,WK
Schopf,WK
Schöpf,LS,WK
Schöpfer,LS,WK
Schöpflin,WK
Schöplein,WK
Schopp,GL(68,344, 387,504),WK
Schöppacher,WK
Schoppelrey,WK
Schöpper,WK
Schoppert,WK
Schor,WK
Schora,WK
Schordgen,WK
Schorg,WK
Schorich,WK
Schork,WK
Schörle,LS
Schorlemer,MM
Schorn,WK
Schorr,HW(29),LS,WK
Schorrin,WK
Schors,WK
Schorter,WK
Schortie,WK
Schorzmann,GL(108)
Schosan,GL(112)
Schosberger,LS

Schoseph,W#(2.29)
Schosler,LS
Schosseler,WK
Schosser,WK
Schoßler,LS,WK
Schoten,MM
Schott,LS,SW(26),WK
Schotta,WK
Schottenhamel,WK
Schotter,LS,WK
Schottermayer,LS
Schöttle,HW(22,25, 63,67)
Schoy,WK
Schoysss,W#(6.23)
Schözle,WK
Schrabbe,WK
Schrack,LS
Schrader,K1(167B),MM
Schraek,WK
Schrag,LS,WK
Schram,LS,WK
Schramegger, W#(7.105)
Schramm,K1(167B), KL(18),LS,MM,WK
Schrank,HS(38),WK
Schraub,WK
Schraudner,WK
Schraz,WK
Schreck,LS,WK
Schred,WK
Schreder,WK
Schrederin,WK
Schredinger,WK
Schreer,GS(91A),MM
Schrefer,WK
Schreiber,HW(179, 208),LS,MM,WK
Schreiberin,WK
Schreider,WK
Schreier,LS,WK
Schreiner,LS,SW(12), W#(1.11),WK
Schreiter,W#(5.98)
Schrempf,WK
Schrenk,GL(446,508)
Schrettl,WK
Schreuder,MM
Schrey,IE(90),LS, SW(14)
Schreyer,LS,WK
Schreyner,LS
Schringmann,W#(4.70)
Schrins,WK
Schriz,W#(1.28)
Schrod,WK
Schroder,WK

Schröder,BU,HS(75),
 KL(18),LS,MM,
 SW(21),WK
von Schröder,MM
Schröderin,WK
Schroeck,WK
Schroeder,KL(32)
Schröhr,SW(26)
Schrok,LS
Schrom,WK
Schröpf,LS
Schrot,GL(220)
Schröter,BU,WK
Schroth,GL(365)
Schrott,LS,WK
von Schrötter,MM
Schrötz,WK
Schrupp,GL(505)
Schrupp-La Force,
 GL(391)
Schtang,GL(401)
Schu,W#(1.62)
Schub,WK
Schuber,WK
Schüber,WK
Schuberin,WK
Schubert,GS(18,91A),
 HS(75),LS,WK
Schübert,WK
Schuberth,WK
Schubertin,W#(3.68)
Schubien,WK
Schuch,LS,WK
Schuchardt,MM
Schuchmacher,WK
Schuck,LS,WK
Schücker,WK
Schuckler,WK
Schudi,WK
Schüdich,WK
Schué,WK
Schuf,WK
Schuff,WK
Schuffler,WK
Schügler,WK
Schuh,GL(430,431),
 HW(10 entries),
 LS,WK
Schuhardt,MM
Schuhbauer,WK
Schuhg,WK
Schuhi,WK
Schühlin,GL(474)
Schuhm,WK
Schuhmacher,LS,MM,WK
Schuhmacherin,WK
Schuhmann,LS,WK
Schui,WK

Schük,WK
Schukow,MM
Schul,WK
Schulcz,WK
Schulderer,WK
Schuler,GL(194),LS,
 WK
Schüler,GL(69,303),
 WK
Schulerus,WK
Schulgen,WK
Schulhauser,SW(16)
Schulkosi,GL(494)
Schull,WK
Schullberg,WK
Schuller,LS,
 W#(7.62),WK
Schüller,WK
Schullian,WK
von Schulmann,MM
Schult,WK
Schulte,MM,WK
Schulter,WK
Schultes,WK
Schultheis,WK
Schultheiß,WK
Schultus,WK
Schultz,GS(11,18,
 90A),LS,MM,WK
Schultze,LS,MM,WK
Schulz,BU,GF(133B),
 GL(195,282,446),
 GS(14,91A),
 HS(75),HW(23,39),
 LS,MM,W#(7.117),
 WK
Schulze,GL(408),LS,
 MM,WK
Schulzer,WK
Schum,WK
Schuma,WK
Schumacher,GF(133B),
 GL(186),LS,MM,
 SW(26),WK
Schumak,LS
Schumann,LS,WK
Schumer,WK
Schumm,IE(98),WK
Schummer,LS,WK
Schumppen,WK
Schun,WK
Schunder,WK
Schünemann,MM
Schuner,WK
Schüning,MM
Schunk,WK
Schuntenberger,WK
Schuntz,WK

Schup,WK
Schupfer,WK
Schupp,LS,WK
Schur,MM,WK
Schüren,WK
Schurger,WK
Schuriwar,WK
Schuriwer,WK
Schürn,WK
Schurr,GF(133B),WK
Schurt,WK
Schurtz,LS
Schury,WK
Schürzinger,WK
Schuß,LS
Schüssel,WK
Schüßer,SW(27)
Schußler,WK
Schüßler,WK
Schuster,HW(14),LS,
 SW(16,38),WK
Schusterin,WK
Schutgen,WK
Schütt,HS(75),MM
Schutter,W#(5.80,
 6.56),WK
Schüttgen,WK
Schüttler,LS,SW(35)
Schutz,GL(446),WK
Schütz,BU,GL(342,
 401,430),GS(91A),
 HW(29),LS,MM,WK
Schverbel,WK
Schvörin,WK
Schwaab,WK
von Schwaan,MM
Schwab,GS(57,91A),
 HW(26),LS,SW(38),
 W#(8.25,8.31),WK
Schwabe,MM
Schwabenhausen,WK
Schwabentagin,WK
Schwabin,WK
Schwaderer,GL(18
 entries)
Schwager,LS,WK
Schwäger,WK
Schwägler,GL(316),WK
Schwagten,WK
Schwahn,WK
Schwaitzer,WK
Schwakob,WK
Schwakop,LS
Schwalbe,HW(87)
Schwaler,WK
Schwalge,WK
Schwaller,WK
Schwallie,WK

Seifert,WK	Semler,WK	Seuberlich,MM
Seiff,WK	Semmer,WK	Seufert,WK
Seiffart,MM,WK	Semmlow,MM	Seuffert,WK
Seiffert,MM,WK	Semmrau,K1(167B)	Seufzer,SW(21)
Seifridt,WK	Semroch,K1(167B)	Seuß,WK
Seifried,LS	Sen,LS	Seutter,GL(488)
Seigel,LS	Sender,WK	Seuyberlich,MM
Seigl,WK	Sene,WK	Sevbott,WK
Seil,LS	Senen,WK	Severien,MM
Seiler,LS,WK	Senf,LS,SW(34),WK	Severin,WK
Seiller,WK	Senft,GF(93B),LS,WK	Severing,WK
Seinn,WK	Seng,WK	Severus,MM
Seip,WK	Sengbusch,MM	Seweke,MM
Seipel,LS,WK	von Sengbusch,MM	Seybert,WK
Seipeth,WK	Sengeisen,WK	Seybold,HW(18,39,81,
Seipl,LS	Sengelmann,MM	89)
Seipolt,LS	Sengle,GL(427),LS	Seyer,MM,WK
Seippel,WK	Senicki,LS	Seyfang,WK
Seiß,GF(92A)	Senison,LS	Seyfert,WK
Seissiger,WK	Senn,WK	Seyffert,WK
Seistein,WK	Senner,WK	Seyfrid,WK
Seit,LS,WK	Sennft,WK	Seyfried,WK
Seitz,GL(40,299),	Senon,WK	Seyler,WK
IE(89),LS,WK	Senpht,LS	Shubert,IE(98)
Seix,HW(18)	Senser,WK	Shukow,MM
Seiz,GL(279)	Senß,WK	Shürmann,WK
Sekel,LS	Sensse,WK	Siber,WK
Sekira,WK	Sent,WK	Siberin,WK
Sekl,WK	Senteff,WK	Sibert,WK
Selb,WK	Sentif,WK	Sibeth,MM
Selber,WK	Senz,LS	Sibler,WK
Selchinger,WK	Sepl,WK	Sibold,WK
Selchow,HS(26)	Seppelt,WK	Sibra,WK
Seleiter,LS	Serafin,LS	Sibrand,MM
Seler,WK	Seras,WK	v. Sibrand,MM
Selge,MM	Seraß,WK	Siburg,WK
Selgenrath,WK	Serasse,WK	Sichler,WK
Selgra,WK	Serde,WK	Sichrist,WK
Selis,LS,WK	Sereck,WK	Sick,WK
Sell,KL(37)	Serenz,WK	Sickeberger,WK
Sellentin,MM	Serfas,LS,SW(33),WK	Sickenberger,WK
Sellius,MM	Serff,WK	Sieb,WK
Sellmann,MM	Serger,LS	Siebel,WK
Sellschopp,MM	Serier,WK	Siebenaler,WK
Seln,WK	Serkall,MM	Sieber,LS,WK
Selt,WK	Serket,MM	Siebert,BU,HW(208),
Seltenreich,WK	Serkolewa,MM	MM,WK
Seltner,WK	Sermetinger,WK	Siebler,WK
Seltz,W#(4.81)	Serni,WK	Siech,WK
Seltzer,LS,WK	Serr,GL(251,409,495)	Sieg,MM
Selzer,LS,WK	Sertel,WK	Siegel,LS
Selzerin,WK	Sertz,MM	Siegelbach,LS
Sem,WK	Servaux,WK	Siegenthaler,WK
Sembery,W#(8.100)	Servay,WK	Sieger,WK
Sembler,WK	Sessin,IE(94)	Siegers,WK
Sembri,WK	Seswey,WK	Siegfrid,WK
Semer,WK	Setter,WK	Siegl,WK
	Setzer,WK	

Siegle,GL(105
   entries)
Sieler,WK
Sielmann,MM
Siemens,BU
Siering,LS
Sierot,WK
Sieß,GF(93B),WK
Sießmayer,WK
Sievers,MM
von Siewers,MM
Siewert,MM
Sifenborn,WK
Sifert,WK
Siffermann,GL(82,
   405),WK
Siffert,LS
Siffrich,MM
Sifrid,WK
Sigel,WK
Sigelbach,LS
Sigelkow,MM
Sigellkow,MM
Sigl,WK
Sigle,GL(299)
Sigles,W#(2.73)
Sigmund,WK
Sigrünn,WK
Sigry,WK
Sihle,GL(285)
Sihler,WK
Sika,K1(167B)
Sikocki,K1(167B)
Silagy,W#(8.102)
Silagyi,WK
Silberberg,MM
Silberhorn,WK
Silberhuber,WK
Silchen,LS
Siligan,WK
Silingen,WK
Silla,WK
Silli,WK
Silmann,W#(8.79)
Silzer,LS,WK
Siman,WK
Simani,GL(276,497)
Simater,LS,WK
Simborn,MM
Simegh,WK
Simkele,WK
Simko,WK
Simman,WK
Simmo,WK
Simon,GF(92B),LS,MM,
   WK
Simone,WK
Simonet,WK

Simoni,LS,WK
Simonin,WK
Simono,WK
Simpfendörfer,HW(51)
Simpli,WK
Simsch,MM
Simson,WK
Sinckel,WK
Sineg,WK
Sinen,WK
Siners,WK
Singele,WK
Singer,GL(261,451),
   LS,W#(8.14),WK
Single,LS,WK
Sinkel,WK
Sinlaub,LS
Sinn,WK
Sinner,WK
Sinnstein,WK
Sino,WK
Sinz,WK
Sipmann,WK
Sippel,WK
Sips,MM
Sir,WK
Siren,WK
Sires,WK
Sirier,WK
Siriker,WK
Sirouger,WK
Siska,WK
Sislerin,WK
Sitinger,WK
Sitkowski,K1(167B)
Sittenthaler,WK
Sitter,WK
Sitterle,WK
Sittner,GL(492)
Sittow,MM
Sitz,IE(94,95),
   KL(54),WK
Sitzmann,WK
Siwrin,WK
Six,WK
Skalla,WK
Sklenars,WK
Sklinarsch,W#(7.51)
Skoda,WK
Skotschko,GL(483)
Skowronski,GL(112)
Slabik,WK
Slarz,WK
Slaun,WK
Slavicsek,WK
Slesak,WK
Słowiński,K1(167B)
Sluchinski,GL(350)

Smacsek,WK
Smedia,MM
Smekal,WK
Smerczle,WK
Smereczański,LS
Smetana,WK
Smicz,WK
Smidin,WK
Smidt,MM,WK
Śmigielski,K1(167B)
Smigraski,MM
Smit,MM,WK
Smitauer,WK
Smith,GL(496)
Smolholcz,WK
Snehveiß,WK
Sneider,GF(93A),WK
Sneiderin,WK
Sner,WK
Sniczler,WK
Snoderpech,WK
Snur,WK
Sobat,WK
Soder,LS
Söderberg,MM
Sodomka,SW(24)
Sodorf,MM
Sohl,GF(133B)
Sohn,LS,WK
Sohrbeeren,MM
Sois,WK
Sokolow,MM
Sokolowski,MM
Sola,WK
Solbach,WK
Sölbach,WK
Soldau,MM
Soldner,WK
Söldner,WK
Soling,WK
Soll,WK
Solling,LS
Sollner,LS
Solmon,WK
Solms,LS,WK
Soltow,MM
Soly,WK
Som,WK
Sombach,WK
Somer,WK
Someray,WK
Sommer,LS,MM,SW(63),
   WK
Sommerfeld,K1(168A),
   MM
Sommerfeldt,BU
Sommerin,WK
Sommerrock,LS

Sommerrok,WK
Somogyi,WK
Son,LS
Sondag,WK
Soneck,WK
Sonitsch,WK
Sonnabend,LS
Sonnberger,WK
Sonnenberg,HS(33,
    38),MM
Sonnenfeld,GL(491)
Sonnet,WK
Sönnke,GL(181,356)
Sonnleuthner,WK
Sonntag,LS,SW(67)
Sonß,WK
Sonst,WK
Sontag,LS,WK
Sopha,MM
Sorg,GF(91A),WK
Sorgen,WK
Sornet,WK
Soro,WK
Sörös,WK
Soulier,LS
Soy,LS,WK
Spaal,WK
Spachinger,WK
Spachingerin,WK
Spaczek,WK
Spad,LS
Spahn,LS,WK
Spalinger,WK
Spaltenstein,LS,WK
Span,WK
Spanering,LS,WK
Spang,LS,WK
Spanger,WK
Spanheimer,LS
Spanier,LS
Spanig,WK
Spaniol,WK
Spaniolin,WK
Spannagel,GF(113,
    114,126),MM,WK
Sparer,W#(8.60),WK
Sparr,MM
Spat,LS
Spath,LS,WK
Späth,GL(198),
    SW(12),WK
Spätin,WK
Spatt,WK
Spatz,WK
Specht,GL(437),LS,WK
Speck,WK
Specker,WK
Speckermanin,WK

Speckermann,WK
Speckmann,WK
Spee,GF(95B)
Speer,LS,WK
Speichel,WK
Speicher,LS,WK
Speichler,WK
Speidel,LS
Speidelsbacher,
    GL(311)
Speidl,LS,WK
Speiger,LS
Speiser,WK
Speitel,LS
Speitelspacher,LS
Spelz,WK
Spendel,LS
Spenger,WK
Spengler,GF(93B),WK
Spenn,WK
Spenst,BU
Spenz,WK
Sper,WK
Sperber,KL(18),LS
Sperer,WK
Sperl,SW(16)
Sperr,WK
Speß,WK
Spesserter,WK
Spet,WK
Speycher,WK
Spichl,LS
Spickermann,GS(91A),
    WK
Spicznogl,WK
Spiegel,MM,WK
Spiegelhalter,LS
Spiel,LS,WK
Spier,WK
Spies,GF(93A),WK
Spiesen,WK
Spieß,LS,MM,WK
Spießlerin,WK
Spigl,WK
Spiglhalter,WK
Spilker,IE(98)
Spiller,WK
Spillmann,WK
Spindeln,WK
Spindler,MM,WK
Spingler,LS
Spinner,WK
Spircker,WK
Spiry,GL(494,511)
Spisin,WK
Spiß,WK
Spitz,MM,WK
Spitzbarth,WK

Spitzbarthin,WK
Spitzenmacher,WK
Spitzner,LS
Spitzschuh,SW(27)
Spizenstader,WK
Spizinger,WK
Splitt,HS(75)
Spohn,LS
Spohner,GL(401)
Sponer,GL(401)
Sponhauer,WK
Sponheimer,WK
Sponhold,MM
Sponsheimer,LS,WK
Spoor,MM
Sporer,WK
Spörke,MM
Sprauerin,WK
Spreen,IE(95)
Spreitzensch,WK
Spreitzer,LS
Spreler,WK
Spreng,LS
Sprengard,WK
Sprenger,GL(312,499)
Sprewitz,MM
Spriestersbach,WK
Spring,HW(18,29,82,
    89),LS,WK
Springarth,WK
Springborn,MM
Springburg,MM
Springel,WK
Springer,GL(455,
    476),LS,WK
Springfeld,MM
Springmon,WK
Sprink,WK
Sproker,LS
Sproß,WK
Sprötter,WK
Sprung,MM,WK
Spuch,WK
Spuhler,LS
Spuler,LS
Spuller,LS
Środziński,K1(167B)
Srzeczka,WK
Ssatin,MM
Staab,LS,WK
Staader,WK
Staalschmid,WK
Staats,WK
Stab,LS
Stabel,LS,WK
Stablan,WK
Stacheler,WK
Staches,WK

Steinbach,GL(13 entries),LS,WK
Steinbacher,WK
Steinbauer,WK
Steinbeck,MM,WK
Steinberg,HS(75),MM
Steinberger,LS,WK
Steinborn,WK
Steinbrenner,GL(215)
Steinbrunn,WK
Steincken,MM
Steindl,WK
Steinecker,LS
Steineckerin,WK
Steinemann,WK
Steiner,LS,W#(4.56), WK
Steinfeld,MM,WK
Steinfelder,WK
Steinfest,WK
Steingart,BU
Steinhard,WK
Steinhart,WK
Steinhauer,WK
Steinhof,W#(8.122)
Steinik,WK
Steinin,WK
Steininger,LS, SW(35),WK
Steinke,HW(63), Kl(166A)
Steinko,WK
Steinkönig,LS
Steinkopf,MM
Steinl,WK
Steinlin,WK
Steinmann,WK
Steinmetz,GF(91B, 93A,95A,122B, 133B),LS,MM,WK
Steinmitz,WK
Steinmüller,WK
Steinn,WK
Steinpacherin,WK
Steinpartzer,WK
Steinruck,WK
Steinwand,HW(207),WK
Steinweder,WK
von Steinwehr,KL(33)
Steinwend,W#(7.96)
Steir,WK
Steitzer,WK
Stekel,WK
Stekle,WK
Steknek,WK
Stelczer,WK
Stelczin,WK
Steler,LS

Stellenberg,HS(26)
Steller,LS,WK
Stellwanger,WK
Steltz,WK
Steltzer,WK
Steltzner,WK
Stelz,WK
Stelzer,WK
Stelzig,LS
Stemetz,WK
Stemler,WK
Stemper,WK
Stenbek,MM
Stender,MM
Stengel,LS,WK
Stenger,WK
Stengers,WK
Stenin,WK
Stenkamp,WK
Stenner,LS
Stentzel,WK
Stentzl,LS,WK
Stenzel,HS(70)
Stenzl,WK
Stepanek,WK
Stepfan,WK
Stepfes,WK
Stephan,HW(5 entries),LS,MM,WK
Stephani,WK
Stephanie,SW(27)
Stephanus,WK
Stephes,WK
Stepkin,HW(16)
Steppan,WK
Stepper,GL(5 entries)
Stepperin,GL(168)
Steppinger,WK
Ster,SW(38)
Sterbing,WK
Stercz,WK
Sterczingerin,WK
Sterkler,WK
Stermer,LS
Stern,WK
Sternbeck,MM
Sternberg,MM,WK
Sternecker,WK
Sterntaller,WK
Sterz,WK
Sterzheiser,WK
Stesmann,WK
Stetzer,W#(7.25)
Steub,WK
Steuer,LS,WK
Steuerl,W#(8.28)
Steuerman,WK

Steuerwald,WK
Steuger,WK
Stever,MM
Stewenel,WK
Steyber,WK
Steyer,LS,WK
Steyert,W#(5.93),WK
Steyrer,W#(4.17)
Stiber,WK
Stich,LS,WK
Stichelberger,WK
Sticher,WK
Stichter,WK
Stickel,HW(11 entries)
Stieber,WK
Stiebinger,WK
Stief,WK
Stiefbold,LS
Stiefel,HW(6 entries)
Stiefmayer,WK
Stiegelmár,GF(119B)
Stiegelmayer,GL(210, 466)
Stieger,WK
Stiegler,WK
Stiehl,MM
Stielze,WK
Stiepp,WK
Stierling,WK
Stifler,WK
Stift,WK
Stiger,WK
Stiglbauer,WK
Stigler,WK
Stihr,WK
Stilimuneus,W#(2.46, 2.87,2.91,2.92)
Stillbauer,WK
Stiller,GS(90A)
Stilling,WK
Stiltie,WK
Stimmel,LS
Stimmer,WK
Stingl,LS
Stinglbauer,W#(8.40)
Stintmann,MM
Stinzing,LS
Stirion,WK
Stirm,GL(299)
Stirmer,WK
Stitz,WK
Stitzl,WK
Stix,WK
Stjernsträla,MM
St. Main,GL(276)
Stobbe,BU

Strohmann,WK
Strohmayer,WK
Strohmenger,LS
Ströle,GL(263)
Strom,LS,WK
Strömer,MM
Strömich,LS
Ströpling,K1(167B)
Strowl,WK
Stroz,WK
Strub,WK
Strüber,MM
Struberth,WK
Struck,MM,WK
Struemke,HS(26)
Strumez,WK
Strümke,HS(26)
Strumperger,WK
Strumpf,LS,WK
Strunck,WK
Strunk,GF(91B),WK
Struphart,WK
Strupp,WK
Strußnik,WK
Struwe,MM
Strychulski,GS(18)
von Stryck,MM
Strycki,K1(167B)
Strzembski,K1(167B)
Strzyplewski,
  K1(167B)
Stub,WK
Stubbe,HS(26),MM
Stübe,MM
Stubenböck,WK
Stubenhofer,WK
Stubenrauch,WK
Stuber,HW(87),LS,WK
Stüber,LS,WK
Stübler,WK
Stuchner,WK
Stuck,WK
Stückel,WK
Stuckerl,WK
Studinzky,WK
Studter,WK
Stüeble,WK
Stuhl,WK
Stuki,LS
Stuky,WK
Stüldt,GS(91A)
Stumerin,WK
Stump,GL(278),HW(20)
Stumper,WK
Stumpf,LS,MM,WK
Stumpfin,WK
Stumph,WK
Stumpillig,WK

Stumpp,GL(136,139,
  174,456)
Stuner,WK
Stup,WK
Stupp,WK
Stuppe,MM
Stuppy,WK
Stuprecht,WK
Stur,WK
Sturciades,MM
Sturcius,MM
Sturem,WK
Sturm,GL(80,446),LS,
  WK
Sturmayer,WK
Sturmer,WK
Stürmer,WK
Sturmin,WK
Sturtz,MM
Sturtzbaum,WK
Stürtzlinger,WK
Sturz,WK
Stuß,WK
Stutinger,WK
Stuttengerd,WK
Stutz,MM,WK
Stütz,LS
Stützer,WK
Stüwe,MM
Stüzel,WK
Subantzki,HS(44)
Süber,WK
Suchatschewskaia,
  HW(87)
Suchsdorf,MM
Suckau,BU
Suckert,HS(24)
Sudermann,BU
Sueboda,WK
Suel,MM
Sufel,WK
Suff,LS
Süffert,WK
Sugel,MM
Sugg,WK
Suhr,MM
Sulfoh,GS(55)
Sultan,WK
Sültz,MM
Sulz,GL(219)
Sulzbach,WK
Sulzer,MM
Sulzner,WK
Sumer,WK
Sumerhausen,WK
Sumpf,MM
Sundag,WK
Sundius,MM

Sunn,WK
Suntag,WK
Suntagh,WK
Supernthall,WK
Suppenmoser,WK
Sur,WK
Surgeon,GL(339)
Surowiecki,K1(167B)
Suschinka,WK
Susemihl,MM
Süss,HW(17)
Süß,LS,WK
Susse,WK
Süßmann,GS(19)
Suszynska,MM
Suter,WK
Sutor,LS
Sutter,LS,WK
Sutterel,WK
Sutthoff,MM
Svab,WK
Svaiczer,WK
Svaigl,WK
Svarcz,WK
Svarczinger,WK
Svarczvalder,WK
Sveger,WK
Sveiczer,WK
Sventner,WK
Sverkart,WK
Svoboda,WK
Svobodarin,WK
Svonenberg,WK
Swarzbarter,WK
Sweitzer,IE(95)
Swenk,LS
Swesch,LS
Swester,GL(246)
Swiderek,GS(91B)
Świderski,K1(167B)
Świeczkowski,
  K1(167B)
Świętek,K1(167B)
Swoboda,LS,W#(8.61),
  WK
Syring,LS
Szabo,WK
Szalit,MM
Szaran,WK
Szauer,WK
Szecsanin,WK
Szedlak,WK
Szegedy,WK
Szeiler,WK
Szelczner,WK
Szep,WK
Szepan,GS(91B)
Szerkal,WK

Szeska,WK
Szesula,W#(8.64)
Szetele,WK
Sziber,WK
Sziborowski,LS
Sziegielowska,MM
Szikora,WK
Szimecsek,WK
Szimmer,WK
Szinn,WK
Szmidecki,K1(167B)
Szmidowicz,K1(167B)
Szmitka,K1(167B)
Sznycerz,K1(167B)
Szoblek,W#(8.59)
Szotka,GL(503)
Szramowski,K1(167B)
Sztoltz,WK
Szücs,GF(133B)
Szulborski,K1(167B)
Szwankowski,K1(167B)
Szwemiński,K1(167B)
Szymański,K1(167B)
Szymonek,LS
Szynka,K1(167B)
Szyw,K1(167B)
Taback,MM
Tabar,WK
Tabbert,GL(390)
Taber,WK
Tabernier,WK
Tabner,WK
Tachritter,GL(311)
Taer,GL(406)
Taetz,MM
Tafelmayer,WK
Tafelmeyer,GF(92B)
Taffe,GF(92A,95A)
Taffen,WK
Taffernerin,WK
Tägl,WK
Taglieber,WK
Taier,GL(406)
Talal,GL(112,150)
Talberger,WK
Talinger,WK
Taller,LS,WK
Tallier,WK
Talmin,WK
Talweil,WK
Tanck,MM
Tanda,SW(17,56,72,
73,74)
Taner,WK
Tängel,WK
Tanhauser,WK
Tann,HW(23)
Tanner,W#(5.4)

Tantl,WK
Tantos,WK
Tantzer,WK
Tanzerin,WK
Tapp,WK
Tapper,LS
Taran,WK
Taretschek,W#(7.43)
Tarin,W#(7.5)
Tarnow,MM
Tasch,WK
Taschler,WK
Tätich,LS
Taub,IE(88,89),
SW(4),WK
Taube,K1(166A),LS,WK
Tauber,WK
Taubner,GS(22,89B)
Tauenhauer,WK
Tauenheimer,LS
Tauer,WK
Tauhamer,WK
Taus,WK
Tauscher,WK
Tausser,WK
Tauzenberger,WK
Taychert,GS(18)
Tayer,WK
Tebald,WK
Tebel,MM
Techald,WK
Techen,MM
Tede,MM
Tege,MM
Tegelmeister,MM
Tegetmeyer,MM
Tegg,MM
Tegtmeyer,IE(98)
Teiber,WK
Teibert,WK
Teichgräb,BU
Teichgräf,BU
Teichgräff,BU
Teichgräw,BU
Teichgref,BU
Teichgreff,BU
Teichgröw,BU
Teichler,WK
Teichmann,K1(167B),
W#(7.26)
Teichner,WK
Teidler,LS
Teifl,WK
Teig,WK
Teiger,WK
Tein,LS
Teippel,WK
Teis,WK

Teisch,W#(5.23)
Teischer,LS
Teiß,WK
Teissen,WK
Teister,WK
Teitenbach,LS
Telfer,WK
Telicky,BU
Teller,LS,WK
Tellich,WK
Tellmann,LS
Telschow,MM
Temenin,WK
Temerot,WK
Tempel,LS,WK
Templ,WK
Tengler,WK
Tenk,WK
Tenner,BU
Tensch,WK
Tentchen,WK
Tentel,WK
Tentelew,MM
Teperth,WK
Tepp,MM
Tepweiler,WK
Ter,WK
Teres,WK
Terflinger,WK
Terian,LS
Teries,WK
Terner,WK
Ternes,WK
Ternow,MM
Ternus,WK
Tertinger,WK
Tertl,WK
Tesch,WK
Tescher,WK
Teschker,WK
Teschner,HS(59)
Teschter,WK
Tesdorff,MM
Teska,HS(33)
Teske,HS(33,38,55)
Tessényi,GF(117,118,
119,120)
Tetl,WK
Tetter,WK
Tetz,MM
Tetzlaff,HS(65),
IE(98),KL(37)
Tetzner,MM
Teuber,W#(7.38)
Teubler,MM
Teuchern,MM
Teuchert,GS(22,89B)
Teuer,LS

Teuerer,LS,WK
Teufel,GL(473),WK
Teuffl,W#(4.74)
Teurer,GL(406)
Teuring,GL(40)
Teuscher,IE(90),
  SW(14)
Teutsch,WK
Texter,MM
Teylacher,WK
Tezler,WK
Thal,LS,WK
Thaler,LS,W#(6.88)
Thalgott,WK
Thalhamer,WK
Thalhamerin,WK
Thalheimer,WK
Thalheimerin,WK
Thalinger,WK
Thalingerin,WK
Thall,LS
Thaller,WK
Thallinger,SW(42)
Tham,WK
Than,WK
Thaner,WK
Thanerin,WK
Thanhofer,WK
Thannenpfälzer,WK
Thanner,WK
Thayer,GL(495)
Thebacher,W#(4.28,
  5.85)
Thecz,WK
Thegen,WK
Theilmann,IE(90),LS,
  SW(19)
Theim,LS
Thein,LS
Theiner,LS
Theis,WK
Theisen,WK
Theisin,WK
Theiß,SW(21,27),WK
Theisse,WK
Theissen,WK
Thel,WK
Thellen,WK
Thentz,WK
Theobald,LS,WK
Theowald,WK
Thepacher,WK
Theriar,WK
Theunert,W#(7.107)
Theurer,GL(443)
Thewald,LS,W#(2.38)
Theyer,GL(251)
Thiede,HS(26)

Thiedemann,GL(350)
Thiekau,MM
Thiel,LS,MM,WK
Thielatym,LS
Thielen,WK
Thiell,WK
Thiellen,WK
Thielmann,BU
Thiem,HS(43)
Thierbach,GL(206)
Thierfeld,HS(26,31)
Thies,LS,WK
Thieser,WK
Thiessen,BU
Thil,WK
Thill,LS,WK
Thillier,WK
Thillman,WK
Thillmann,WK
Thilmayer,WK
Thiost,WK
Thir,WK
Thirian,LS
Thiry,WK
Thiß,W#(1.46),WK
Thöden,MM
Thol,WK
Thöl,MM
Tholio,WK
Tholl,LS
Tholmayer,WK
Tholmer,LS
Thom,LS,WK
Thoma,LS,W#(5.15,
  5.18),WK
Thoman,WK
Thomar,WK
Thomas,GF(92B),
  HS(44),LS,MM,
  W#(5.52),WK
Thomasi,SW(27)
Thomasin,W#(7.4)
Thomaß,WK
Thomayer,WK
Thome,WK
Thomen,WK
Thomi,WK
Thoms,MM
Thon,WK
Thona,WK
Thönslen,WK
Thor,WK
Thormann,MM
Thorn,W#(7.94),WK
Thors,WK
Thorschend,WK
Thot,LS
Thott,WK

Thouuenel,WK
Thron,LS
Thühl,LS
Thul,WK
Thull,WK
Thum,WK
Thuma,WK
Thumi,WK
Thun,BU
Thuren,WK
Thurn,WK
Thurnbläßer,GL(416)
Thüsen,WK
Thym,MM
Thyme,HS(52)
Thyry,WK
Tibau,WK
Tibell,WK
Tibl,WK
Tibo,WK
Tibold,WK
Tibolt,WK
Tich,WK
Ticz,WK
Tiebmann,WK
Tiede,GL(496),
  K1(167B),MM
Tiedemann,MM
Tiedjens,MM
Tiefbold,LS
Tiefenbach,LS,SW(34)
Tiefenbacher,WK
Tiefenbacherin,WK
Tiefenthäler,WK
Tiel,WK
Tier,WK
de Tierenkrantz,MM
Tierr,W#(2.47)
Tierstein,WK
Tiesche,WK
von Tiesenhausen,MM
Tiessen,BU
Tietz,GS(89B),LS,MM
Tiff,GL(337)
Tiger,WK
Tik,WK
Tilch,WK
Tildgen,WK
Tilger,WK
Tiling,MM
Tilinger,WK
Tilitzki,BU
Tilk,LS,WK
Till,LS,W#(8.35),WK
Tillieke,BU
Tillin,WK
Tillitzke,BU
Tillitzky,BU

Trautinger,WK
Trautman,WK
Trautmann,GL(76,
 303),LS,
 W#(8.88),WK
Trautwein,GL(200,
 332)
Trawniczek,LS
Traxler,WK
Traxlin,WK
Trebbow,MM
Trebel,LS,WK
Trebinger,WK
Trebl,WK
Trebnitz,HS(55)
Trebus,WK
Trech,WK
Treer,WK
Treff,WK
Treffinger,GL(190),
 HW(18,82)
Treffler,LS
Treffs,WK
Trefz,GL(109,316,
 345,438)
Trefz-Ware,GL(501)
Tregel,WK
Treher,WK
Treib,LS,WK
Treiling,WK
Trein,LS
Treinzen,WK
Treister,WK
Treit,LS
Treith,LS
Treitz,WK
Tremel,WK
Tremer,WK
Tremlin,WK
Trenck,WK
Trendle,WK
Trendli,W#(4.45)
Trenklerin,WK
Trenkman,WK
Trenkmann,GL(305)
Trenkwalter,LS
Trennbak,LS
Trenner,WK
Trens,WK
Trenz,WK
Trepper,WK
Trer,W#(4.13,4.29)
Treschl,WK
Treschler,WK
Tresler,WK
Treß,WK
Tressel,LS,WK
Treßler,WK

Trester,WK
Treter,LS
Trettel,WK
Trettin,MM
Treu,WK
Treuer,WK
Trexler,WK
Trey,WK
Treyborn,LS
Treyer,W#(4.115),WK
Treyerin,WK
Treyin,W#(6.95)
Treymann,WK
Trichbe,WK
Tricht,LS
Triebe,GS(90A,91B)
Triebsees,MM
Triedner,BU
Trier,GF(93B),WK
Tries,WK
Trießler,WK
Triffo,SW(15)
Trifon,LS
Trinkel,LS
Trinkl,WK
Trinzler,WK
Trisson,LS
Tristel,GL(189)
Tritt,LS
Tritthart,LS
Trobsch,LS,WK
Trocksner,LS,WK
Trodner,LS
Troester,GL(508,509,
 510)
Troll,WK
Trom,WK
Trombach,LS
Tromer,WK
Tromkort,WK
Trommershauser,LS
Troneker,WK
Tronitzer,WK
Tronwell,WK
Tröscher,WK
Trost,HW(22,24),WK
Tröster,GL(116
 entries),WK
Trottnow,MM
Trotz,WK
Trübler,WK
Trufanovich,WK
Truha,WK
Truhart,MM
Trumpold,WK
Trunkner,WK
Trunkwalter,WK
Truntz,WK

Truringer,WK
Trusl,WK
Tschedi,W#(5.115)
Tschek,HW(12)
Tschernobrowkina,
 GL(404)
Tschischewski,MM
Tschritter,HW(29)
Tschudi,W#(5.32,
 5.107)
Tuba,WK
Tubiantz,WK
Tubil,WK
Tubner,WK
Tück,MM
Tuczek,LS
Tüer,LS
Tulikowski,GS(18)
Tulius,WK
Tuller,WK
Tullus,WK
Tum,WK
Tumbruch,WK
Tumeltinger,WK
Tüncker,WK
Tunfinger,LS
Tunler,LS
Tupf,WK
Tüpke,MM
Türck,WK
Turczanowicz,LS
Turek,LS
Turk,WK
Türk,LS,MM,WK
Türkin,WK
Türkow,MM
Turnna,WK
Türring,WK
Tusch,LS,WK
Tuschner,WK
Tuß,LS
Tusseg,WK
Tussill,WK
Tust,W#(8.76)
Tuster,WK
Tutle,WK
Tutler,WK
Tutsch,W#(7.97)
Tutzmann,WK
Twaas,MM
Twietmeyer,MM
Tychsen,MM
Tyda,K1(167B)
Tyl,LS
Tynf,K1(167B)
Tyri,WK
Tyrion,LS
Tyriot,WK

Völkel,GF(91B)
Völker,LS,WK
Völkl,LS
Volkmuth,WK
Voll,WK
Vollenbeer,WK
Vollendorff,MM
Vollert,LS,WK
Völlm,GL(280)
Vollmann,MM
Vollmar,WK
Vollmer,GL(26,453),
  LS,WK
Vollmuth,SW(17,68)
Vollrath,WK
Völm,GL(280)
Volmar,MM
Völpel,LS,SW(33)
Volper,WK
Volrath,MM
Volthelm,WK
Voltman,WK
Voltrauer,WK
Voltz,LS,WK
Volz,LS,WK
Volzin,WK
Vombohr,GF(92B,125A)
Vonau,LS,WK
Vonbanck,WK
Vonbohr,WK
Vonderbul,WK
Vonhuben,WK
Vonhuber,LS
Voormann,MM
Vorann,WK
Vorgang,WK
Vornwald,WK
Vorreiter,LS
Vorreuter,WK
Vorreuther,WK
Vorßky,WK
Voss,K1(166B)
Voß,MM,WK
Voßky,WK
Vossler,HW(6
  entries)
Voter,WK
Votgen,WK
Voth,BU,MM
Votrova,WK
Vranovich,WK
Vrucser,WK
Vrzeteczka,WK
Vuillaume,WK
Vulpius,MM
Vulsan,WK
Vunder,WK
Waasen,WK

Waats,WK
Wabel,WK
Waber,LS
Waceck,WK
Wach,LS,WK
Wachendorfer,WK
Wachinger,WK
Wacht,LS,WK
Wachtel,K1(167A)
Wachter,WK
Wächter,LS,WK
Wachtler,WK
Wackenhuth,WK
Wacker,LS,WK
Wackerbauer,WK
Wackshut,GL(360)
Wacter,WK
Wadel,WK
Waechter,WK
Waegner,MM
Waeschke,GS(57,58)
Waffenschmied,WK
Wag,LS
Wagemann,LS,WK
Wagenblass,GL(245)
Wagenblast,GL(267),
  WK
Wagener,MM,WK
Wagenheim,WK
Wager,WK
Wagg,IE(95)
Wagman,WK
Wagmüller,WK
Wagner,GF(91A,92A),
  GL(75 entries),
  GS(19,90B),HW(10
  entries),IE(88,
  89),LS,MM,SW(4,
  14),W#(2.37),WK
Wagnerin,WK
Wagruschew,GL(407)
Wahl,GL(7 entries),
  LS,MM,WK
Wahlach,MM
Wahlen,WK
Wahlenmajer,GL(464)
Wahlenmayer,GL(5
  entries)
Wahlenmeyer,GL(40,
  43,44)
Wahler,WK
Wahlfart,WK
Wahlt,GL(510)
Wahnschaff,MM
Wahrheit,WK
Waibel,WK
Waidel,LS
Waidl,LS

Waig,LS
Waigel,LS
Waiz,WK
Wajdacherin,WK
Wakerlin,GF(96B)
Waky,WK
Walch,WK
Walcher,WK
Wald,GL(444,459),WK
Walde,BU,WK
Waldebach,WK
Waldeck,LS,WK
Waldel,WK
Waldenmayer,WK
Walder,WK
Wälder,WK
Waldhauer,WK
Waldmann,W#(8.78),WK
Waldmayer,WK
Waldner,W#(2.94)
Waldpeck,WK
Waldschmid,WK
Waldschmidin,WK
Waldt,GL(444)
Waldung,WK
Walesser,WK
Walfert,MM
Walheiser,WK
Walicz,LS
Walker,LS,WK
Wall,BU,GL(75
  entries),LS,WK
Walla,LS,WK
Wallau,WK
Walle,WK
Waller,GF(104A),
  GL(434),WK
Wallern,LS
Wallewein,GL(480)
Wallinsky,MM
Wallmer,LS
Wallner,IE(95,98),WK
Wallnowsky,MM
Wallrabenstein,WK
Wallraub,WK
Wallrich,WK
Walls,WK
Walmar,LS
Walmer,LS
Walmritter,W#(4.32)
Walner,WK
Walraub,WK
Wals,WK
Walser,WK
Walster,WK
Walt,GL(108)
Walter,GL(251),
  GS(18,26),HW(7

Welzel,WK
Welzenbach,WK
Welzinger,WK
Wemer,WK
Wencel,WK
Wenclaw,K1(167B)
Wend,WK
Wende,GS(18),WK
Wendeker,LS
Wendel,LS,WK
Wendelin,LS,WK
Wender,WK
Wendisch,GS(12,14,
  16,19,22,89B)
Wendl,WK
Wendland,HS(75),WK
Wendling,IE(92,93,
  94,95,97,98),LS,
  SW(19),WK
Wendorff,MM
Wendt,MM
Wener,GL(387),WK
Wenerin,WK
Wengelmüller,WK
Wenger,GL(424),WK
Wengert,GL(358),WK
Wenglar,WK
Wenglerin,WK
Wenhardt,LS
Wenig,WK
Wenigand,WK
Weninger,WK
Wenisdörfer,WK
Wenk,LS,WK
Wenkelmeß,WK
Wenner,LS,WK
Wensel,LS,WK
Wenser,WK
Wenske,GS(61)
Wenson,WK
Wentin,WK
Wentz,WK
Wentzel,LS,WK
Wentzke,K1(167B)
Wentzler,WK
Wenz,GF(92A,127B),
  GL(265,402,496,
  497),WK
Wenzel,GL(215),
  GS(18),LS,SW(27),
  WK
Wenzl,WK
Wenzler,GF(103),WK
Weran,WK
Werb,IE(94,96,97,
  98),LS
Werber,WK
Werbitzki,MM

Werdes,MM
Weres,WK
Wergau,GS(26)
Werhäuser,LS
Werker,WK
Werkhauser,LS
Werkhäuser,WK
Werkheißer,WK
Werkirsch,WK
Werla,WK
Werle,LS,WK
Werlen,WK
Werlet,WK
Werley,LS
Werlüng,WK
Werly,WK
Wermann,WK
Wermuth,WK
Wern,WK
Werndter,WK
Werne,LS
Werneccius,MM
Wernemond,WK
Werner,BU,GF(91B,
  93B),GL(504),
  GS(18),HS(43,44,
  48,55,65),LS,MM,
  W#(3.45),WK
Wernick,WK
Wernie,WK
Wernik,HW(67,152)
Wernitz,GS(89A)
Wernle,HW(17)
Werny,W#(1.82)
Werschim,WK
Werschinger,GF(93A)
Werschler,LS,WK
Werschner,LS
Wersem,WK
Wersio,WK
Werter,WK
Werth,LS,WK
Werthmann,WK
Wertin,WK
Wertle,W#(4.40)
Wertmann,WK
Wertz,HW(18)
Werz,GL(450),LS,WK
Wesan,LS
Wesche,WK
Wesel,HS(26)
Wesele,LS,WK
Weselle,WK
Wesenberg,MM
Wesler,LS
Wesner,LS
Wesołowski,K1(167B)
Węsowski,K1(167B)

Wespy,WK
Wessan,LS
Wessel,MM
Wesselik,WK
Wessinger,WK
Westberg,MM
Westendorf,MM
Westenmayer,LS,WK
Wester,WK
Westerheide,MM
Westerkamb,WK
Westermayer,LS,
  W#(5.63)
Westermayerin,WK
Westermeyer,LS,WK
Westphal,HS(58),
  KL(25),MM
Weth,WK
Wetie,WK
Wetterich,MM
Wetterling,MM
Wettmeyer,LS
Wetz,WK
Wetzel,HW(16,19,81),
  WK
Wetzelers,WK
Wetzer,WK
Wetzl,WK
Wetzler,GL(308,418)
Weudik,WK
Wex,MM
Weyandt,WK
Weyant,WK
Weyer,MM,WK
Weyerich,WK
Weyermüller,WK
Weygar,WK
Weyher,WK
Weyler,WK
Weymar,WK
Weynacht,WK
Weynerowski,K1(167B)
Weyrich,WK
Weysann,WK
Wezel,WK
Wgl,LS
Wiber,WK
Wibich,WK
Wichert,BU,LS
Wichmann,MM
Wicht,WK
Wichter,WK
Wichterig,WK
Wichtner,WK
Wick,LS,WK
Wicke,WK
Wickel,W#(1.9)
Wickenhäuser,LS

Wiloth,WK
Wilpert,MM
von Wilpert,MM
Wilske,HW(63)
Wiltermuth,WK
Wiltfang,MM
Wilthirl,LS
Wiltmann,WK
Wiltzer,MM
Wilwers,WK
Wilwert,WK
Wilwerts,WK
Wilwisch,WK
Wilz,WK
Wimmer,LS,WK
Winandi,WK
Winathall,WK
Winätzer,WK
Winblad,MM
von Winblad,MM
Winck,LS,MM
Winckler,WK
Wind,WK
Windelband,MM
Windenberger,WK
Windheißer,WK
Windholz,SW(64)
Windisch,LS,WK
Windler,WK
Windschihel,WK
Wingarthen,WK
Wingels,WK
Wingendorf,WK
Winger,GL(73,74),
  HW(207,208)
Wingert,GL(358),LS,
  WK
Winiarz,MM
Winkelmann,MM
Winkler,GL(6
  entries),HW(15,
  20,52),LS,MM,
  W#(8.22,8.24),WK
Winklerin,WK
Winne,WK
Winnheim,WK
Wins,BU
Winscha,BU
Winschel,GL(454)
Winschu,GL(454)
Winsenbach,WK
Winsperger,WK
Winte,MM
Winter,LS,MM,WK
Winterfeldt,MM
Winterhalter,WK
Winterich,WK
Wintermayer,WK

Winterrot,GL(490)
Wintger,WK
Winther,WK
Wintherin,WK
Wintisch,LS
Wintrich,WK
Wintscher,WK
Winz,BU,WK
Winzel,WK
Winzeron,WK
Wip,WK
Wippler,WK
Wirdle,WK
Wire,MM
Wires,LS
Wirich,WK
Wirig,WK
Wirl,LS
Wirlein,WK
Wirmsee,WK
Wirner,WK
Wirrich,WK
Wirsch,WK
Wirschen,WK
Wirsching,LS,WK
Wirschinger,WK
Wirschner,WK
Wirt,HW(27),LS
Wirth,GF(93A),
  HW(13),IE(89),LS,
  WK
Wirthin,WK
Wirths,WK
Wirtle,WK
Wirtz,WK
Wiry,WK
Wirz,LS,WK
Wirzler,WK
Wisberg,LS
Wischader,WK
Wischann,WK
Wischert,WK
von Wischmann,MM
Wiser,WK
Wiserner,WK
Wisig,WK
Wisinger,WK
Wislbacher,WK
Wisler,WK
Wisner,LS,WK
Wiśniewski,K1(167B)
Wisnowska,MM
Wisotzki,LS
Wiß,WK
Wissel,MM
Wißgarber,WK
Wißkopf,WK
Wißlerin,WK

Wister,W#(5.12)
Wistinghausen,MM
Wistmer,WK
Witaschkin,GL(386)
Witenberg,WK
Witermiller,WK
With,WK
Witie,WK
Witisch,LS
Witkowski,SW(24)
Witlach,WK
Witman,WK
Witmann,LS
Witmer,WK
Witmeyer,WK
Witpert,WK
Witt,LS,WK
Wittboldt,MM
Witte,MM,WK
Wittenberg,BU
Wittenburg,MM
Wittensellner,WK
Witthmer,MM
Wittich,GL(375)
Wittig,LS
Wittin,MM
Witting,MM
Wittinger,WK
Wittingk,MM
Wittink,MM
Wittlinger,WK
Wittmann,GL(490),LS,
  WK
Wittri,WK
Wittrock,MM
Wittstock,MM
Witz,MM
Witzel,MM
Witzig,WK
Wiwie,WK
Wiza,K1(167B)
Wochner,WK
Wodke,K1(167B)
Wodopi,LS
Wodsinsky,MM
Woehl,GL(192,491)
Woelck,BU
Woelcke,BU
Woelke,BU
Wöffle,WK
Wog,WK
Wogen,WK
Wogur,WK
Wohl,GL(313)
Wöhl,GL(191),MM
Wohlbrück,MM
Wohleb,W#(4.83)
Wöhler,MM